Eight Rant Eight Rant Eight Rant Eight Rant Eig

A rant is a polemic, a forceful argument and in Scots "a noisy frolic". When Norman Finkelstein was told on the Today Programme that his book was "a bit of rant", he replied that all the great polemics such as Edmund Burke's *Reflections on the French Revolution*, Thomas Paine's *Rights of Man* and the *The Communist Manifesto* were rants, and his was just another. They are necessary voices in our national debate, but in this series we also like to keep in mind the gaiety and mischief of our noisy frolic. *Barking up the Right Tree* is a fine example.

Barking up the Right Tree 2019

Paul Kavanagh

Vagabond Voices
Glasgow

Vagabond Voices Publishing Ltd.,
Glasgow,
Scotland

© Paul Kavanagh April 2019

First published in April 2019

ISBN 978-1-908251-89-3

The author's right to be identified as author of this book under the Copyright, Designs and Patents Act 1988 has been asserted.

Printed and bound in Poland

Cover design by Mark Mechan

Typeset by Park Productions

For further information on Vagabond Voices, see the website, www.vagabondvoices.co.uk

To Peter, for green through the asphalt.

Barking up the Right Tree 2019

Brexit is all fluffy kittens for the Tories

Ever since Theresa May became PM on the tautological promise that Brexit means Brexit, the country has been trying to find out what Brexit means Brexit actually means. Now we know. Brexit means Brexit is one of the Zen koans that means both everything and nothing. Whatever you want Brexit to mean, at least if you're a member of the Tory cabinet, that's what Brexit means. It means all things to all Tories. As a means of keeping a fractured Tory Party together, it's genius. As a means of giving the country some security and confidence in the face of the storms of uncertainty ahead, it's as much use as a pair of open-toed wellies, although a whole lot less stylish.

This week in Westminster Theresa May's guy in charge of Brexiting, David Davis, was more than happy to say what he thought Brexit meant. It means fluffy kittens, happiness and joy, for everyone who isn't foreign. Mainly what Brexit means for David is leaving the Single Market and not letting any more foreigners into the country. It's going to be great-Britulous, the sort of thing that proves that British nationalism isn't remotely nationalist at all. Oh no.

If you're a Tory, not letting any more foreigners into the country is what the Brexiteers meant when they said they wanted to make the UK an outward-looking country that's engaging with the rest of the world and not just with Europe. And if building a big wall around the UK to stop unBritish types getting in means leaving the Single Market then oh dear how sad never mind. It's far more important to prevent the sprouting of foreign food shops in Farnham than it is for the British economy to have free access to the European market, and if the Tories can do that by isolating the British economy from the rest of the globe and destroying job opportunities then that's a price worth paying. After all, it's only the working classes who're going to suffer.

The following day, Theresa May told Westminster that Brexit didn't mean what David had just said it meant after all. It means something entirely different, but she's not going to tell us what that might be precisely, because that would spoil the surprise. It's still going to be great-Britulous, and will probably come draped with a Union flag, and it will still stop foreign types coming into the country, and because it's British it's still most definitely the non-nationalist kind of nationalism however xenophobic it gets. Brits don't do xenophobia anyway, when it comes wrapped in the red white and blue it's not xenophobic, it's merely exclusive. Brexit will be a bespoke solution for a bespoke country. We'll be having none of that off-the-shelf nonsense that sufficed for the Norwegians and the Swiss. Theresa's glad to have cleared that up for us.

Meanwhile Jezza, the last person in the country who still believes in the British Labour Party's parliamentary road to socialism, neglected to press the PM on the topic during PMQs this week, doing absolutely nothing to clear up the lingering suspicion that he's really quite happy with this whole Brexit thing. Instead he asked a question sent to him on Twitter by Martin of Gloucester, asking about the best way to remove wine stains from a rug. Theresa replied with some snarky jokette written for her by someone without much of a sense of humour, and slapped JC down with an even more snarky Tweet from a guy who turned out to be a notorious Twitter troll. All the Tory backbenchers laughed uproariously. None of us were left any clearer about what's actually in store for us over the coming months and years. But who cares, what's really important is that the Conservative member for Foxhuntingshire got a few good guffaws in.

During the Scottish independence referendum, the Unionist parties and their followers in the press insisted that

4

the Yes movement provide exquisite detail on every single aspect of an independent Scotland, up to and including how much a first-class stamp was going to cost. How could Scotland possibly become independent when Alicsammin couldn't even tell the people of Scotland what was going to be on the television instead of *Bake Off*? The kind of people who would struggle to answer the questions on a daytime quiz show demanded a level of detail that they wouldn't have been able to understand even if they'd got it. Which of course was kind of the point. Either way, the case for independence was going to be condemned.

Eleven weeks on from the EU referendum vote, there's still precious little clarity about what's awaiting us in the future. All those people who were demanding every tiny detail about Scottish independence are quite happy to wait for Theresa May to tell them when they can unwrap their Brexit present. What they're going to find is a boxful of disappointments and shattered illusions. That's the real reason that Theresa isn't for saying what Brexit really means.

10 September 2016

Goodbye Davie, you were the worst ever

Davie Cameron said before the EU referendum that he wouldn't stand down as prime minister if he lost. After he lost he stood down as prime minister and said that he'd continue in post as the MP for Witney until the next general election because he didn't want to be remembered like Blair, who immediately stood down in order to spend some more time with Central Asian dictators. Then on Monday Davie announced he was resigning as an MP with immediate effect, saying he didn't want to continue as a backbencher. It's typical of Dave. He's leaving politics – in one almighty mess.

In between his petulant announcement to resign as PM when he said he wouldn't and his pettit-lipped announcement to resign as an MP when he said he wouldn't, the only work he managed to do was to give awards to some of his pals and his wife's stylist. So it's not exactly like we're facing a grievous loss to British public life. Now he's triggered a by-election in one of the safest Tory seats in the country, and if we're really really lucky they'll offer it to Ruth Davidson and we can hear a whole lot less of her going on and on about another independence referendum instead of doing her day job. Sadly, Ruth has said no.

Poor Davie, he'll go down in history as one of the worst prime ministers that Britain has ever had. He was such a disaster that the day he resigned as PM he had been responsible for national catastrophes of such proportion that his resignation only made it as the third item on the TV news. And then a few weeks later when he announced that he was leaving politics for good, he got upstaged by the revelation that *The Great British Bake Off* will be disappearing from the

BBC screens. You know you're a rubbish prime minister when people care about the loss of a soggy-bottomed sponge cake more than they care about the loss of a soggy-bottomed ex-prime minister who accidentally cut the UK off from Europe. If nothing else, Cameron is the undisputed winner of the Great British break off.

Doubtless he'll be appearing in ermine in a House of Lords nowhere near you sometime soon as he moonlights for a series of lucrative consultancies and speaking engagements. He leaves a country that's divided, broken and diminished, and now he's walking away from the mess he's made, leaving the rest of us to cope with the consequences. What you can be sure of with Dave is that his personal wealth will insulate him and his family from the negative fallout of the calamities he's inflicted on the country. That's the kind of leadership you get taught on the playing fields of Eton.

Cameron is the worst prime minister this country has ever had, in a field with some very strong competition, after all he succeeded Gordie Broon, and by this time next week he'll be a respected elder statesman. A couple of years ago he could have gone on to some highly paid post in the EU, now he'll have to console himself with making piles of money with some consultancies in the City. So very much like the Tony Blair whom he said he didn't want to be remembered as being like. Nae worries there Davie. You'll be remembered as being even worse than Blair, and that's quite a spectacular achievement.

The EU referendum is looking suspiciously like the Scottish independence referendum, because it doesn't seem as though any of the promises made by Westminster's politicians during the campaign need to be kept after the result is in. Cameron broke the vows he'd made during the Scottish referendum campaign, and he broke the vows he'd made during the EU referendum campaign. You've got to admire his consistency. To be fair though, he probably lost the EU referendum deliberately and inadvertently created the conditions for a second Scottish independence referendum that will lead to the end of the UK just so he will be remembered in the history books for something other than the pig thing.

Ruth Davidson tweeted that she was sorry to see Cameron stand down. "He transformed the party and country," she said. Well that's one way of putting it. You could just as easily say that someone with a wrecking ball, a demolition crew, and who then let loose a herd of feral pigs to scrabble in the ruins for fetid scraps has transformed a historic building. All this would probably be a much better way to transform the Palace of Westminster than anything Davie Cameron has done with it. Although to be honest, the feral fetid scrabbling bit is not an unfair description of what the House of Lords is like right now.

Davie came to power claiming that Britain was broken, and he left politics leaving it smashed into tiny pieces and less able to be put back together again than Humpty Dumpty. His gamble on a Scottish independence referendum didn't silence the demand for Scottish independence. Instead his arrogant disdain for the promises Better Together made during the 2014 independence referendum has left an indy movement which is revitalised, energetic and angry. His contempt for the country led him to put the short-term needs of his party first, and so he took us into a needless EU referendum that was hijacked by the very worst proponents of the narrow xenophobic insularity that characterises the basest aspects of British nationalism. Oh sorry. I forgot. There's no such thing as British nationalism. There's just jolly bunting-bedecked patriotism.

Cameron's legacy is a widening gulf between rich and poor. He left almost a million people dependent on food banks while the richest thousand grew even richer. The man who claimed he'd lead the greenest government ever derailed the renewable energy industry. He said the NHS would be safe in his hands, and he left it wrecked, being privatised by the back door, with doctors driven to strike action. He said he'd control the deficit and ran up more debt than under thirteen years of Labour. He told Scotland that we'd be a respected and valued partner in the UK, and then in response to the indy referendum result he reduced our MPs to second-class status. His legacy is a UK that's parting from its friends and allies in the EU, and a UK which will itself part in two. The only reason he's not the last PM of the UK is because he didn't hang around long enough.

14 September 2016

A Gaelic map isn't 'Gaelic imperialism', it's a restorative act for the language which created Scotland

I studied Gaelic when I was a teenager, but after many years living outwith Scotland my command of the language got very rusty. When I was still living in Spain, I decided that a good way to get back into the language would be to draw Gaelic maps of Scotland. It's a project that's kept me occupied for the past five years. Unfortunately what I've now discovered is that while I've got pretty good at Gaelic mediaeval agricultural terminology, I'm still not very good at holding a conversation. There's only so many times you can drop words like dabhach ("the area of land that can support a head of forty cattle") into a modern conversation. On the plus side, I've now got some detailed Gaelic maps of a number of Scottish regions.

I put a few excerpts from the maps on social media a few days ago. The response was hugely positive from most, but I also found myself subject to attacks and abuse from people who identified as Unionists. Prominent Unionist Tom Gallagher referred to me as a nationalist demagogue, and said that a Gaelic map of Glasgow was a form of Gaelic imperialism. He claimed I was only doing this project in order to make a lot of money. Clearly Tom has a more optimistic view of the commercial potential of Gaelic maps than I do. Which does make me wonder why he's so opposed to them. Others weighed in to call me a blood-and-soil nationalist and a fascist, drawing a Gaelic map of Glasgow means you must be narrow-minded or insane. Some simply responded with pig-ignorant personal abuse.

Yet others were very keen to inform me that Gaelic has never been spoken in Fife, or Edinburgh, or Dumfries and Galloway, despite the fact that the language was once widely spoken in all those areas. Gaelic was at one time the language of all of Fife, and it was widespread in Edinburgh, as Gaelic place names like Corstorphine, Balerno or Inveresk attest. Galloway Gaelic survived into the eighteenth century.

In fact at the time of its greatest extent, around 1100, Gaelic was at one time the dominant or sole language of all of mainland Scotland west and north of a line drawn approximately from Edinburgh to Lockerbie. It was even spoken in parts of the modern English county of Cumbria. Yet despite being very keen to inform me how little they cared about Gaelic, my critics were equally keen to insist that they knew more about the language than those who have studied it seriously, those whose works I used as sources for the maps. In Scotland, ignorance about Scottish languages is passed off as lofty erudition.

It's a peculiar paradox. Those who claim that Gaelic and Scots are irrelevant are often those who put the most energy and enthusiasm into attacking those of us who do see the relevance of Scotland's traditional languages. Those who say they don't care about the languages all too often care deeply that other people do care about them. This proves that contrary to the assertions of their attackers, there is in fact a use for Gaelic and Scots. The languages are useful as cringe detectors, and as such they're incredibly accurate. Scotland's languages are the epicentre of the Cringe.

The critics of Scotland's languages claim that spending public money on them is a waste, yet they don't object to the state spending public money to protect and foster other parts of our national heritage. Intangible assets like Gaelic and Scots are as much a part, indeed arguably more a part, of Scotland's heritage than tangible aspects of our heritage like castles or museums. The languages are responsible for the creation of Scotland. It was the use of Gaelic that created the Scottish nation, the mediaeval Latin word *Scotti* meant Gaelic speaker. The nation those Gaelic speakers created formed a state, the Kingdom of Scotland, and for much of its history that state expressed itself through the medium of Scots. Without the Gaelic and Scots languages there would be no Scotland.

And that's precisely why modern Unionists object so vehemently to a part of their own history, culture and heritage. The existence of Scottish languages puts a lie to the myth that there is no content to Scottish culture except an atavistic hatred of the English. They prove that Scotland is capable of discussing itself and looking at itself without reference to the English language.

Maps are inherently political. A map is a statement of ownership and possession. The British colonial enterprise painted much of the globe in the blood red of Empire. Native languages were extirpated, native place names corrupted. That's real cultural imperialism. And Scotland didn't escape, our modern English-language maps consist of names made up of nonsense syllables, written down by English-speaking surveyors who neither knew nor cared about their meanings. When you draw a map of Scotland in Gaelic, you're reclaiming the sense of Scotland, and that's threatening to those who want Scotland to remain firmly locked within the Great British shortbread tin. A Gaelic map of Glasgow isn't Gaelic imperialism, it's an act of restoration.

Gaelic maps do not replace English ones, but they do return meaning to the Scottish landscape. A Gaelic map is a meaningful map. It unleashes the story of the land. It tells us who we are. And while there were certainly critics who attacked and belittled the idea of Scottish maps in Scottish languages, the response from the great majority was one of excitement and pleasure. Most people in Scotland want to know the story of this land, they want to hear the voices locked into the place names of our landscape. Modern Scots want the chance to view our country through different eyes.

And that's what really frightens the Unionists who howl in derision, because once you look at Scotland through a different and Scottish lens, you might very well decide that Scotland doesn't need the UK to teach it about itself.

1 October 2016

Life's a brawl for UKIP, but maybe not much fun for the rest of us

Want to become a doctor? If you have an O Grade in biology and a British passport, you are eminently qualified. In years to come, patients might be left to die in neglect and agony on a trolley in a hospital corridor, but they'll die in a British neglect and agony safe in the knowledge that they've preserved this great country of Theresa May's from the horrors of qualified medical staff who eat pierogi. Because we now know what Brexit means, Brexit means hating on foreigners and calling it British patriotism. It means listing foreign workers so that their employers can be shamed. It means making the armed forces immune from prosecution for human rights violations, because it's more offensive to insult the integrity of the armed forces than it is to commit war crimes.

The Tories have now completed their transition into a full-on blood-and-soil ethnic nationalist party and have adopted the UKIP manifesto wholesale, and gone further in some respects. Even Nigel Farage didn't propose forcing companies to draw up lists of their foreign employees. Now the only difference between the Tories and UKIP is that the Tories don't settle their leadership disputes by having a square go and a punch-up after a cabinet meeting. Although to be fair, Fluffy Mundell already serves as everyone's punchbag as his job is to take the beatings that the Tories dole out to Scotland and then tell us that we serve a valuable purpose. The Tories are far more civilised than the barroom brawlers of UKIP. They just knife one another in the back instead.

According to some of the frothier Unionist commentators, the cancerous growth of vicious xenophobic nationalism in the Tory Party is the fault of the SNP for allowing national-ism to gain a foothold in politics. But then everything is the fault of the SNP. See that probe that crashed on the surface of Mars a few years ago? That was the fault of the Scottish transport minister and it caused hard-working commuters to miss the 7.47 to Dalmuir. Bloody SNP, why can't they do the day job eh? Somewhere in the constellation of Cygnus there's an alien civilisation that's on the brink of extinction, and what's Nicola Sturgeon doing about it? Nothing. That's what.

The blame for xenophobic British nationalism lies with those people who rail against Gaelic maps and road signs but were silent when Unionist thugs went on the rampage in George Square. It rests with those people who try to draw a moral equivalence between the desire for a country to be gov-erned by those who choose to live there and who identify with it, and those who wish to exclude, deport and demonise. It belongs to those who condemn a Scottish pro-independence politics that speaks of inclusion and welcomes migrants, and yet accept without demur an exclusionary British politics that preaches to those it calls indigenous. The only place that this British politics recognises for Scotland is a subordinate one in which Scotland is stripped of everything that makes it distinctive, where consultation means doing what you're told, and where being an equal partner means having no say. There's no place for foreigners, and Scots are permitted on sufferance.

The fault for the growth of xenophobic nationalism in the Tory Party lies squarely with British nationalists who are incapable of recognising that British ethnic blood-and-soil nationalism is exactly that. They're the people who can't see that it's a very short step from describing your telly contests as Great British to imagining that your country is better than any other. These are the same people who claimed that there's no such thing as British nationalism, there's only patriotism. They're the people who condemned the open, tolerant and civic nationalism of Scotland, while being blind to the neo-fascism of the worst of the Union. They're the people who can't recognise that they are in fact nationalists, that their support for the British state is every bit as much a form of nationalism as wanting an independent Scotland. In fact it's a far worse form of nationalism, because it rests upon the belief that Britain is somehow special because it's magically immune to nationalism.

Because the worst nationalism of all, the most dangerous, the most vile, is the nationalism that refuses to recognise that it's nationalism at all, because that's a nationalism that knows no moral boundaries. That's British nationalism, and that way fascism lies.

But the point isn't so much to throw around blame for the rise of the nasty and exclusionary self-aggrandisement and xenophobia that the Tories want to make the centre ground of British politics. The point is to do something to protect ourselves from it. And the Unionist hand-wringers have no answers. The only answer is for Scotland to hold another independence referendum and escape this dysfunctional mess. That's the only way in which we can protect the values of tolerance, acceptance and social justice that we hold dear. Scottish independence has become a moral imperative.

8 October 2016

Who said Andrea Leadsom was plain crackers?

After almost four months of a dog's Brexmess, our Conservative overlords are slowly shaping a plan to reboot the UK's economy after the country leaves the EU in one almighty xenophobic sulk. Britain is going to be butter together. According to Andrea Leadsom, Minister of State for Energy, Climate Change and *The Great British Bake Off*, Britain is going to storm the world with its food and drink products.

Speaking at a food trade event in Paris as she sipped on a cup of Earl Grey and nibbled a patriotic sandwich, Andrea told the French that British food was grand. Never mind France and its different cheese for every day of the year, Britain's got biscuits. The UK exports over £10 billion a year in food and drink products, and all across the world when people think of a Brexit Britain, they think "crackers".

The great food plan also conveniently settles the dispute between those who want a hard Brexit and those who want a soft one. All you need to do is dunk your hard Brexit in your tea for a few seconds and it will soften. Everyone is happy in this new land of Great British opportunities. Well, everyone except migrants and foreigners. And the poor, and the disabled, and the low-paid, and everyone else who's going to have to pay for Conservative idiocy. But apart from that, everyone is going to be happy.

Warming to her theme, the Minister of State for Clutching at Strawberries explained how Brexit brings amazing opportunities to the British biscuit and conserves industry. We'll export innovative jams to France. Now Britain has a beef with the Europe we are free to export beef to the rest of the world, at least those parts of it which haven't banned it due to mad cow disease. When the world thinks of Britain, it thinks of tea, said Andrea, and tea will be Britain's salvation. Obviously this is great British tea from the tea plantations in the Peak District, and not tea that the UK is going to have to import from abroad that will cost far more due to the collapse of the pound. And we will sweeten our tea with sugar refined from the treacle from the Lancashire treacle mines. A nice cup of tea fixes everything, including British economic collapse.

She warmed to her theme as the tea cosy on her head overheated her brain. We'll wow the Walloons with our waffles. We'll drench Japan in gin. The Brexiteers will silence the mockers who claim that there's no plan to deal with Brexit and send honey to Hungary as part of the Great British plan bee. The UK might no longer be a part of the world's largest and richest trading block, but we'll always have our scones and jam. Who needs Europe when you've got the Ukipshire branch of the Women's Institute and royalist sponge cakes.

Britain no longer has an empire, but we will always have empire biscuits and the world will flock to our door for them. We will fight those Europhiles on the peaches, we shall fight on the coffee grounds, we shall fight on the peeled fruit and the sugar beets, we shall fight in the chilli; we shall never surrender. Our tea exports will take over the world, never have so many owed so much to a brew.

Can you imagine the reaction if a prominent supporter of independence announced that independence would herald marvellous opportunities for Scotland's shortbread and teacakes trade? There would be howls of derision and outrage. Yet this is all that we've heard so far from the British government about how the UK is going to make its way in the post-Brexit world. Well, that and the insistent claim that the EU will cave in to Theresa May's every demand because the Germans want to sell us cars. But we should be grateful to

Andrea Leadsom for clarifying what Brexit means. It means rhubarb. It means nuts. It means a raspberry. These are the broad shoulders of the UK that Scotland is told it is better for us to rely on, and we discover that they carry a head that's a fruitcake.

The interesting thing about the UK's £10 billion worth of food and drink exports is that over £5.1 billion of them are Scottish, according to the most recent statistics published by the Scottish government. The Scottish whisky trade alone brings in around £4 billion annually, and Scottish fish exports bring in another £613 million. And when Scotland becomes independent, we'll be taking those export industries with us. Proportionately, food and drink exports make up a larger proportion of Scottish exports than UK exports, but it would be considered ludicrous for a Scottish minister to stand up and make a speech like Andrea Leadsom made this week. Britain has fallen to such a ridiculously low level that Andrea's crackers plan is the best that we've got.

22 October 2016

It's obvious that May's government lacks Brexit strategy

Theresa May met with the leaders of the devolved administrations this week, and had a face-to-face with Nicola Sturgeon and the Scottish government. It was the second time in a week that the UK prime minister was indulged by people who hold more cards than she does. The prime minister has called for a "grown-up" relationship between Whitehall and Holyrood, by which she means that Whitehall is the grown-up and Holyrood the child which will do as it's told.

Scotland has been told that it's not to try and speak to the grown-ups of Europe without adult permission. It's to eat up its big bowl of Brexit cereal, the one with the unspecified ingredients. Scotland won't be allowed to undermine Downing Street's Brexit strategy, but Downing Street refuses to tell anyone what that strategy is. It's becoming more obvious that the reason May won't discuss her strategy is because she doesn't possess one.

The truth is that it's the Scottish government which is making the running, and all Number 10 is willing to do is to offer a few worthless platitudes. If we're really lucky, Theresa will throw in some beads, mirrors and pox-ridden blankets to sweeten the deal. And that's exactly what she's done. May has offered to give the devolved administrations a "direct line" to David Davis's office in the belief that Scotland will be happy that its wishes will be respected because 10 Downing Street has said, "Don't call us, we'll call you. But you can speak to our semi-trained monkey."

Davis would be the guy who came to Scotland last week

to throw poo at the idea that Scotland could get any sort of special Brexit deal. He's the guy who stands up before the House of Commons to tell everyone that Brexit means Brexit means Brexit. He's not actually sure what it means in any detail, and even if he was he wouldn't tell anyone else. But Brexit is going to be grand. It's going to be fabulous. It's going to involve lots of bunting and patriotic feel-goodness.

David Davis is blessed with many skills and talents, foremost amongst them the ability to make Fluffy Mundell seem like a reasonable human being. Davis is the Brexit robot, utterly convinced by the sound of his own voice, programmed to tell us what marvellous opportunities Brexit will unleash irrespective of what question is asked of him in the vain hope that if he keeps saying the same thing the rest of us will be convinced by it too. Scotland is just a minor irritation that keeps complaining, the kid that wants to play a different game, a grown-up game.

A direct line to an ideologue like Davis is as much use to Scotland in getting a special deal on Brexit as plugging an Internet router into a pile of horse manure and hoping to get connected to the world. In fact all it's going to get you is Restore Sovereignty Take Back Control on a repeating loop. The Conservatives better be careful or they are going to find that the Scottish government will take them at their word.

According to the BBC, sources close to Number 10 say that the Conservatives intend to play hardball with Nicola Sturgeon. Which is an interesting tactic from a UK government which has no plan, no strategy, no game and certainly no balls. The prime minister is convinced that the Scottish government is bluffing, said the eager BBC reporter, there's no appetite in Scotland for a second independence referendum, and because Westminster has comprehensively trashed the Scottish economy the entire place is a basket case. All that Theresa May needs to do is to act tough, and those spineless Scots will back down.

The City of London can have a special EU deal. Other

sectors of the economy whose directors have ties to the Tories can have a special EU deal. But Scotland can do what it's told. There will be no special deal for Scotland, despite the fact that during the first independence referendum campaign Theresa May was one of those who assured us that Scotland was an equal partner amongst the nations of the UK. It turns out that statement is as meaningless as Brexit means Brexit.

Earlier this week the think tank Institute for Government published a report warning that the failure of the British government to respect the different desires and needs of the devolved nations of the UK risked breaking up the Union. Theresa May can have her hard Brexit, or she can have her UK. She can't have both. Despite that, May's government has already ruled out allowing Holyrood to have more powers over trade and some control of immigration, it's said no to a Holyrood vote on Brexit, and it's set its face against allowing Scotland to remain in the single market while the rest of the UK leaves. It's adopting this hard-line stance because Theresa May's government is infected with the same disease that has afflicted all previous British governments in modern times, the same disease that has brought the UK to its current sorry state of affairs – the arrogant and unfounded belief that it holds all the cards when all it clutches is a joker and a memory of kings and queens of an empire long past.

Theresa May is about to discover that she wants to play hardball with a government which does actually have a ball to play with. This is what happens when you rely on Fluffy Mundell and Buffalo Ruth for directions to negotiate your way across the Scottish political landscape. Ruth is only capable of negotiating her way to her next hilarious photo op, while Fluffy still needs someone to hold his hand so he can cross the road.

Despite what Ruth and her pals say, there's a mandate for a second independence referendum. There's a majority in the Scottish parliament for a second independence referendum. There's a good half of the Scottish population that supports independence. There's a Scotland which has the most politically aware and active population in Europe, and the knowledge and skills and experience to mount another grass-roots movement that can reach the entire country. That's before the banks and other businesses have started to relocate to other EU countries. That's before the pound has completed its plunge in value. And most importantly of all, that's before a revived and reinvigorated independence movement has even started to campaign formally.

26 October 2016

How to win indyref2? By demonstrating that the British state is a threat to our future

There's only one real question which preoccupies the Scottish independence movement these days. And it's not whether there will be another referendum. We're already taking that pretty much as read. No, the real question is, how do we win that second independence referendum? How does the independence movement persuade soft No voters of the case for independence?

There are a number of schools of thought on this vital question. Some believe that we can win by doing what we did the last time, once more with feeling. After all, what we did last time was very successful in persuading hundreds of thousands to come over to the dangerously radical idea that a country is best governed by people who actually know where its largest towns and cities are, because they live or work in them. This strategy was highly successful in persuading people in Scotland that the abnormal thing isn't independence. What's abnormal is that we have a government made up of out-of-touch Conservatives from outwith Scotland who would struggle to distinguish between Balmoral and Balornock, at least when it comes to locating them on a map. Even a map that's in English. Although to be fair, Jacob Rees-Mogg knows how to tell the difference. He just needs to ask his nanny. She knows how to work the satnav.

During the first independence referendum campaign the Yes movement was characterised by wish trees, paintings of butterflies and unicorns, and a relentless positivity that would make a glee club seem as morose as our national fitba team's fans after yet another drubbing by a small country in Central Asia that not even Jacob Rees-Mogg's nanny knows how to find. It was a refreshing change from the more typical Scottish approach to things, which is to start off miserable and get gradually more torn-faced as things proceed.

This was of course the strategy adopted by the Better Together campaign, and one which they've pursued with gusto as they've continued to get even more torn-faced after their victory in 2014. Just look at Fluffy Mundell and his increasingly strident attempts to stave off another referendum. He's not doing it by being happy and cheerful.

But although the Unionists won, they've also seen support for the Union decline from over two-thirds of the population to a majority that's as lacking in substance as Donald Trump's comb-over. So even though the Yes campaign didn't quite make it over the finish line, adopting the kind of positivity that you more normally associate with US football cheerleaders instead of the moroseness of Scottish fitba is a strategy that works well.

The question is, will it work well enough the next time to get us over that magic fifty-per-cent figure and really knock the stuffing out of the po-faced plush toy who occupies the post of Secretary of State for Telling Scotland What to Do? Will it make the leader of the Ruth Davidson Selfie Party pose with a sad face on a buffalo? It could be that we were so concerned to paint a positive and glowing picture of an independent country of butterflies that fly free, of unchained unicorns, and wish trees bearing fruit that we neglected to warn people of the downsides of remaining a part of a UK which isn't going to respect Scotland's needs, which will lie, deceive and dissemble in order to get its way and then attempt to lock us back in the shortbread tin.

It's certainly the case that the dangers and uncertainties of staying in the UK are far more stark in this post-Brexit world. The Unionists can no longer claim that it's the independence movement which is narrow-minded and parochial nationalism, because that's Brexit Britain. Independence will allow Scotland to rejoin the world, staying in the UK will isolate us. They can no longer claim that it's only by remaining a part of the UK that we can protect jobs and public services, or that it's only by relying on the broad shoulders of the UK that we can achieve stability. Those broad shoulders have no head on them and they're carrying us in a headlong rush over the cliff of Brexit.

We were threatened the last time that we'd not be allowed to use the pound. During the next independence referendum we will see the Chancellor of the Exchequer come to Scotland to threaten us that we'll have to keep using it. The pound is no longer a byword for stability, it's lost twenty per cent of its value since the Brexit vote and could well fall even further. The Better Together threat that Scotland would have to adopt the euro is looking a whole lot less scary.

With Brexit, there's precious little stability or security in the UK, and during the next independence referendum campaign we need to be a lot more assertive about getting that message across. Your job, your pension and your NHS will not be safe in a Tory state which is facing a massive shortfall due to a shrinking economy. There's a Heisenberg Principle that's more certain than the future of the UK. Or to paraphrase Albert Einstein's saying about mathematics, as far as the laws of the UK refer to reality, they are not certain; and as far as they are certain, they do not refer to reality.

There's only a minority of Scots for whom Britishness is a core belief. For most people in Scotland, Britishness and the British state were supported because they were seen as being useful to Scotland. Being a part of the UK allowed Scotland access to a larger world. It provided us with security and economic stability. That's no longer the case. We'll win the next independence campaign by demonstrating that it's by becoming an independent member of the European Union that Scotland will attain access to a larger world, that will provide us with security and economic stability.

Britishness survived as long as it has done because it was useful to Scotland, in the post-Brexit world it's no longer useful. We'll win the next independence referendum, in part, by demonstrating that the British state is a hindrance to Scotland's opportunities, a danger to our stability and a risk to our future.

2 November 2016

Remember they told us that only the Union could protect our pensions? Another Better Together lie

This week the United Kingdom has sunk even further into the cruel, compassionless, chaotic confusion that the government calls Conservatism. Over the weekend there were calls from the House of Commons Work and Pension Committee to scrap the triple lock on state pensions. So if you're an older person who voted No in 2014 because you thought that your pension was only going to be safe if Scotland remained a part of the UK, you were sadly mistaken.

The Tories are looking for ways to ensure that the UK state pension, already one of the worst in Europe, becomes one of the worst in the developed world. The Conservatives are taking an axe to state social security provision and the elderly aren't going to escape either. It doesn't matter if you lived through World War II. It doesn't matter if you did your National Service getting shot at in the jungles of Malaya or on the banks of the Suez Canal, you can have a poppy instead of a pension. There's respect for you.

Having bribed us last week with the news that some of the ships promised by the MoD would actually be built on the Clyde after all, although not as many as originally promised, another of Better Together's promises collapsed like a UK benefits payment. Eight defence sites in Scotland are due to close despite Scotland being assured that the only way defence jobs in Scotland could be safe was for us to vote No to independence. The scale and extent of the closures is far greater than anyone had forecast, and it's clear now that last week's announcement about the ships on the Clyde was an attempt to sweeten the bitter pill of Britain. The MoD giveth, and the MoD taketh away. That's us feeling safer and more secure in the United Kingdom.

Then on Monday the new benefits cap came into effect, stripping income from some of the poorest families in the country and increasing the risk that they go hungry, lose their homes or sink further into debt and despair. Irrespective of the size of your family, how many mouths you have to feed or whether you live in a high-rent area, outside of London the total amount your family will be allowed to receive in a year will be capped at £20,000. When you're already struggling to make ends meet, all the own-brand baked beans in the world aren't going to make up a further shortfall of £70 a week in your income. That's the amount that the likes of Iain Duncan Smith can cheerfully spend on lunch. If you voted No in 2014 because you were hopeful that the Labour Party would protect you from the excesses of Tory contempt, think again. 184 Labour MPs didn't vote against the benefits cap, including Red Morningside's Ian Murray.

The social security net is shredded and frayed. This latest measure threatens to destroy what's left. We've already got a system where random cruelty counts as an incentive to employment. The benefits cap encourages people into work in the exact same way that sticking a petrol bomb through the letter box of a slum landlord's property encourages people to seek better-quality housing. There's a fine line between a disincentive and degradation, and the UK is miles across it. But never mind, you can always Call Kaye on Radio Scotland and say how bad the SNP is.

Also on Monday the United Nations published a report showing that people with disabilities are seeing their human rights violated by a British government which is slashing support. People with terminal illnesses are being assessed as fit for work, people with chronic degenerative conditions or congenital disorders are having to prove that their health hasn't improved. If you've got terminal cancer, in the UK you can still be assessed as work-shy. The UN report concludes, "There is reliable evidence that the threshold of grave or systematic violations of the rights of persons with disabilities has been met."

And as the very poorest families in the country wake up to the realisation that they face a greater chance of homelessness, that they're going to struggle to feed their kids, and as people with disabilities bear the burden of austerity, another pensioner on benefits is getting a pay rise of £2.8 million a year. Under the Sovereign Grant Act of 2011, the amount that the Queen receives from the state every year can never be less in cash terms than the amount she received the previous year. So that's OK then. Never mind that people are starving and if you're poor the government will strip you of your dignity along with your income, we've got poppies and a well-fed monarch.

Meanwhile over in India, Theresa May is hoping to make a good impression on Narendra Modi, the only prime minister in the democratic world who's possibly more of a xenophobe than she is. In the post-Brexit world it's vital for the UK to strike trade deals with growing economies like India, only India has already signalled that in return it will seek a loosening of the strict visa requirements that the UK imposes on Indian citizens. Britain has agreed to a bespoke deal, a phrase we've been hearing a lot of late, for Indian business people and their families which will smooth their path through UK immigration. So there's going to be less immigration from Europe but more from India. How's that getting out of the EU so we can crack down on immigration looking for you Theresa? The closet racists of UKIP will be thrilled.

The Tories say that the Brexit vote was all about cracking down on immigration, and they're doing all they can to reduce immigration by turning the UK into a cold, harsh, unwelcoming country. The Conservatives are destroying all the good parts of Britain that attract people to come here. It's the only thing they're succeeding in. And what we know

now is that paradoxically, if we seek to preserve the good parts of Britain, the positive and progressive achievements of the British state, we're going to have to seek independence in order to do so.

9 November 2016

It's a grave new world for the US... and for us

It's been a pretty dreadful year. It was bad enough that 2016 has been characterised by the deaths of dozens of celebrities who were actually talented, leaving us only with reality TV stars, baking shows and people with unnaturally white teeth, but now the reality TV stars have taken over the world. The shock of Brexit was pretty dreadful, but America refused to be beaten and wrested the title of World Champion Political Stupid back from the UK after defeating Boris Johnson in the category of Scary Clown.

A man who thinks veracity is a township in Kansas will be the most powerful US president for a decade. A man who actually managed to bankrupt his own casino won the election by citing his business acumen. It's said that gambling is a mug's game, but it's not supposed to be the bookie who's the mug. Unless you're the Donald.

The world woke up on the morning of the ninth of November to discover that the brash and boorish star of the American version of *The Apprentice* now has the ability to tell US nuclear missiles that they're fired. The only thing thinner than the gold leaf that adorns every surface of Trump Tower is Trump's skin, and after January he'll have his finger on the nuclear trigger. And here we are in Scotland with one of the biggest collections of nukes just a few miles down the road from our largest city, making us a prime target. Don't you feel really safe as a part of this glorious United Kingdom?

If you voted No in the 2014 referendum because you were afraid about your pension, it's not going to reassure you to know that you won't be able to collect it in the wasteland of the post-nuclear apocalypse when Donald goes to war with

Mexico because the Mexican president has sworn at him again. But look on the bright side, your grandweans will be cannibal mutants so they won't worry too much about the shortage of employment opportunities. And then there's the other plus that instead of having to worry about the nuclear fallout drifting up from down south, that half of Scotland's population living on the banks of the Clyde will be evaporated in the first strike. Aberdeen will envy Glasgow for possibly the first time in Scottish history. So it's not all bad.

Not everything will change. We can be quite sure that as Ruth Davidson emerges from her bunker surrounded by a bunch of mutants, she will blame it all on the SNP. Although to be honest it's not sure whether Ruth will notice much of a difference, as she's surrounded by mutants every time she goes to a Tory Party conference.

The first black American president will concede the White House to an artificially tanned xenophobe who was endorsed by the Ku Klux Klan. Just let that sink in for a wee minute. And you thought *Orange Is the New Black* was just the title of a TV show – turns out it was a prediction. We've got a simple-minded bigot in the White House, the most complex thing that goes on in Donald's head is his hair. The closest thing he ever described to an actual plan during the election campaign was when he advised that you should suck on a Tic Tac before you force yourself on a woman. His other plans include covering the White House in gold leaf and converting the Oval Office into a roulette table. That would be Russian roulette.

All those independence supporters on social media who went on and on about how terrible Clinton was now have as a US president a thin-skinned man whose brain can't hold a fact for longer than five minutes but which can hold a grudge for decades. And he's got a very big grudge indeed with Scotland. Hillary would have opposed Scottish independence, but she'd have opposed it in much the same way that Obama did. Donald's opposition to Scottish independence will be personal, vicious and vindictive. The only silver lining in this very dark cloud is that Trump is so widely despised in Scotland that his opposition to independence is likely to be counterproductive. But that won't stop it being plastered all over the front pages of the Unionist newspapers and being the lead item in the BBC news for days on end.

Criticise Trump on social media and immediately you have to fend off hordes of people demanding to know why you're behaving just like the BBC and backing Hillary Clinton. The truth is that you don't have to have a very high opinion of Clinton in order to come to the conclusion that Trump is a whole lot worse. It's a sad indictment of the world's most powerful democracy that the voters were faced with a choice between Clinton and Trump. Especially for minorities, it's frightening that America chose Trump. Just as we saw with Brexit, his victory is likely to legitimise the hatred of the far right. For America's black, Hispanic and Native American communities, for women's rights, for gay and transgender rights, things have taken a very dark and serious turn for the worse. Welcome to the grave New World.

12 November 2016

These social injustice warriors
must not be given a platform

The Brexmess and the Trumpageddon were bad enough, but the forces that they've unleashed and legitimised are even worse. Since the English and Welsh parts of the UK voted to leave the EU there has been a surge in hate crimes as bigots interpreted the vote as a legitimisation of their discriminatory views. In the USA there's likewise been a reported rise in hate crimes since Trump's victory. And likewise on both sides of the Atlantic we have also seen a triumphalist and energised extreme right which is now being normalised by sections of the media. Although to be honest you'd be hard-pressed to distinguish between certain right-wing newspapers in Britain and the views of Alf Garnett. They're bigoted and intolerant, they're stuck in the past and they're works of fiction.

We've been led to this sorry state of affairs by those parts of the traditional media which specialise in the demonisation of migrants and social security claimants, and something called political correctness. This last is a phrase that only ever occurs in right-wing commentary and which is inevitably followed by the words "gone mad". Examples cited include the mythical abolition of Christmas so as not to offend non-Christians. Although, as we view Christmas adverts earlier and earlier every year and the piling up of Christmas merchandise in supermarkets from the end of summer, the abolition of Christmas doesn't seem like such a bad idea. Then having invented an entirely fictitious left-wing enemy to rail against, an enemy existing purely in their own fevered imaginations, the same commentators complain about the rise of post-truth politics.

Many have suggested that the malign influence of UKIP on British politics is not unrelated to the fact that its leader Nigel Farage is constantly indulged by the media and is rarely off our TV screens. By giving him publicity the media has legitimised and normalised his views, and that has in turn made it more acceptable for the public to embrace the intolerant views that so many in UKIP espouse. Over the past couple of weeks sections of the media have ceased to pretend that they're challenging or arguing against the far right and have instead been giving it a platform.

A few days ago *Sky News* invited Milo Yiannopoulos to comment on its press review. Yiannopoulos is far-right commentator and editor of Breitbart News, the "alt-right" commentary platform beloved of neo-racists. After the Orlando attack on a gay club he was suspended from Twitter for apparently being unable to distinguish between Muslims in general and psychopathic murderers, and later permanently banned for allegedly inciting his followers to send racist and sexist tweets to African-American actress Leslie Jones. He enjoys being offensive and claims that he's challenging elites, but his offence is in the service of the rich and the powerful. It's all just a hilarious joke, he claims.

Twitter is a cesspit at the best of times, getting banned from it requires a special kind of offensiveness. Yet there he was on *Sky News*, leafing through newspapers as a serious and respected commentator on current affairs. Next week on *Scotland 2016*, the Unionists' favourite Twitter troll Brian Spanner will be giving us his opinion on global warming and political uncertainty in the Baltic States. It's all the fault of the SNP, in case you were wondering. Mind you there are differences between North Britain's very own Brian Spanner and Yiannopoulos. Yiannopoulos is brave enough to be offensive under his own name.

The week before Yiannopoulos appeared as a newspaper reviewer on *Sky News*, the French far-right leader Marine Le Pen was interviewed on *The Andrew Marr Show*. You could at least argue, as the *Marr Show* tried to, that Le Pen was being interviewed so that her extremist views could be challenged and countered, although the effect was to give her a platform to further spread her noxious hatred. That's not the case with inviting someone like Yiannopoulos on to *Sky News* as a newspaper reviewer. That's normalisation. That's propagating extremism. That's normalising hatred.

Yiannopoulos and the alt-right rail against so-called social justice warriors. For them the fight for social justice and equality ended when they got theirs. Yiannopoulos is gay, and the only reason he and other prominent right-wing lesbian and gay political types enjoy their positions and privilege is because older generations of LGBTI people were proud to come out as social justice warriors and upset established views in order to right injustice and challenge discrimination. That's the generation I belong to myself. If it wasn't for the ageing LGBTI social justice warriors that Yiannopoulos affects to despise he'd still be hiding in the closet leafing through a men's underwear catalogue hoping to get his jollies. The modern generation of alt-right social injustice warriors delight in offensiveness in order to perpetuate inequality and entrench discrimination.

Now the champions of the alt-right are being appointed to positions of power and influence. Trump has given the post of attorney general to a man who was rejected as a federal judge during the Reagan era because of his offensive views. Senator Jeff Sessions's appointment was applauded by the former Ku Klux Klan leader David Duke. Sessions himself is on record as saying that he only had a problem with the KKK after he discovered that many of its members smoked marijuana. He also once stated that the highly respected African-American civil rights organisation NAACP was "un-American".

In an attempt to defend themselves from their critics, the social injustice warriors of the alt-right invented the hashtag #AltRightMeans. It backfired, as Twitter users decided that #AltRightMeans racism for potheads and fighting for a future where ghostbusters are white and male. Basically, what alt-right means is an adolescent fascist who can't get laid and who blames his unattractiveness on feminism. Alt-right means social inadequates banding together to blame black people for making them uncool. They're white supremacists who can only reign supreme in a forum for gamers. Let's just call them what they are, they're racist bigots who have no business appearing as neutral commentators on newspaper review shows.

23 November 2016

It's panto time and the EU isn't on the side of the Brexit Brits

The EU is establishing its negotiating team for the Brexit talks. It's panto season, and more and more it's looking like the EU is getting together a band of Europeans who're going to point and laugh at the idiocies of the brick-footed Brexit Brits who're trying to pass Boris Johnson, David Davis, Liam Fox and Theresa May off as dwarfs in order to save money. Which to be fair is perfectly reasonable as they're intellectual dwarfs. Sadly they're going to end up costing us a fortune.

It's bad enough for supporters of the red white and bleugh that the EU's lead negotiator has hinted that the Brexit talks will be held in French. Because as the French proverb has it, *C'est le ton qui fait la chanson* – it's the tone which makes the song. The tone that's coming from Europe isn't pleasing to Brexitish ears and the song is one which Westminster doesn't know the words to and silently makes mouth movements when it comes to the chorus in the hope that no one will notice.

The tone of the negotiations will be determined by the people whom the EU is choosing to do the negotiating. The EU Parliament will be represented in Brexit negotiations by Guy Verhofstadt, a man who has already expressed his support for Scottish independence and agreed with Nicola Sturgeon that if Scotland votes for independence before the Brexit process is complete then Scotland's entry into the EU will be automatic. Europe is singing a *chanson d'amour* for Scotland, and giving null points to the Brexiteers.

Then this week we learned that one of the twelve-person team of MEPs who will oversee the Brexit process for the EU

Parliament is to be the Catalan MEP Josep Maria Terricabras, who will be joined on the group by Sinn Féin MEP Martina Anderson. The group is being chaired by Martin Schulz, the current president of the European Parliament, who met with Nicola Sturgeon when she was in Brussels in the immediate aftermath of the Brexit vote.

Important members of the EU Parliamentary group are unlikely to look favourably on a UK government which seeks to deny Scotland another independence referendum in order to maintain its membership of the EU and forge a different path from the isolationists of Brexit. Terricabras is a member of the Esquerra Republicana de Catalunya party, a left-wing pro-independence party from Catalonia which is one of the closest allies of the SNP in the European Parliament. He's also the president of the European Free Alliance, the bloc of pro-independence and regionalist movements to which the SNP belongs and which is allied with the Greens in the EU Parliament.

Irritatingly for those who are insistent that Spain is going to block any moves by Scotland towards independence, Terricabras will be the only Spanish representative on the EU Parliamentary Brexit negotiating body. Even more irritatingly for the red white and blah faction in Scottish politics, after being selected for the negotiating team Terricabras told the Spanish press that he saw his role in the team as being "to see how [Brexit] evolves and what possibilities there are for an understanding with Scotland, and for a new relationship for Scotland with Europe, and for the Catalans this seems to me to be extraordinarily important".

The latest development comes hot on the heels on Nicola Sturgeon's visit to the Irish Senate, where she got a standing ovation and a series of Irish senators queued up for selfies with her. One after another, senior members of the Irish Senate stood up to tell her how they supported Scottish independence and supported Scottish membership of the EU as an independent state. That was the Scottish Furst

Meenister being snubbed by the way, in case you're of a Unionist persuasion.

The response of the more frothy section of Unionist support on social media, which is most of it, to be honest, was to trawl the Rangers' Supporters True Blue Book of Irish Insults for epithets to hurl at the Irish Republic. Because that's really going to endear the British to the Irish government during Brexit negotiations. This even included a certain prominent Unionist supporter and apparent academic who described Ireland as a "potato republic", because that's not racist at all. Oh no. But then the person in question is already frothier than a Fairy Liquid cappuccino and independence supporters should encourage the Unionist campaign to keep using them as a spokesfoamer as every time they open their mouths another bit of the Union drowns in the spume. Meanwhile Tory MSP Murdo Fraser tweeted passive aggressively about how the Irish were no great friends of the British, despite all that Britain has done for them. You know, like causing a famine that resulted in the deaths of over one million Irish people and driving three million more into emigration. Because that's really the way to make friends and influence people.

And that's the real problem for the UK during Brexit negotiations, and the real strength of Scotland. The UK relies on bullying and bluster, but bullying and bluster won't work when your opponents are the ones in the strong position and know that they're the ones in the strong position. Scotland, on the other hand, knows how to make friends, and that will pay off for us in the longer term as the rUK declines into its self-imposed irrelevance.

3 December 2016

Westminster's arrogance will
be the death of the Union

This week the Supreme Court is hearing the British government's appeal against the recent High Court ruling that Article 50 to leave the EU can only be triggered after a parliamentary vote. The Scottish government is making submissions too, in an attempt to ensure that the Scottish parliament must be consulted during the Brexit process. The Tories are pretty torn-faced about this, although to be fair they're torn-faced about most things and it's not always easy to tell the difference.

Despite having spent the entire EU referendum campaign insisting that control had to be returned to the British parliament, after a Leave vote the Brexiteers don't want the British parliament to be consulted. When the High Court ruled that the prime minister doesn't have the constitutional right to overrule an entire body of law by fiat, the take-back-control mob immediately launched an appeal so that the parliament they demanded should be in control wouldn't have any control at all. This is the only context in which Theresa May, Boris Johnson, David Davis and Liam Fox could ever possibly be described as appealing.

Naturally the *Daily Mail* was outraged, and blamed the decision on openly gay Olympic fencing judges. But then outrage is the baseline state for the *Daily Mail*. Just this weekend it was outraged that voters in Austria had rejected the far-right candidate for the country's presidency in favour of a pro-EU Green candidate. The last time an Austrian fascist was elected the *Daily Mail* was thrilled. If Brexit isn't a project for the far-right, you do have to wonder why it is that the *Daily Mail* thinks that a victory for a right-wing extremist in the Austrian presidential elections would have been a victory for what it likes to describe as "the Brexit revolution".

One of the striking features of 2016, other than the mass celebrity die-offs, Brexit and the non-dumping of the Trump, is how language is being perverted by right-wing extremism and how parts of the media are complicit in it. We're not supposed to call the far right fascists any more. The approved term is "populist". Night after night on the TV news, out-and-out fascists are being described as populists. Left-wing political movements never seem to be described as populist. The Syriza movement in Greece, Podemos in Spain, or the Corbyn Momentum in the UK aren't populist, possibly because they're not popular with newspaper proprietors. The Scottish independence movement is only ever described as populist when British nationalists seeks to link Scottish independence with far-right extremism.

We also have a new term, "alt-right", which is 2016's synonym for nasty white supremacist – spotty middle-class white adolescents who are upset that the advances in social equality and civil rights over the past few decades mean middle-class white men have to compete on a playing field that's marginally more level than it was before. Because when you're the oppressor, equality feels like oppression, and it's far easier to blame feminism for the fact that you can't get laid than to stop being a whiny middle-class brat with an entitlement complex. The alt-right rails against the establishment, but what they're really opposed to are minorities and women becoming a part of the establishment.

What the UK government's appeal against the High Court decision tells us is that the supposedly populist right wing isn't about returning control to the people at all. It's a rearguard move by the establishment to retain control and to reverse the progress achieved by the social democratic civil rights movements of the late twentieth and early twenty-first centuries. The far right, Brexiteers and the Ukipised

Tory Party are the opposite of populist, they're exclusionary and inward-looking reactionaries who dress their elitism in a veneer of mass appeal.

There's certainly no control being conceded to the people of Scotland by the unlayable reactionaries of Conservative Ukipification. Ukipised populism is markedly unpopular in Scotland. You might imagine that when the voters of Scotland decided that they wanted to remain in the EU, and decided by a considerably larger margin than they decided that they wanted to remain in the UK, that the British government would go out of its way to appease the rebellious Scots in order to get us on board with their supposedly populist project. Quite the reverse. Because only some populaces are popular with the populists of Westminster.

The digital journal *Scottish Legal News* reported that Scottish legal commentators have described the UK government's legal response to the Scottish government's submission to the Supreme Court as "fantastically rude", "unnecessary" and "inappropriate". The British government is essentially arguing that when the Unionist parties vowed back in 2014 that the permanence of the Scottish parliament would be enshrined in the British constitution and that changes could only be made to the devolution settlement with the consent of Holyrood, they were telling a big fat lie to the voters of Scotland. And moreover they're annoyed that the Scottish parliament should have the audacity to complain that they were lying, and come close to calling the Scottish parliament stupid for complaining, because the sovereignty of Westminster means that Westminster has the constitutional right to lie through its teeth. Promises to voters mean nothing at all. That's British populism for you. How dare you want something different.

The argument hinges on the word "normally". The law says that Westminster will not "normally" legislate on matters that are devolved. But the British government is arguing that it's entirely within their gift to decide what is or is not normal, and they have decided that Brexit isn't normal. In other words, the guarantee that they gave the voters of Scotland back in 2014 was a guarantee of absolutely nothing at all.

We'll have to wait and see what the judges say. But one thing is perfectly clear. This is no Union that Scotland is in, it's the death embrace of a centralised state that has no respect for the different nations of which it's composed. Britain isn't a Union, British nationalism is an intolerant arrogance where difference is to be crushed not accommodated. Only some peoples are allowed to be popular with our supposedly populist government. The British state has no intention of accommodating the will of the Scottish people, and that means that its days are numbered.

7 December 2016

Farewell to 2016, pin number of the Beast

There're only a few hours to go now before the worst year for decades finally ends. 2016 is 666 + 666 + 666 + 6 + 6 + 6, which means that 2016 is the pin number of the Beast. 2016 saw a slew of unexpected celebrity deaths, carrying away those who had made a genuine contribution to humanity's happiness and well-being. There's still time for an unexpected celebrity death, but those celebs who do make it alive and kicking into 2017 will be slightly disappointed at the realisation that they weren't quite as talented or famous as they'd hoped they were.

Most disappointed of all are those columnists and pundits who this time last year wrote their predictions for 2016. In the wise words of Mark Twain, or possibly someone else, never make predictions, especially about the future. A year ago we all thought that Ed Balls would fade gracefully into obscurity and wouldn't sear our consciousness with his rendition of "Gangnam Style" on *Strictly*. Some of us are still waking up in the middle of the night in a cold sweat.

This time last year we comforted ourselves with the knowledge that the Remain campaign was a safe bet to win an EU referendum and Nigel Farage was destined to spend the rest of his life appearing on *BBC Question Time* complaining that he'd been robbed. Instead the UK is leaving the EU and Nigel Farage makes his frequent appearances on *BBC Question Time* being even more smug than he was before, something that no one could have believed was humanly possible. Nigel has broken the smug barrier, and has disappeared so far up his own fundament that he's come out the other side and straight into the panel for an episode of *BBC Question Time* coming to you from a quiet and leafy racist corner of Little Englandshire. Which by some bizarre coincidence seems to be every single episode of the show.

No one could have believed that there were so many people in the country who believe every word of a *Daily Mail* editorial, but then no one believed it was possible for a single individual to make so many appearances on *BBC Question Time*. However this is a programme which manages to find an overwhelmingly Unionist majority audience every time that it deigns to make an appearance in Scotland, so we shouldn't be too surprised. It's a safe prediction for 2017 that Nigel will continue to be best pals with the producers of *BBC Question Time*, and that it will keep on making its broadcasts from an alternate universe where everyone treats the *Daily Mail* as gospel and no one in Dundee has a Scottish accent.

Also this time last year smart money was telling us that Donald Trump had as much chance of becoming president of the USA as there was of Ruth Davidson passing by a tank without leaping on it for a photo-op. He'd be doomed to spending the rest of his life spouting conspiracy theories to zoomers. Now he'll be spouting conspiracy theories along with the zoomers in his cabinet.

Clearly, making predictions is a bit of a mug's game, but we can be pretty certain that the Donald will fail in his determination to Make America Great Again. Although that won't stop him claiming that he's succeeded. Truth and Donald Trump are two concepts that usually only appear in the same sentence when there's also a negative there too, like that one. The Donald will simply claim that "great" means something different to whatever everyone else thinks it means, and so claim he's been vindicated.

This is pretty much the same strategy adopted by Theresa May, who says Brexit means Brexit, and that Brexit means Brexit means the crumbs she'll be left with after the EU has eviscerated her negotiating position and the UK is cast out into the wilderness of an uncertain future. Then she can say that it's a great victory and that whatever it is that she ends up with is what she'd been planning all along. We might be going down the Great British pan, but we're being flushed away with red white and blue toilet duck. And because the Tories will have destroyed the economic prospects of everyone in the UK who isn't a banker, no one will want to come to live here and they'll be able to claim that their anti-immigration measures are an outstanding success.

Another thing guaranteed to be a feature of 2017 is the British government swearing that it's going to listen to Scotland and take Scotland's views into account, and then ignoring us completely and telling us to be happy with whatever it is that they're imposing on us. This isn't so much a prediction as an immutable law of the British state. This goes hand in hand with another feature of 2017
, which will be the Scottish government seeking a means of protecting the benefits Scotland enjoys as a part of the EU even though everyone and their granny knows that nothing will happen without the collaboration and consent of Westminster, and they're not about to give it.

The surest prediction of all is that the political cracks will continue to widen between Scotland and the rest of the UK. And sooner or later, not in 2017 but certainly within the lifetimes of most of us, Scotland will be rejoining the family of independent states.

31 December 2016

Oh baby, you can't object to this box idea

You might think that giving the mother of every newborn baby in the country a box that doubles as a crib, which contains some necessities to help get the baby off to a decent start in life, would be universally seen as a good thing, a kind thing, a thing to gladden the heart of even the most cynical soul. But no, this is Scotland, and on Scottish social media those who believe that absolutely everything that the SNP does is evil managed to find reasons why it's evil to give mothers and newborns a few useful bits and pieces, a starter kit for infancy. If the SNP managed to find a way of adding fifty years of healthy life expectancy to everyone in the country, these are the same people who would complain that the Scottish government is putting hard-working undertakers and gravediggers out of work. Will no one think of the crematoria eh?

The baby box scheme is projected to cost just £6 million a year. A similar scheme has been running in Finland for seventy-five years where it has been claimed to help tackle infant mortality. The Scottish baby box was immediately criticised by the Labour Party. Although you'd have thought that a party that's dying in its own cradle might not rush to attack the scheme. Meanwhile Tory MSPs were gutted to realise that acting like infants having a tantrum on Twitter didn't make them eligible. It's outrageous, spending £6 million on a universal benefit for infants. The Tories believe we should be spending the money on sensible things instead, like renovating Buckingham Palace, renewing Trident or paying for the costs of registering foreigners after Brexit.

Like the Finnish baby box, the Scottish box contains

nappies, clothing, a changing mat, a mattress and blanket, books and other items which are essential in early infancy. The Scottish box also contains a poem in Scots by the Makar, Jackie Kay, which led some of the zoomier and froth-ier Unionists on social media to assert darkly that filling the heads of infants with linguistic propaganda is the "real" reason behind the boxes. This claim was made on the first of January, so the year had hardly started and already we'd reached peak yoonzoom. These are the people who probably believe that the only reason the Scottish government wants to tackle infant mortality is because independence support-ers tend to be younger and the more children who survive infancy the quicker it will be to outbreed the Unionists.

We can only be grateful that the baby box didn't also contain a poem in Gaelic, or NHS Scotland would have been bankrupted by the spannerbags of zoomers who required emergency treatment for apoplexy. As it was, we only had to endure those who quoted Adolf Hitler as though somehow that was a reason for the Scottish government not to assist mothers and infants, and who railed against the £6 million annual cost of the scheme. £6 million is how much it costs to install two Gaelic road signs on the A9, at least that's how much you think they cost if you're a Tory MSP in Holyrood with a burning need to feel that English monoglots are oppressed. Although it's a well-known fact amongst the spanneresque brigade that the original draft of Mein Kampf was written in Lewis Gaelic and supporting anything related to Scottish languages is just one step away from advocating genocide.

Others were outraged because the scheme is universal. Every mother of every newborn will receive a box. Somehow this was perverted in the eyes of the more vehement nawbags into an attempt by the SNP to lay claim to every Scottish child. Others thought that the baby box was just another SNP lie, because it doesn't actually contain a baby. Meanwhile the Tories are threatening to investigate whether the baby box counts as an extra bedroom for the purposes of the bedroom tax.

The claim has been made that the introduction of baby boxes in Finland helped to reduce infant mortality in that country. However the introduction of baby boxes in that country also coincided with the introduction of universal social services, universal social security benefits, a comprehensive health service accessible to all, and the extension of workers' rights and maternity rights, all of which no doubt played a vital role in reducing Finnish infant mortality to one of the lowest rates in the world. The key factor in ensuring a low rate of infant mortality is the introduction and maintenance of social democratic policies. The kind of policies, in other words, that are increasingly at threat in a Brexit Britain that's heading out of the door of Europe.

What reduces infant mortality, what reduces poor health outcomes for the disadvantaged, what reduces poverty and deprivation, is universality of social provision. Labour has abandoned its traditional commitment to universality, but when a benefit becomes means-tested it not only adds to the costs of administering the scheme, it also means that it becomes second class and low quality. The baby box scheme is a small and welcome return to universality. We're aw Jock Tamson's bairns. It's only Tories who think that means that only Jock Tamson should pay for them. Means-testing the boxes would add a fortune to the administration costs of the scheme, meaning that fewer women would receive a poorer-quality box which would then be seen as a poor box, not a baby box. It would be seen as a symbol of exclusion and deprivation, not as a symbol that all children deserve an equal welcome to the world.

Baby boxes themselves won't have a huge impact on Scottish infant mortality rates. But that's not the point. The point of baby boxes is to demonstrate that as a society we value and support new mothers and that every child in this country deserves to be valued and supported equally.

That's what baby boxes are for, and it's by continuing and developing the universalist ethos that baby boxes represent that Scotland will reduce infant mortality and give every child in this country the best start in life.

4 January 2017

There's nae need tae cringe - Scots is oor mither tongue

Earlier this week, this newspaper published its front page entirely in Scots, and provoked an outbreak of serial harrumphing on social media. Many were outraged that a respectable publication had dared to produce a front page in an unrespectable language. It's an embarrassment, they screeched, while simultaneously denying that they were embarrassed. Scotland's home-grown languages, Scots and Gaelic, are routinely dismissed, disparaged and disdained by a large segment of the Scottish population, a segment which has been educated in ignorance and taught that a lack of knowledge and awareness is something to be proud of. Scotland's languages are ground zero of the Cringe.

The most common complaint about Scots is that it's not a language at all. People whose knowledge of the science of linguistics fills a dictionary from A to Aardvark all of a sudden turn into Noam Chomsky when the subject is Scots. It's just a nationalist attempt to manufacture a language to have a grievance about, they sniff, dismissing centuries of Scots literature with an airy wave of contempt.

Linguists, people whose profession is the study of language and how it functions, have no doubt that Scots is a language and that the collection of dialects which make up the language are clearly differentiated as a group from anything else that is often regarded as English by the linguistically naive. Linguists know what is English and what isn't. Scots very clearly isn't.

The truth is that people who say that Scots is just some kind of English are as ignorant of English as they are of Scots.

Yet in Scotland, these same people wear their ignorance as a badge of pride and demand that the rest of us should be ignorant too. We live in a country where linguistic ignorance is something to aspire to, where attitudes to language formed in Victorian times are still current, where inward-looking English-language parochialism passes for cosmopolitanism.

Let's clear up one myth right away. The legal status of Scots as a language was not decided by the SNP, it was decided by the UK government at Westminster when it signed up to the European Charter for Regional or Minority Languages and included Scots as one of the languages of the UK which the British government made a legal pledge to protect. As a result of this treaty, which was signed by a Labour administration, the UK government and its agencies have a legal obligation to protect and foster the Scots language.

Most people in Scotland have some degree of passive understanding of Scots, and because they understand it but don't regard themselves as being bilingual, they assume that Scots can't be a language. Moreover, Scottish people naturally compare Scots with Scottish Standard English, a variety of English which is distinguished by the strong Scots influence it contains. These people have a faulty understanding of what bilingualism entails, but they assume that it's not their understanding that's at fault, it must be the fault of Scots.

Another common complaint is that Scots doesn't have words for important concepts like referendum, physics or government, but neither did English until they were borrowed from Latin, Greek and French, respectively. When new words are created by Scots writers, words like *wabsteid* for website, the same critics howl in derision that they're artificial words. But all literary languages are artificial. Catalan, Czech and other languages have official academies which invent new words for modern concepts. These words are every bit as artificial as Scots neologisms. New vocabulary is not magicked into being by the Vocabulary Fairy, someone sat down and created it. But Scots isn't to be allowed access to the same processes of enrichment enjoyed by any other language. The critics of Scots insist it's not a fit tongue for the modern world, and want to do all they can to ensure it stays that way.

What is killing the Scots language is snobbery and the peculiar belief that if your head is full of Scots then it prevents you from acquiring English. The reality is that the more languages you speak, the easier it becomes to acquire others, but in Scotland English-language monolingualism is regarded as praiseworthy and command of Scots is a sign that you're a ned. It seems that English is such a delicate flower that if you speak another language then you'll magically forget how to speak and write English. Speaking Scots does not prevent you from speaking good English as well. In fact a good education in Scots would help Scots kids to distinguish Scots from English, and that would improve their command of both languages. However we also have to contend with the out-and-out snobbery that if you speak a stigmatised language like Scots then you must be lacking in education. The way to improve linguistic standards is not to pander to these prejudices, it's to change them through education.

No one should be shocked that a Scottish newspaper printed its front page in a tongue that was the official language of the Scottish state during the centuries Scotland was independent, a language which is still spoken by a million and a half Scots and understood by many thousands more. What we should be shocked by is that there is not a single newspaper published in the language, that there is not a single TV or radio station devoted to broadcasting in it, that in our schools not a single subject is taught in the medium of it. That's the real Scots embarrassment, and it will continue as long as we allow our language and cultural policies to be determined by arrogant ignoramuses who believe that a dose of middle-class prejudice counts as erudition. If we want to rid ourselves of the Cringe, we need to start treating our languages with the same respect that other modern European countries grant to theirs.

9 *January 2017*

Where does Scotland stand in the UK? It doesn't

We've got a prime minister who has just announced that everyone is a Ukipper now. The concerns of the 48.1 per cent who voted to remain are ignored. Scotland is ignored. Northern Ireland is ignored. Gibraltar is ignored. We have a government that says it's striving for a deal for all, but which doesn't understand the difference between democracy and majoritarianism.

Theresa May made her Brexit speech, she closed her eyes, stuck her fingers in her ears and started singing "Rule Britannia" at the top of her voice. She's been doing that ever since. She can't hear the outraged opposition to her xenophobic Little Britain plans, nor see how the rest of the EU is laughing at the UK. And she doesn't care either. This is how she aims to achieve national unity and restore national pride. If this is supposed to make us proud to be British, Theresa May is doing a very poor job of it. The UK is an utter embarrassment.

We heard a lot about pride during the last independence referendum, although rarely from independence supporters who felt that their pride in Scotland was self-evident and so didn't feel the need to state it overtly. Saying that you want independence for your country, that you want to make your own decisions and to accept the responsibility for their consequences is an implicit declaration of pride. That's real pride, a quiet pride, the pride of confidence. It was invariably Unionists who were keen to assure us loudly and vocally how proud they were to be Scottish. Their statements that "I'm a proud Scot" were equally invariably followed by a but.

"I'm a proud Scot, but I don't think Scotland is capable of making its own way in the world." "I'm a proud Scot, but I think we're too poor to manage by ourselves." "I'm a proud Scot, but believe that uniquely amongst the countries of this world, Scotland is incapable of having a currency." "I'm a proud Scot, but my declarations of pride are a compensation mechanism for a bad case of the Cringe." If you need to tell people how proud you are, you're really just covering up for your insecurities.

Brexit has shown us exactly where Scotland stands within the UK. It has shown us that Scotland doesn't stand at all. It lies prostrate and face down, crushed by the boot of right-wing English nationalism. There can no longer be any doubt about where Scotland is in relation to the rest of the UK, the contempt and arrogance of a Tory government and its hard-as-nails Brexit has shone a harsh light on the realities of the so-called United Kingdom. It's just a veneer for a state in which Scotland counts for as much as an English local authority. The UK is not a partnership. It is not a joint project in which the four nations cooperate and collaborate. The UK means that Scotland is subsumed in English political priorities and a dying Labour Party will do nothing to help.

If Scotland wants to preserve our traditions of equality, tolerance and justice, our sense that we're all Jock Tamson's bairns and we are all collectively responsible for the well-being of society, that we must ensure that there are measures in place to assist those of us who struggle with ill health and misfortune because any one of us could be in the same position, we can only do so through independence. The UK has turned its back on the post-war social contract. Britain is the land of exploitation, of tax breaks for the rich, of public services that have been hollowed out to the point of collapse. Britain is declaring it's no longer a European country, but a poundland USA with worse food and worse weather, where the rich can live comfortably but the poor are left to fend for themselves and the working classes are low-paid and exploited. The irony is that if Scotland wants to preserve and defend the good things that the British state has created, the NHS, our public services, our education system, we can only do so with independence. Britain isn't interested in them any more.

In the next referendum let's have no more proud Scot buttery nonsense, and call it out for the pathetic cringing that it really is. Because if you genuinely believe that Scotland ought to remain a part of a post-Brexit Britain which runs roughshod over Scotland's will, you're not proud of Scotland at all. If you want Scotland to be isolated and impoverished by a mad Brexit plan to turn the UK into a tax haven for Russian oligarchs, you're not proud, because you are saying you are proud of wanting to turn Scotland into a beggar that hopes to receive a few crumbs from the Westminster table. You're declaring pride in a Scotland that's been told in no uncertain terms that its concerns, needs and desires are of no consequence in Westminster. You're saying you're proud of a Scotland whose role in the UK is to serve as the tartan window dressing which allows xenophobic English nationalists to pretend that their nationalism isn't nationalist at all. That's not pride. That's the Cringe. Real proud Scots have more self-respect.

21 January 2017

There is no fight in Jeremy Corbyn but the same can't be said for Scotland

"The real fight starts now," said Jeremy, after capitulating to the hard Tory Brexit in return for a concession that boils down to having a choice between jumping off a cliff or being pushed off it. There are rabbits frozen in headlights which have got more fight in them than Jeremy Corbyn's Labour Party. Some of those bunnies can be vicious and can give a nasty nip, which is a whole lot more than you can say for the Labour Party's ability to wound the Tories. The tragedy for the country is that Theresa May's government's Brexit position is as solid and well formed as a blancmange in a tumble drier, and yet still Labour can't make an impression on it.

The only fight Labour's got is the fight against gravity as Britain plunges on to the rocks of a hard Brexit. That's a fight they're going to lose. But hey, they can always change things as they hurtle towards their doom. The real fight starts as you flail your arms about wishing that they were wings. The real fight starts when you wonder why you didn't start it before you fell off the cliff. The real fight starts when you're lying broken and bleeding on the rocks. It's just that then you're in a fight for your life and it's a fight you can't win because you've smashed your arms and legs in the fall and the NHS has been sold off to American health corporations.

We're in a time of enormous uncertainty, but a couple of things are clear. It's clear that the Tories have morphed into UKIP and are bent on taking the UK into the hardest possible Brexit in which Scotland, along with everyone else, will be subject to the sort of right-wing regime that Liam Fox with his cold dead eyes and his compassion the size and shape of a dried-up prune that's been left under the sofa for six months daydreams about when he's cosying up to Adam Werritty. We can deregulate the labour market, whispers Liam. Which sounds very adult and grown-up except that it's code for slashing the minimum wage, abolishing statutory leave, and weakening trade unions even further. Liam's dream is to see Britain turning into a Sports Direct warehouse. And it's equally clear that Labour is as much use at protecting us from that nightmare as waving a torn plastic shopping bag will help to break your fall.

We're living in a country which has decided it's not going to give shelter to child refugees from the countries that we've bombed. We're not going to give any reassurances to EU citizens who're living here, condemning them to a life of uncertainty as pawns in a Tory game. And it's all to placate a right-wing press that was spouting fake news and alternative facts before the terms were invented. That byword for unreliability, Wikipedia, has announced that it's no longer going to accept pieces in the *Daily Mail* as sources for its articles, because the newspaper is too unreliable. We've got an unreliable source that does care banning an unreliable source that doesn't. Not even *Russia Today* or *Fox News* have been banned by Wikipedia. That puts the Brexit cheerleaders in the same category as *The Chronicles of Narnia* as a record of fact. But that's fair enough, because Narnia is where the Brexiteers have been telling us we're heading. Right into the dungeons of the Ice Queen's palace where it's winter every day.

Meanwhile there are reports that Theresa May's government is making plans to fight a second independence referendum. It's likely to go along the lines of, "Scotland, it's true that we lied to you all the way through the independence campaign. We told you the only way you could ensure your continuing membership of the EU was by voting No. We told you that Scotland was going to be an equal partner in this family of nations, and that you would always be listened to and would always have a voice. We promised you all sorts of things that never got delivered, but I'm sure we can agree that everything that has happened is the fault of the SNP. Because they're bad. The stepson of the third cousin of Nicola Sturgeon's husband's sister's ex-husband's former neighbour once taunted a homeless man, what more proof do you need?

"Anyway, there's the possibility that we might be open to discussing the chance of having talks about ideas for what we could suggest that could be on the table in the future. We're calling it devo-phantomax because it doesn't really exist. So... can I put you down for a No vote then?"

Or you can decide that the real fight for Scotland starts now. We can take the moral high ground, although to be fair when we look down into the selfish sink where British policymakers are taking us that's not very difficult. Life in Brexit Britain is like living in the BBC *Question Time* audience, jeering at migrants, the poor and Scots, with a grinning Ukipper at the top table.

The real fight is between a Scotland that makes its own decisions, a Scotland that's open to the world and which knows the difference between morality and a headline in a right-wing tabloid, or a Scotland that meekly does what it's told while its people are impoverished, its resources drained off and its wealth squandered on the bonfire of British nationalist vanity while we turn our backs on the homeless in our streets and starving children in countries that our armed forces have helped destroy. The real fight is a fight between humiliation and dignity. Let's choose the dignity of making our own decisions.

11 February 2017

Cynical Unionist word play is fooling no-one

That's us telt then. Supporting Scottish independence and wanting an escape from the xenophobic madness of Brexit is exactly the same as snuggling up in your bed at night with a nice cup of cocoa and a copy of Mein Kampf. So said Sadiq Khan and opinionistas in the Guardian, so it must be true. How dare white Scottish people object when an Asian guy says something about racism?

Only those white Scottish people were not rubbishing what Sadiq Khan or some random *Guardian* columnist had to say about racism, they were rubbishing what was said about Scottish nationalism. That part got lost in the British Unionist moral outrage. There are no bounds to the shameless hypocrisy of supporters of the British state, they decry an open inclusive Scottish indy movement that welcomes migrants and refugees, and say nothing about a xenophobic and nasty British state that is basing its entire future on a desire to put up walls against foreigners.

The condemnation is based upon a simple trick of words. The English language lacks the nuances that other languages possess when it comes to discussing independence movements. I'm fluent in Spanish, and when discussing Scottish politics with my Spanish-speaking friends I would never describe myself as a *nacionalista escocés*. The Spanish term *nacionalista* calls to mind a nasty right-wing authoritarianism. It suggests someone who believes in the moral and political superiority of their own particular ethnicity. The party of the late dictator Franco were the *nacionalistas*. This is the kind of nationalism that Unionists want us to associate with the Scottish independence movement. It's why one of the most common jibes against independence supporters is that nats equal Nazis. It's why, during the first independence referendum campaign, the *Scotsman* newspaper printed that shameful photograph of a saltire that had been photoshopped with a swastika.

It's a straw man argument. The overwhelmingly dominant force in the drive for Scottish self-determination is the political opposite of what Francisco Franco stood for, it is social democratic, progressive, left-wing, democratic, and it celebrates its diversity. Mainstream Scottish nationalism doesn't make the claim that the Scottish ethnicity is morally superior or better than anyone else. It doesn't even concern itself with defining Scottishness in ethnic terms. Scottish nationalism is a civic nationalism which defines Scottishness in terms of the future not the past. Ethnic nationalism is about the past. It's about who you are descended from. Civic nationalism is about the future. It's about welcoming everyone who wants to share in the journey that Scotland can take as a country. Scottish nationalism seeks the establishment of a Scottish state. It is nationalist only in so far as it recognises the existence of a Scottish nation, which is a bit like saying that recognising the existence of matter makes you a materialist.

In Spanish espousing this kind of politics doesn't make you a *nacionalista*, it makes you an *independentista escocés*. Sadly however, if you try to call yourself by the closest direct equivalent in English and say you're an independentist, people just ask you how much you charge for orthodontic work. But the fact that the English language happens to conflate two very different political ideologies under the same term, "nationalism", doesn't mean that the two share anything much in common.

English, like most languages, contains many words which have different and sometimes contradictory meanings. It's rather like the word "bolt", which also has two very different and contradictory meanings. Bolt can mean to secure, or to flee. Left can mean remaining or departed. To be a peer can mean that you are someone's equal, or it can mean that you've been given the legal power to lord it over the rest of us, don fancy costumes and continue to influence our laws even though no one voted for you. Just ask Michael Forsyth.

Dust can mean to wipe away fine particles, or to cover something in small particles. The one word contains opposite meanings, but if your maw tells you to dust the living room and instead you open up a bag of flour and scatter it all over her new rug you'll soon discover that there's a very big difference indeed. That's exactly what those who equate Scottish nationalism with fascism are doing though. They scatter a bag of ground-up dried crap all over Scottish politics and claim that they're cleaning.

Words which contain contradictory meanings are called contronyms, and in English the word "nationalism" comes very close to meeting that definition. A political movement which is seeking a state for a country which currently doesn't have a state and which doesn't have the political powers associated with statehood is a very different creature from a political movement which seeks the aggrandisement of an ethnicity which already possesses a state and the full range of political powers that go along with statehood. The arguments of Unionism very often depend upon convincing us that the different definitions of the English word "nationalism" are indeed describing the exact same phenomenon. It's just a cheap trick of words that comes from people who are either unaware that they're confusing two distinct phenomena or, more worryingly, just don't care.

The word "nationalism" isn't the only political contronym in English. There's also the term "Labour Party". Labour can mean to work very hard, but in politics it refers to a party which achieves nothing at all. Conserve means to keep something the same, but Conservative means to rip up social protections and kick away a disabled person's crutches while telling them to stand on their own two feet.

And then there is the greatest contronym of all. There's the brutish xenophobic nationalism of the British state and its desire to define itself by its hatred of migrants, and those who defend it with lies, deception and mendacity deny that they are nationalists at all. British nationalism is the nationalism that doesn't exist at all despite the bunting-bedecked military parades and its royalism and arrogant belief in its own exceptionalism. The real racism that Scotland faces is the racism of Brexit.

In plain and simple language, the British state and its supporters are terrified, because they know that their precious nationalist state is in its final days. And the days of the British state are numbered because of the actions and inactions of those selfsame British nationalists who think they don't exist.

1 March 2017

Empire 2.0 drive takes the biscuit
when it comes to delusion

Liam Fox, whose official title is the Disgraced Minister of State for Adam Werritty, has an ambitious plan to strike trade deals with former British colonies after Brexit. Sadly for Liam, his amnesia about the evils of Empire has led him to believe that former British colonies hold some measure of affection for the UK, instead of remembering that the reason so much of the map was coloured red was because of all the blood that Britain spilled. His plan to strike trade deals with Commonwealth countries has been dubbed Empire 2.0 by sceptical civil servants who've got a rather more realistic view of the world than the one Liam sees through his Union Jack-tinted sunglasses.

We now have a government whose idea of the post-Brexit future of the UK is the plot of *Star Wars*. Liam is clearly angling for the role of ruthless trader Jabba the Hutt, although rumour has it that it has already been promised to Michael Gove since he would need to spend far less time in make-up. Naturally the idea of Empire 2.0 was thoroughly ridiculed on social media. The Empire Strikes Flak, you could say. Britain is now very firmly in the grip of the dark side of the farce. This sort of nostalgic apology for racism is at the heart of every Brexit proposal.

Liam said recently that the UK is the only country in Europe which doesn't need to bury its twentieth-century history, drawing a convenient cut-off date that allows him to quietly bury all the genocide, mass murder, exploitation, rape, despoliation, pillage and destruction that Britain was responsible for in the centuries that went before. You know, trivial little things like the Irish Famine, the genocide of Native Australians, the reduction of India from one of the richest countries in the world to one of the poorest, the theft of land and resources from Africa, and other tiny wee instances of things that don't sully the history of Britain as long as you look the other way and ignore them.

The history of Britain in the twentieth century however, well that's just grand. It's unsullied. It's a spotless record of bunting-bedecked good, unlike that of the shameful Danes, Swedes or Czechs. Well, Britain's twentieth-century history is absolutely impeccable as long as you overlook the Amritsar Massacre, or the Bengal Famine of 1943, when the British authorities chose to believe that there was plenty of food available in Bengal despite abundant evidence to the contrary, leading to the deaths of between 1.5 and 4 million people. Then there's the Irish and Indian partitions, white rule in South Africa, concentration camps and torture in Kenya, the mass deportation of the Chagos Islanders, institutionalised sectarianism in Northern Ireland as a means of maintaining British rule, setting off the chain of events that has led to the Israel-Palestine dispute, and on and on in a litany of disgrace that would make any serious student of British history acknowledge that the UK has no moral high ground from which to lecture anyone.

Britain was of course very much on the side of the good guys in WWII, but then we were up against your actual Nazis. Citing Britain's role against Hitler as evidence of the UK's unalloyed goodness is a bit like claiming that you're really a good guy despite the fact you're a serial wife beater who made a living stealing bread from the mouths of orphans because you once helped to beat up a child abuser.

Empire 2.0, the Revenge of the Brexsith, comes in the week that Indian historian and politician Shashi Tharoor publishes a new book called *Inglorious Empire*, which critically examines Britain's imperial and colonial past. It's a story that isn't taught in British schools, and it's a story of exploitation, theft and atrocities. Liam Fox is the perfect exemplar of the historical amnesia that Shashi Tharoor describes.

It's not just that Liam's Empire 2.0 plan is ridiculous because it is deaf to historical truths, it's also ridiculous because it is blind to modern economic and political realities. The Commonwealth countries with which Liam seeks preferential trade deals used to have preferential deals with the UK, but then the UK left them high and dry when we joined the EU. Those countries now have their own trade deals with the EU, and they're not about to put their access to a market of 500 million people at risk in order to do a favour for an old colonial master which has done them few favours. The British Empire was the opposite of the free trade that Liam claims to espouse. It was an exercise in creating captive markets, and imposing duties and tariffs on colonised nations in order to enrich Britain.

Apparently the British High Commission in Commonwealth countries is now to seek preferential trade deals saying, "Yes, we're terribly sorry about all those massacres but they were just a misunderstanding. We're sorry about abandoning you when we joined the EU, but do have some innovative jam and cake. The French love our cakes, no, really. Oh don't worry about that Empire 2.0 thing, we just meant it like the biscuit."

Britain's attempt to seek preferential trade deals with countries it once colonised and exploited is symptomatic of Brexit. The entire exercise is an exercise in Empire nostalgia, a hankering back for the days when Britannia ruled the waves. That power was built on the backs of the poor and dispossessed of the colonies, and the poor and oppressed in working-class slums within the UK. Tories like Liam seek to bring it back and call it "free trade". He might be a historical illiterate, his problem is that the rest of us aren't. The Empire is dead and so are the UK's pretensions to be anything other than a middle-sized European nation with very limited influence. The harsh realities of Brexit will expose that. The emperors of Brexit have no clothes.

8 March 2017

The Tories' benighted kingdom
will be a dark, dark place

It's the weekend of the SNP party conference, and Theresa May has made a preemptive strike to tell Scotland that we can't have an independence referendum until it suits her, because she's got a plan for us. The plan is that Scotland will be bought and sold for English innovative jam, there's no gold any more. At least it looked like Theresa May, although it could very well be a waxwork figure from Madame Tussauds with a tape recording stuck on a loop. It's very difficult to tell the difference with Theresa. All you get are sound bites on repeat.

This means we're forced to translate Theresese into human language. When Theresa May, or her waxwork figure, says there can be no Scottish referendum so that she can ensure that Britain can get the best Brexit deal, what she means is that she needs Scotland's resources so she can sell them out. If Scotland is having a referendum, it will be much harder for Theresa to trade away Scotland's fisheries in return for access to the European Single Market for the financial sector of the City of London. The EU will curtly inform her that the fish aren't hers to bargain away. And Theresa will reply with "Brexit means Brexit. Now is not the time. I've been very clear."

Theresa wants Scotland to wait until after Brexit is completed so that EU citizens won't have a vote. It's a means of gerrymandering the vote in order to produce an outcome that's more favourable to the Union. We cannot allow the Conservatives with the xenophobic narrow-minded nationalism to tell Scotland who can or cannot have a view on Scotland's future. That's a choice that must be made by all who live in Scotland, whether they are Scots, English, Welsh or Northern Irish or from anywhere else in the EU. And if I had my way I'd allow non-EU citizens resident in Scotland to vote as well. Everyone who has chosen to throw their lot in with Scotland is Scottish. Britishness is restrictive and nostalgic, Scottishness is open and it looks to the future.

The Conservatives are lying to us, yet again. The proposal is that Scotland has another referendum after the Brexit deal is struck, but before it is ratified by the parliaments of the twenty-seven EU members. We will know by then what sort of deal is on offer. The Tories want to delay the vote until it's too late.

Theresa has just inadvertently told us what the new name of the United Kingdom is going to be after Scotland leaves. It will be the Benighted Kingdom, because Theresa's taking it into the darkness. Her intransigence has just made it all the more likely that Scotland will vote for independence when a referendum is finally held.

There was us thinking that it was just David Cameron who loved pig-headedness, but it seems that Theresa enjoys it too, at least metaphorically if not literally as in the case of her predecessor. There's a word for a politician who doesn't have a mandate who blocks a politician who does have a mandate, and that word is "despot". Actually there are a number of words. There's "Fluffy Huffy", in the case of our governor general, the not so honourable Member of Parliament for beard-snacking and foot-stamping. And there's "rank hypocrite", in the case of a Ruth Davidson who said not so long ago, on more than one occasion, that if there is a majority in the Scottish parliament for a second referendum then there is a clear mandate for that referendum. But the Unionist media isn't about to call out Ruth for making more U-turns than a slinky, even though like a slinky her rhetoric only takes her downwards. Ruth and Fluffy keep telling us that a majority of Scots don't want a referendum, but a majority of Scots don't want Tories telling us what to do and that doesn't seem to shut them up.

What makes May's action all the more arrogant is that she can't actually prevent Scotland from having a vote. She only thinks that she can. However there are other paths to a referendum that don't require Theresa's permission. Holyrood only requires Westminster's consent to a Section 30 Order to make a referendum legally binding. There is nothing to prevent it pressing ahead with a consultative referendum. The EU referendum was also a consultative referendum, and once a clear result is produced it takes on a political imperative of its own.

Alternatively there can be early elections for a Scottish parliament, and those elections can be turned into a plebiscite on independence. That would require close collaboration between the SNP, the Greens and the rest of the independence movement. It would throw up some very difficult questions for the Labour Party, do they throw their lot in with the Tories, or do they fight for Scotland?

If a Conservative government with a single solitary MP in Scotland continues to block the democratic will of a Scottish parliament enacting a clear manifesto commitment, the Scottish government should make it clear that it will pursue a referendum regardless. This isn't about Nicola Sturgeon. This isn't about the SNP. This is about democracy in Scotland, and whether we will consent to it all being traduced by a Westminster government which has the support of less than a quarter of Scottish voters.

Watch and learn Theresa. Scotland's going to teach you how democracy is done. One way or another Scotland will have its say, and May's arrogance and high-handedness only make it more likely that when Scotland does vote again, it will vote to leave this Benighted Kingdom. Scotland holds the cards here, not Westminster.

18 March 2017

Theresa May – the ideologue without any ideas

Theresa May came to Scotland, and according to preliminary reports she was going to offer Scotland some special temporary powers which we were assured were going to be so fabulous that we'd all decide that there was no point in pursuing that self-determination lark. Who needs independence when you can have a handful of temporary powers, said no one ever. Who needs self-determination when we have Theresa's determination eh?

Sadly it turned out that the only special power on offer was the power of invisibility, which is the exact same special power that Scotland got granted after the 2014 referendum. But now is not the time for that superpower. Now is not the time for talking about a second referendum, said Theresa, talking about a second referendum. Now is not the time for tautological sound bites. Now is not the time for a prime minister who comes to Scotland on a PR exercise and says absolutely nothing of any substance at all. Now *is* the time for meaningless buzzwords, but then it's always the time for those with Theresa.

We're supposed to be getting a Brexit deal that's so good that we won't want independence. Which is as inviting and tempting an offer as telling us that we'll have a swimming-with-sharks experience that's so great that we won't need a metal cage. But then it's senseless to expect sense from Theresa May. Our prime minister says she comes in search of consensus with the Scottish government. And that is true, but only if you redefine "consensus" to mean "give up on your mandate, forget the policies which you were elected on, abandon your voters and do exactly what I tell you".

There was precious little in the way of a search for consensus. All we got were a few new variations on Theresa's favourite gnomic tropes, although no reporter was brave, or foolhardy enough, to ask her what Brexit means Brexit actually means. We did learn that now is still not the time, and that now is not the time for telling us when she thinks the time is, and that's a sentence which makes more sense than anything that came out of Theresa's gob on her visit to Scotland.

The Union is still precious, which seemingly means that she wants to lock Scotland in an airless vault and keep the key herself. And we got a new one, the Union of the four nations of the United Kingdom is an unstoppable force. Although Theresa told us nothing about the purpose to which that force is directed, other than a headlong rush off a Brexit cliff. Although we all know that the unstoppable force is directed by Theresa all by herself. She told us nothing about the constitutional crisis that's going to happen when Theresa's unstoppable force meets the immovable objections of Nicola Sturgeon and a Scottish parliament vote for a second referendum. Nothing that is, other than more tautological and content-free sound bites. It takes a very real political skill to make David Cameron seem statesmanlike and serious, but Theresa May managed just that. She's a rare and special breed of politician, an ideologue without any ideas.

She delivered her collection of vacuities in front of a captive audience of civil servants in the Department for International Development in East Kilbride, who were allegedly told by their managers beforehand to applaud her. Their faces said it all though. They looked like they'd far rather be sitting through a seminar on reinforced concrete, complete with a video of it drying. Reinforced concrete has better listening skills than the prime minister. After the speech, her staff issued a press release tagged from "East Kilbridge", and then they wonder why people say she's out of touch with Scotland.

Kilbridge, for those as geographically challenged as the prime minister's office, is just outside Basildon. Perhaps they were just longing to be in Basildon because they'd have felt more welcome.

East Kilbride is the same town where thousands of civil servants had jobs in the tax office, jobs which we were told would only be safe if Scotland voted No in 2014. So Scotland voted No and the jobs went anyway. It's hardly surprising the workers in the DFID had to be instructed to applaud. It was a speech with no substance, no details, no plans, no ideas, just a collection of assertions and empty assurances about how important Theresa's Union is to Theresa. She was so interested in engagement and discussion that she didn't take any questions.

The swimming with the Brexit sharks doesn't seem any more attractive than it did before she came to Scotland. The only reason she bothered was so that she could make like she is paying heed to Scottish concerns, so she can tell her supporters that she's listening and consulting when she's merely going through the motions. There she was, delivering a speech about the importance of a union, how we are stronger together, how we are interconnected, just before she triggers the process of leaving a union. But then Theresa's only interested in unions in which she gets to be in charge. But we're being ungracious. It was terribly thoughtful of her to tour the constituent parts of the UK to tell us that we're getting a hard Brexit whether we like it or not. If only she'd bothered earlier.

After her lecture to the bored civil servants of not-Basildon, Theresa had a meeting with Nicola Sturgeon in which she did an impression of Darth Vader trying to persuade Luke to the dark side of the Brexit farce. Nicola gave her one of those typically Scottish "Aye. Right. Ye think so?" looks in return, and that was about as close as minds got to meeting.

The much-hyped new powers came to nothing at all. Theresa blew her last chance to save her precious union. Her visit was a PR exercise designed to allow her to pretend that she's listening and consulting, when she came to lecture and command. The unstoppable force was stopped in its tracks, and the Scottish parliament voted for a second independence referendum, because when an unstoppable force meets an immovable object, it's the immovable object which always wins.

29 March 2017

Repeal Bill may well be Act
of Union's death knell

We've finally been thrown off the Brexit cliff by our prime minister, and if you can hear a whooshing sound it's the attempt to explain the disastrous consequences going straight over Theresa's head. But Theresa doesn't care, because Brexit gives the office of the prime minister the opportunity to make the greatest power grab in history. When Theresa speaks about taking back control, it's her own control that she's got in mind.

Just one day after Brexit, when the Tories were telling us to celebrate Britain's taking back power, we discovered that they're introducing legislation that will enable them to take back power from Scotland, and from everyone who isn't Theresa. The Great Repeal Bill is so called because it's really about repealing any opposition to Theresa May. When she stood up this week in the House of Commons and said that she would represent every person in the UK, she meant it. She meant that whatever she decided would represent everyone else.

The Great Repeal Bill contains a provision for what's called Henry VIII powers, which basically means giving the prime minister and her cabinet appointees the right to chop the heads off laws and pillage the ministries. Without having to bother themselves with parliamentary scrutiny or oversight, the government will be able to change legislation. This is what taking back control means in practice. It means the final transformation of the UK into an elective dictatorship, and moreover one in which the elections are carried out according to an unrepresentative system. And then the

Tories will cheat the electoral process anyway.

Scotland certainly won't be taking back any control if Theresa and her little helpers in Holyrood have anything to do with it. But then she had to be reminded during PMQs that Scotland is actually a country. Theresa and her pals don't want to allow Scotland a say. It's unfair, say the architects of an unplanned and chaotic Brexit, to ask Scots to vote before every single consequence of Brexit has played itself out. They may deign to permit Scotland to have a vote, sometime in the unspecified future long after Brexit has reduced us all to living in caves, but in the new taking back control UK it's the party that came a very distant second in the Holyrood elections which has the control. But even then they'll only countenance another vote if it can be proven beyond any doubt that there are still some straight bananas in Asda.

All the Unionist parties are quite definite about the rectitude of bananas as the only fair way of judging whether Scots have all the information about Brexit that they require, although to be fair UKIP hasn't voiced an opinion as they've been far too busy with their commitments to the BBC. UKIP don't do very well at elections, but they do have one safe seat. That's the one on the panel of BBC *Question Time*.

For Scotland, the Great Repeal Bill is all about repealing Scotland's ability to resist Brexit. For all that the Conservatives say that there could be more powers for Holyrood after Brexit, these are the same people who refuse to recognise the legitimacy of a vote in the Scottish parliament. They want us to trust them to deliver more power to a parliament that they don't believe in.

The Westminster government insists that it's not going to take powers back from Holyrood, but the reality is that if it does not repatriate all the devolved powers currently exercised by Brussels then it's doing just that. A power that is not specifically reserved to Westminster is a devolved power, that's what the Scotland Act says. If Westminster unilaterally decides to retain any of those powers for itself, it is effectively taking power back from Scotland. It is a Westminster power grab which weakens and undermines the Scottish parliament. And Westminster will not engage in any negotiations with Scotland about which powers it seeks to retain. Scotland will get the leftovers from the table after Westminster has decided what it wants to keep for itself. So much for all the extra powers that Leavers promised Scotland during the EU referendum campaign. They're going the exact same way as all the extra powers and security within the EU that Scotland was promised in return for a No vote in 2014.

As Mark Elliott, professor of public law at the University of Cambridge, points out, the Great Repeal Bill gives "no guarantee that repatriated EU powers will go to devolved institutions, even in relation to subject areas that are currently devolved". He adds, "Implication seems to be *new* reserved matters will be carved out of existing devolution settlements. Raises some questions of constitutional politics."

In order to retain these powers, Westminster will have to make changes to the Scotland Act, and to the equivalent legislation in Wales and Northern Ireland because according to existing law these powers should automatically come to the devolved parliaments. The devolved administrations will certainly refuse to give consent, and while Westminster has the legal power to overrule them, it puts the final nail in the coffin of the idea that Scotland's consent is a vital part of its government within the UK. The Great Repeal Bill will go down in history as the beginning of the repeal of the Treaty of Union. Unionists might think it's an April Fool for Scotland, but in the longer term the joke will be on them.

1 April 2017

I told you so: the 'Spanish veto' was always a myth

It's funny how things change. Just a week ago, Spanish Prime Minister Mariano Rajoy was the guy who was going to save the Union. He was the superhero with the superpower, he was Vetoman, and he was going to shoot across the grey Scottish skies telling us "Naw, ye cannae", only in Spanish, if we continued to have ideas above our lowly North British station about joining the European Union in our own right. Yet here we are, just a few days into the Brexit negotiations, and already Spain has ripped several key pages out of the British Unionist Big Book of Scary Stories, and now it's a UK's Brexit that includes Gibraltar that faces a Spanish veto while the country has confirmed that it won't veto a Scottish application to join the EU.

Spain's announcement was a red rag to some British bull. Temper tantrum Unionists on social media and their slightly more grown-up representatives in politics were outraged and left clutching at the straw that the Spanish foreign minister Alfonso Dastis had said, at least in some English translations of his comments, that there would be no "automatic" veto of Scotland. The actual phrase he used in Spanish was *de entrada*, which means "to start with". What his words really meant was that Spain would treat the Scottish application just like the application of any other state. Spain will still veto Scotland! The Unionist trolls insisted, despite the fact that Spain had just said it wouldn't.

But it's a tough gig being a Unionist these days, one by one it's the Tories who have destroyed every single argument that was wielded by the Better Together campaign in 2014 – the safety of the UK economy, gone, the stability of the pound, gone, job security, gone, EU membership, gone, the NHS, going. So to see the Spanish veto threat argument destroyed by someone who's not actually a British Tory was a bit of a kick in the cojones.

Tory MEP Ian Duncan was reduced to plaintively arguing that it had never been about a Spanish veto of Scottish membership at all, despite the fact he'd been arguing just a couple of weeks previously that we faced that very threat. But at least he was arguing from some semblance of reality, even if it was a reality that was 180 degrees opposed to the reality he'd been arguing for previously. This was very unlike the Lib Dems' Wullie Rennie, who had the misfortune to publish a piece in a Scottish national newspaper warning of the Spanish veto on the very day that the Spanish foreign minister confirmed that there was no such veto. There's yer Lib Dems there, with their finger on the pulse of politics.

The news was presented in many Unionist outlets as a change in Spain's position. It's only a change in position if you have spent the last couple of years interpreting everything that comes out of Spain through the prism of "a blow for Nicola Sturgeon". In fact it was no change at all. Spain is now merely making explicit what anyone who has been paying attention to what Spanish politicians really say has known all along. Spanish politicians have always said that the cases of Scotland and Catalonia are entirely distinct. The Spanish veto story was always a myth, invented by Unionist politicians and gleefully repeated by Unionist journalists who failed in the very first principles of journalism. And then they wring their hands and wonder why people are losing faith in the media. There was never any prospect of a Spanish veto of Scottish membership of the EU, I said as much in the pages of this newspaper back in July 2016. It's not Scotland that needed to fear a Spanish veto, it was any Brexit deal that involved Gibraltar.

The veto power that Spain now has over the status of

Gibraltar has provoked the ire of British nationalists outside of Scotland. All weekend pundits and politicians lined up to say how unexpected it was. The genuinely surprising thing is that they were genuinely surprised by something that anyone who had been paying attention had seen coming. The then Spanish foreign minister José Manuel García-Margallo had warned of a veto over Gibraltar last year. The only thing it proves is that the British establishment and its media apologists aren't paying attention. I've spent the entire week going "Told you so. Told you so. Told you. Told you. Told you so". Which at least makes me marginally more mature than the Unionists, if no one else.

A politician who threatens war with Spain over Gibraltar is acting like a toddler who's worried about losing a toy that they never play with anyway. In the few days since Brexit was triggered, we've had Theresa May taking on the powers of an absolute monarch with her Great Repeal Bill and the so-called Henry VIII powers it confers on the government. And then over the weekend we've had threats of war with Spain. It's all terribly sixteenth century. In the sixteenth century Scotland was an independent state, so if that's where the UK is heading perhaps independence supporters shouldn't be too upset about it. We can escape to the twenty-first century as an independent state. The madness that has befallen the UK makes Scottish independence more necessary than ever.

The EU doesn't do things without gaining the agreement of its member states, so it's significant that the Gibraltar veto was enshrined in the EU's official response to Theresa May's Brexit letter. The truth is that the other twenty-six EU member countries really don't care much one way or the other about Gibraltar. It's not their issue. The fact that Spain has got them to agree to make it one of the core EU demands was certainly bought at a price. I've got no more information about the inner workings of the EU than anyone else, but it would not surprise me if part of that price was making sure that Spain isn't obstructionist on the question of Scottish independence. It's very much in the interests of the EU to ensure that the British negotiating position is as weak as possible, and now when Theresa May attempts to sell out Scotland's fisheries, or any other Scottish asset, the EU can say that those assets may soon not be hers to negotiate away. And that's the other great change, it's no longer Scotland that needs to worry about threats from the EU.

5 April 2017

Want to waste your local election vote?
Then back the indyref-obsessed Tories

The cooncil elections are coming up, and we get a vote on the make-up of the bodies who're going to be in charge of local issues. The Tories have have a carefully and rigorously thought-out set of policies about every area of local government competence. They've got local policies for local people. Well no, actually, that's as much a lie as the statement that Theresa May is listening to the concerns of the Scottish parliament or that Michael Gove isn't really the mutant offspring of a guppy and the Winston Churchill fan club. The truth is that the Tories' local election policy begins and ends with fighting the entire campaign on the basis of opposing that referendum that they're always accusing other people of being obsessed with.

The reason it's wrong for anyone else to be obsessed with the referendum is because that's what the Tories are for. Opposing the referendum is the day job for Scottish Tories. that's why they're constantly demanding that Nicola Sturgeon gets back to her day job, because they feel that they've pretty much got the referendum thing covered all by themselves. They don't have any other job, with the possible exception of getting all apoplectic when confronted with the sight of Gaelic signage. If you give a Tory a railway station sign with "second referendum" painted on it in Gaelic, their head will explode. That's a true fact too. And I'm strongly tempted to try it, just to see what happens.

Voting for a local cooncillor because they're going to oppose a second Scottish independence referendum is a bit like voting for an X Factor contestant because they're opposed

85

to a referendum on the monarchy. The X *Factor* contestant would probably have a greater influence on whether a referendum is held than a Tory cooncillor in North Berwick, because they do get on the telly and could at least croon about it. All the Tories know how to do is crow, and that's never going to make the top ten of the download list from Spotify. Jackson Carlaw, Murdo Fraser and Oliver Mundell would be the worst boy band in the world, Naw Direction. Tory cooncillors only ever get on the telly when they've been convicted of something, and even then it's only for a five-second mention on *Reporting Scotland* because it doesn't do to dwell on the shortcomings of Unionists. Dwelling on the shortcomings of the SNP is far more important.

The Tories want to turn the Scottish council elections into a referendum on a referendum, because they don't have any policies that anyone outwith the comments section of the *Scotsman* newspaper might find remotely appealing. The Scottish Tories begin and end with opposing a referendum, and opposing the SNP. That doesn't mean that they've got any alternatives to the SNP, it's enough to say that the SNP are bad without bothering their not-so-pretty little heads with anything that amounts to substance.

Or at least they don't want the rest of us to consider their substance, because that substance is pretty rank. Tory substance is supporting the rape clause. Tory substance is denying child support to third children. Tory substance is demonising the poor and blaming them for problems created by the rich. So they prefer to concentrate on criticism, without saying what they'd do differently. It's better to concentrate on criticising your opponents because it means people might not realise that you are in fact the incarnation of Satan. Or at least Satan's love child with a goldfish, in the case of Michael Gove.

Take the recent chorus of manufactured outrage about Nicola Sturgeon's trip to the USA. It coincided with the release of figures showing that the UK economy in Scotland wasn't performing as well as the UK economy in London. This is of course entirely the fault of the Scottish government, despite the fact that the Tories and the other Unionist parties have done their utmost to ensure that the levers of macroeconomic control remain firmly in the hands of Westminster. This is why it's misleading to speak about the Scottish economy, and it's far more accurate to talk about the UK economy in Scotland. The poor performance of the UK economy in Scotland was the cue for Unionist after Unionist to line up and demand that Nicola Sturgeon return from the USA and get back to the day job. Although since Holyrood is in recess for Easter, the day job means MSPs being on holiday and sitting at home trying to get to the next level of *Minecraft* on PlayStation. To be fair, this is the closest that a Tory MSP ever gets to doing anything constructive. It's either that or making eejits out of themselves on Twitter.

One after another, Unionist politicians and their media backers lined up to harrumph that Nicola Sturgeon should get back to Scotland and concentrate on the day job and focus on the state of the UK economy in Scotland. Yet, surprise, surprise, not one of them were able to give a single concrete suggestion about what she should do to improve the UK economy in Scotland, other than forgetting about another independence referendum. Because in Unionistland, the uncertainty that Scotland faces is entirely about the prospect of another indyref, and nothing whatsoever to do with the great unmentionable, the looming catastrophe of Brexit. Complaining about the uncertainty of another independence referendum while ignoring Brexit is a bit like getting angry about the rescue helicopter while you're dangling off a cliff on a rapidly fraying rope.

Labour at least has the fantasy fig leaf of federalism, but the Scottish Tories are a single-policy party, and that policy is making an angry face whenever anyone mentions a second independence referendum. So if you want to waste your vote in the coonceil elections, vote Tory. They don't want you to vote on local issues, they don't want you to vote on rubbish collections, dog mess, local schools, local planning decisions, the state of your parks or libraries. They want you to use your vote to say that you don't want a say on your country's future, or indeed on anything else. They want you to use your vote as a meaningless gesture that won't make the slightest bit of difference, because that's what the Tories see Scotland as – a meaningless place that doesn't make the slightest bit of difference. Vote Tory, vote to be irrelevant. It's quite appropriate really.

12 April 2017

Theresa May is dressing up cruelty as Christianity ... this election is when we say enough is enough

It was Easter weekend, the holiest time in the Christian calendar, and our Conservative prime minister took the opportunity to preach at us about the message of the god that she worships. Presumably that would be the one who said blessed are the poor, for they shall inherit a benefits sanction, blessed are the disabled, for they shall have their mobility cars taken away from them, but blessed above all are the high earners, for they shall get a tax break that allows their private-school-attending children to get extra riding lessons and a second skiing holiday this year. But what she didn't tell us was that she was planning another general election on the back of a broken Labour Party in order to silence critics within her own party.

Blessed are the Tories, for they have a crushing majority in England in the opinion polls. This general election isn't about uniting the country, it's about uniting the Tory Party. It gives May the chance to kill off the Conservative Remainers for good and to secure an unassailable majority in a supine Westminster. She doesn't want to unite the country by achieving consensus, she wants to unite it by crushing all opposition, and Scotland is a part of that opposition. There's little that's Christian about her politics.

In the *Gospel According to Theresa May* it says, "And Jesus said: So I say unto you, ask and it shall be given to you; search, and ye shall find; knock, and the door shall be open for you. Except if thou art a disabled benefits claimant, for thou canst take a hike after Theresa hath kicked away thy crutches.

And thou canst take those rape victims and their children with thee as well. For verily this government is united in its determination to get a rich man's camel through the eye of a needle and the rest of you can put up and shut up. For yeah, if we put our fingers in our ears we cannot hear the protests and can tell ourselves that the country is united." That would be the same gospel in which, when it said "suffer little children", Theresa thought it was a commandment. There's a special place in Hell for politicians who dress up cruelty as Christianity.

Theresa is not only reading some version of the gospels that no one else has ever seen, she also seemed to be suffering from the after-effects of a hallucinatory Easter egg. The whole country, opined Theresa, is united in striving to get the best from Brexit. To which the tiny number of people who had made it through Theresa's robotic delivery and were still awake screamed, "No it isn't!" at the telly. Wild buffaloes ridden by Ruth Davidson could not compel most people in Scotland to get behind Theresa May, except possibly if it was to shove her Brexit bus off a cliff, taking her offensive and inhumane policies with it.

The general election to be held in June will give the people of Scotland their chance to have their say on the Tory Party. Despite trying for the past four years to present herself as a caring compassionate modern Conservative who's put the nasty party label to rest, Ruth Davidson and the Scottish Tories have been revealed themselves to be – in all their obnoxious and inhumane horror – apologists for and supporters of the same heartless inhumanity that the Tories have always stood for.

Not only does Ruth refuse to condemn the abhorrent rape clause, forcing women who've been victims of sexual assault to go into the details of their abuse with a potentially unsympathetic and untrained DWP official, she had the sheer gall to try and take the moral high ground, claiming that it was up to the Scottish government to mitigate the policy as though that somehow absolved her party from introducing it in the first place. Now Ruth's name is forever linked with the rape clause. In June if you vote Tory, it's a vote for cruelty.

All that is bad enough, but May's council elections have seen a series of Conservative candidates exposed as supporters or former supporters of some very unpleasant far-right politics. For one candidate to have been revealed as such would have been unfortunate, two would have been embarrassing, three a bit of a PR disaster. But when it's eight or nine or more, it says that there's something systematically wrong at the heart of Tory selection policy. It says that the party finds a far-right past to be perfectly acceptable in its candidates. It says that the Tories seek to normalise the divisive and nasty xenophobia of the likes of UKIP. And then they decry independence supporters as divisive for wanting to engage in civil politics.

In need of something to distract the media from the fact that the Tories are, to put it kindly, a bunch of offensive and morally bankrupt reprobates without any policies other than saying no to a referendum, the Scottish branch of the nasty party are threatening that if the Scottish government presses on with its manifesto commitment to hold another independence referendum, the Tories are going to flounce out of Holyrood in a huff. To which anyone who is opposed to their vile policies can only reply, "Good. And I hope the door slams on your backsides on the way out." Some of us would even start a crowdfunding campaign to pay for their fares so they can go as far away as possible. New Zealand is nice this time of year. That's where TV presenter Neil Oliver went to avoid the SNP. They could join him in petulant hair tossing.

Perhaps it might help the Tories to get some C-list celebrity support from the broader Unionist campaign in order to improve their image. Neil Oliver's not the only TV presenter who opposes independence. Neil opposes independence because he hates nationalism, except for the British variety which is better than any other nationalism because it isn't nationalism at all. Dan Snow opposes independence because his wife's family have a Highland holiday property the size of West Lothian and that's a better metaphor for the British Empire than all of his telly programmes put together. Ben Fogle opposes independence because he thinks he's a mountain in Wester Ross. He'd be Beinn Fhoghail in Gaelic, which means a mountain of offensiveness. Which is an even better metaphor for the British state that Theresa May's government have in mind for us all after June, come to think of it.

There's nothing great about Theresa's Britain, except for a great deal of poverty, inhumanity, inequality and selfish greed. The biggest division in this country isn't the division between independence supporters and Unionists, it's the division between the haves and the have-nots, and those are divisions which are being fostered and made worse by Conservative policies. They have no intention of bridging Scotland's divisions, only in widening them for their own selfish ends. They're divisions which are far worse than divisions of opinion, they are divisions of life chances, of opportunities, of access.

The Tories are highly likely to secure a crushing majority in England in June's election, which they intend to use to force Scotland to shut up and bow before them. That's how Tories propose to achieve unity. This is Scotland's chance to stand up and say that we will not consent, that Scotland will have its say. In June Scotland can vote to say that we reject May's Brexit, we reject her theatre of cruelty that poses as Christianity, and we reject a Westminster that refuses to allow the people of Scotland to determine their own path. We can vote to give the SNP an explicit mandate for a second referendum on Scotland's future.

May's election call will certainly strengthen her position in England, but it will even further weaken her in Scotland. All the polls show that the Conservatives will win a majority of seats in England, and the SNP will win a large majority of seats in Scotland – and that gives an unquestionable mandate for a second independence referendum. This o-called unity election will bring about the end of the Union.

19 April 2017

It's bloody easy to see that Theresa May is putting her country last

This week the United Kingdom has left us in no doubt that it's making its final descent into a crazed delusional la-la land. Last weekend there was a leak in a German newspaper of details of Theresa May's disastrous meeting with Jean-Claude Juncker, during which the President of the European Commission discovered that Theresa May could tell him that the dining table in Downing Street was strong and stable, but her understanding of the Brexit negotiations began and ended with a tautological sound bite. When someone constantly repeats that they're strong and stable, it's a fairly good indication that they're neither.

It was a leak which any sensible and logically thinking person would see as deeply damaging to our secretive and authoritarian prime minister. But then Theresa isn't looking to gain votes from people who are sensible and logical thinkers. She's seeking votes from the red white and blue in the face British nationalists and so she's made great play of the bloody difficult woman tag. In order to secure the votes of the frothing UKIP tendency, Theresa May used the leak as an excuse to launch a verbal war against the European Union, pretty much guaranteeing that when negotiations begin in earnest the rest of the EU will not be disposed to do Britain any favours.

In order to secure a few votes from UKIP, our wrong and unable PM just made it more likely that the UK will crash out of the EU without any deal being struck, potentially causing the loss of tens of thousands of jobs and gravely damaging the living standards of millions. It's a classic example of putting short-term party political interest before the national interest, and the clearest illustration possible of why Theresa May isn't fit for the office she occupies.

It's terribly unfair, said Theresa, that the EU has hardened its negotiating stance by repeating the exact same things that they've been saying for months. They're trying to manipulate the result of the general election, she claimed, because Theresa thinks that Brussels has a deep interest in whether she is re-elected by a majority of fifty or a majority of fifteen. Or at least that's what she wants us to think. Does anyone honestly believe that Theresa May will have a stronger hand in negotiations with the EU because there's a Tory MP in Stafford North? No one in Brussels will notice or care. It makes not the slightest bit of difference to the reality that the EU will ensure that the UK is worse off as a result of leaving the Union than it was as a member. That's not vindictiveness, it's a simple political imperative.

While all this is going on, the only story that the TV news could be bothered with on Thursday was the revelation that Prince Philip is retiring from his job. It's nice to see that ATOS have finally declared someone unfit for work. He's ninety-six, which is the age that we'll all be retiring at after the Tories have destroyed the state pension. Despite the prince's advanced age, the news came as a great shock to hundreds of thousands of people all across the country, none of whom had realised that he'd ever had a job to retire from. The last time he did anything useful was during WWII.

However the prince with his racist remarks, tasteless insults and unerring ability to alienate people has provided Theresa May with an example to follow in her Brexit negotiations. The real reason he's standing down now is because Theresa has taken on full responsibility for insulting foreigners and she reckons that between her and Boris Johnson they've pretty much got it covered.

Who knew that travelling the world and making racist remarks could have been such a laudable career? It's a shame he's retiring just at the very time that being a tactless xenophobe has come back into fashion. But he's having a well-deserved rest now, because all those decades of class prejudice, racism and sexism must have been exhausting. The royals are going to celebrate his retirement with a quiet party to which only close family members will be invited. So Harry won't be going then. But at least Phil won't need to worry about the triple lock on his pension. Still, whatever you think about him, he does represent an example of what an asylum seeker dependent on state handouts can achieve.

The other big news this week wasn't as earth-shattering as the news that a benefits claimant in his mid-nineties was stepping down from his non-job. Or at least it wasn't as earth-shattering to the TV news. After decades another narrow-minded geriatric who hasn't done anything useful since WWII was retired at long last. The Labour Party finally lost control of Glasgow Council, its last great bastion of power in Scotland.

Now we've got the Labour Party out of the way, it's a straight choice between the parties of independence or a Tory Brexit Britain, and that's a choice that's not bloody difficult.

6 May 2017

Scotland's Unionist media are just Tory cheerleaders

Here are some recent headlines in the Scottish press: Marine Le Pen won the French presidential election with a stunning thirty-four per cent of the popular vote; Rangers won the Scottish League by coming third behind Celtic; A wee ginger dug who writes a column for The National had an amazing jackpot lottery win when he managed to get one winning number in a line; Ruth Davidson's Conservatives won last week's Scottish local elections.

It's bad enough when our partisan media rewrites the past. We've got used to self-serving counterfactual interpretations of history from the Unionist parties, like when we're told that Scotland should suck up Brexit because we knew in 2014 when the country voted against independence that Britain was likely to have a referendum on leaving the EU and to vote to leave.

This rewriting of history conveniently overlooks what really happened, such as the remarks of Ruth Davidson herself who assured the country in a debate during the independence referendum campaign that it was vanishingly unlikely that her party would be returned with a majority in 2015's general election. And even if it was, no one expected that England and Wales would vote to leave the EU. But it's now an established alternative fact of the Unionist establishment that Scotland's electorate were, uniquely amongst the peoples of the world, blessed with the ability to foretell the future. Which does beg the question of why I've still failed to win the lottery jackpot. If what the Unionists asserted was true, then Scotland wouldn't need the Barnett Formula or the oil, we could fund all our public services with our massive gambling wins and would have a booming export trade in tarot card readings. The mystic dug is currently predicting that Theresa May will end up more unpopular in Scotland than Margaret Thatcher.

Content with their ability to rewrite recent history, and convinced as they are that the Scottish public has a memory span that makes a goldfish seem like one of those prodigies who can recite ϖ to one million places, the Scottish Unionists and their media fanboys and girls have embarked on a radical new step. Now they're trying to rewrite the present and tell us that something different is happening even when we can see reality unfolding before our very eyes, and so we're told that the Conservatives were the real winners of an election in which they came a very distant second.

We were told that the SNP had lost seven seats and the only winners were the Tories, who made massive gains. The loss of seven seats was touted by the BBC, who mumbled over the small print that the SNP had only lost seven seats in this year's council election compared to the results of an entirely imaginary notional election that only ever took place on a spreadsheet in a BBC office. This is how, in Scottish Unionist arithmetic, the number of seats that the SNP won in this election, at 431, is really a smaller number than the number of seats that they won in the previous council elections, which was 425. So the Tories really won the election because 431 is seven less than 425 and a humungous number less than the 276 that the Conservatives won.

What really happened was that the SNP won. In the actual real election that took place and not the one that only happened in the imagination of someone in Pacific Quay, the SNP won six more seats compared to last time. They really made some modest gains compared to their performance in the previous council elections, nothing dramatic to be sure, but gains nevertheless. Thursday's vote was in fact the SNP's best performance ever in a Scottish local authority election.

Achieving your best result ever is a pretty peculiar definition of a blow for Nicola Sturgeon.

The Tories did do well. No one is disputing that. What's being disputed is how they made their gains. The Conservatives and their media supporters would have us believe that the Tory advances were made at the expense of the SNP and that the doughty Ruth with her propensity for cheeky photo ops has reversed the nationalist tide. This narrative conveniently overlooks the collapse of the Labour Party. The Tory gains came almost entirely at the expense of Scotland's other main Unionist party. The Tories have taken over from Labour as the second largest party in Scottish local government, but whereas in 2012's election Labour ended up marginally behind the SNP, the Tories are still miles behind them.

What happened in the council elections was that the Unionist vote realigned itself. There was a new arrangement of deckchairs around the Unionist bandstand, but there are still no more chairs than there were before. The Conservatives fought a campaign on one issue and on one issue only, saying no to a second referendum, but despite that they only ended up with a paltry 22.5 per cent of the seats in a rigorously proportional election. For all the crowing in the Unionist press, Scotland said no to the Tories.

Scotland has another chance to say no to the Tories in June's general election. June is May's Me, Myself, I election. She's made it all about herself. This is an election in which we are called upon to give Theresa May a blank cheque to interpret Brexit however she pleases, and to interpret the devolution settlement in any way she likes. Theresa May and her little Scottish helper want Scotland to say no to a second referendum, but refuse to tell us what we'd be saying yes to, other than putting all our faith and trust in a prime minister who doesn't trust the people enough to tell us what her plans are.

Barring something catastrophic, the SNP is likely to end

up as by far and away the largest party in June's election, but it's likely that due to the realignment of the Unionist vote the Tories may very well make some gains. You don't need the ability to foretell the future to know that the Scottish Unionist media will be telling us on the ninth of June that the Conservatives are the real winners of the election in Scotland. But what will really have happened is that Labour will have been replaced as the bastion of the Union by the Tories, and that makes independence more likely, not less likely.

10 May 2017

Denying us time with dying loved ones is cruellest cut

Tucked away in a quiet corner of the East End of Glasgow is Lightburn Hospital. It's not a glamorous place. It's not like Holby City, where impossibly handsome doctors and nurses get angst-ridden about their complicated love lives while conducting open-heart surgery. Lightburn is where the essential grind of medicine takes place, the slow hard work of rehabilitation following a long illness, the nursing care required by the elderly and the infirm, and the support and love needed by those reaching the end of their lives.

I'll always have a special place in my heart for Lightburn and its dedicated staff, it's where my late partner Andy spent the last couple of months of his life as he succumbed to vascular dementia, and where he died in early September 2014. The final weeks and days of Andy's time were marked by the care and understanding of the nurses, doctors and auxiliary staff of Lightburn, who made him feel appreciated and understood, and who held his hand and mine as we embarked on the last steps of our journey together. They were there for us when we still had hope that Andy might recover. They were there for us when it became clear that his condition was terminal and the end was approaching. They were there for us in his last hours, making him comfortable, ensuring he was not afraid.

However the hospital is now threatened with closure. The health board in its wisdom has decided that it is surplus to requirements and proposes to shut down the site. Gradually services and funding have been run down. The proposal is to transfer services to Stobhill, but Stobhill is in the north of the city and is poorly served by public transport from the East End, an area which has one of the lowest incidences of car ownership in the country.

In order to get to Stobhill from my flat in the East End of Glasgow, it requires two bus journeys. Lightburn is a walk away, and that meant that I was able to be with Andy every day of his last days, every day of our last days together. If he had been in Stobhill I wouldn't have been able to visit him every day, the cost alone would have been prohibitive, existing as I was at the time on a meagre £70 a week carer's allowance. I couldn't have afforded over £7 every day in bus fares. The East End of Glasgow is an area where there are thousands who survive on low incomes. It's an area which is famously deprived. Closing Lightburn means that potentially thousands of people in the East End will be deprived even further, deprived of the chance to spend a few hours in the company of loved ones whose time remaining is limited. We're used to cuts in public services, but that would be the cruelest cut of all.

The decision of the Greater Glasgow and Clyde health board to close down Lightburn not only strips away a vital community resource from the heart of the East End, it also threatens to strip out the hearts of East Enders and deprive them of time with family members who are dying. That is time that is limited, time that is running out, time that they'll never have again. Economic decisions have a human cost. The cost of closing Lightburn is a cost in grief and tears.

The Greater Glasgow and Clyde health board previously tried to close Lightburn down, but that decision was overruled in 2011 by Nicola Sturgeon who was then Minister for Health in the Scottish government. If she hadn't made that decision, Andy's final days on this earth would have been very different. They'd have been lonely, isolated and fearful because I wouldn't have been able to be at his bedside every day. The reasons she gave for overruling the health board's decision – reasons of access for the local population, reasons of keeping health services as local possible, reasons of providing effective and accessible rehabilitative care – remain exactly the same today as they were in 2011.

In the hours after Andy passed away, while waiting for the necessary paperwork to be completed I stood outside Lightburn Hospital on a bleak September's day and wept as an early autumn leaf fell from a tree and landed on my shoulder. And Lightburn's staff were there for me. Every day, the people who work in Lightburn, who make that hospital what it is, provide that intensely personal service to the people of the East End of Glasgow. They hold our hands in the fearful nights. They're with us as we struggle to recover. They're there for us when all hope is lost and make us know that we are not alone. Lightburn's staff have been at our side, they've always been there for us. Let's be there for them now. Support the campaign to keep Lightburn open.

13 May 2017

Democracy Tory-style ... Ian Duncan
lost the election but still wins the job

In most jobs, in most spheres of life, there's a consequence for failure. If you slave away at a low-paid job in a warehouse and you fail to make up your hours, you'll get sacked. If you answer phones in a call centre and you fail to make your targets, you'll get disciplined. If you miss your bus and are late to your appointment at the job centre you'll get sanctioned and face going hungry and having your power cut off. But that doesn't apply if you're a Unionist politician. If you're a Conservative MEP who's going to lose his job because his party decided to placate its right wing with an EU referendum that went disastrously wrong, and who then stands for a seat in Westminster and fails to get elected, you'll get appointed to the House of Lords and the job in government that you were going to get anyway had you been elected. It's not really much of a consequence for failure, but negative consequences don't apply to Tories. The consequences of Conservative failure are borne by the rest of us.

There's been outrage that Tory MEP Iain Duncan has been rewarded with a seat in the Lords after failing to get elected during the general election. What exactly is the point of having elections if the guy that the voters rejected still gets the government job that he was standing for election for? It makes a mockery of democracy. It's the sort of thing that happens in a one-party state, and it comes from a party which has spent the last few years complaining that Scotland is a one-party state because it hasn't voted for the Tories in sufficiently large numbers. Now the Conservatives have just informed the electorate of Scotland that it doesn't matter who we vote for, we're going to be governed by whomever the Conservatives choose for us. It's a massive two fingers from the Tory Party to the democratic process.

None of this is new of course. Back in 1997 Michael Forsyth led the Scottish Conservatives to their greatest defeat in electoral history. He was the frontman, the leader of the party, Secretary of State for Scotland in the government of John Major, and presented the Scottish Conservative manifesto to the people of Scotland, who took one look at it and regarded it with much the same expression as you'd give to something deeply unpleasant that had been squashed into the sole of your shoe. "Oh no," said the people of Scotland, "we're not allowing that into the house."

The result was that Michael Forsyth lost his own seat, a seat which had been a safe Conservative seat when it was created in 1983, and he lost the seats of every other Conservative MP in Scotland. The people of Scotland told Michael Forsyth that he could stick his manifesto in the nether regions they were booting him in, they didn't want him anywhere near power, and they didn't just want his party nowhere near government, they didn't want it in Opposition either. Democratic rejections do not come any more emphatic or comprehensive.

If Michael Forsyth was a teacher who had failed as spectacularly and extensively, he'd be marched out of the school and would be subject to a restraining order banning him from approaching within 300 metres of any place of education. If he was a plumber, he'd have his wrench wrenched off him and he'd have a suction cup superglued to his head. But Michael is a Tory politician, so he was rewarded with a seat in the House of Lords from which he continues to pontificate and to preach and to influence our laws and public policy. During the EU referendum, Michael actually had the gall to campaign for a Leave vote, because he claimed it was terribly unfair that we're governed by people that we didn't elect and can't vote out of office. You don't say, Michael.

Michael Forsyth is the undead vampire of politics, not even an electoral stake through the heart could finish him off. Dracula would be so impressed. And now he's been joined by Iain Duncan who was resurrected in less time than it took Frankenstein to create his monster. We've already got the hirsute Mundell as Cousin Itt, so now with Iain we've got the full set of Halloween monsters.

At least with Michael Forsyth the Tories had the decency to wait two years after his electoral rejection before appointing him to the Lords. With Iain Duncan they've not even waited two weeks. Iain is the doughboy of politics, knead him down and after a few days he rises again. There hasn't been a quicker resurrection since that Galilean guy. Don't vote Tory, get Tories anyway. Vote Tories out, get Tories anyway. And then our political classes wonder why people are losing faith in the political system.

There is speculation that Iain Duncan was in line for a position in the Scotland Office because Cousin Itt needed assistance from a human brain, even if it's one that was transplanted into a resurrected body. Iain's failure to get elected earlier this month meant that the Tories had to resort to Plan B. We should be grateful that they at least had a Plan B for something, they sure as hell don't have a Plan A for Brexit, for minority government or indeed for much else.

What we're witnessing is a democratic outrage, but it's not as if democracy ever had a great deal to do with the Scotland Office anyway. The Scotland Office was created to give Scotland a voice in the UK government, but it's long since become the voice of the UK government in Scotland. Since we've got a UK government that wasn't elected by the people of Scotland, it makes no real difference that the members of the Scotland Office aren't representatives of Scotland either.

Still, it's nice to see that all those Unionist commentators who complained that Scotland was a one-party state are going to be up in arms about Iain's appointment. I'm sure they'll get around to being incensed about it just as soon as they're finished holding Ruth Davidson to account for voting against the Housing (Scotland) Bill in 2014 and voting down stricter regulation for landlords, or asking her what she thinks about the appointment of a justice secretary who has consistently voted against LGBTQ rights after supposedly getting assurances on that very topic from Theresa May. It's going to be a long wait. Meanwhile what passes for democracy in the UK becomes the laughing stock of the world.

21 June 2017

Cutting off puppy dog tails is
a huge own goal by SNP

I don't usually criticise the SNP. I don't usually criticise them for the same reason that I don't criticise the Greens, the Scottish Socialists or any other groups who are involved in the independence movement. When independence supporters start to have a go at one another, it's the Unionists who benefit. It's not a coincidence that the independence supporters who vocally and frequently make public criticisms of the SNP are the ones who are most likely to find themselves being offered writing gigs in the Unionist press. The Unionist press isn't doing that because it's keen to promote diversity within the wider Yes movement. So generally, I bite my vicious tongue.

But sometimes you do need to point out that your friends are shooting themselves in the foot, and you're particularly likely to shoot yourself in the foot when you get into bed with the gun lobby. This week, the SNP did something which from the perspective of someone outside the party, but who is a part of the wider independence movement, came across as a monumental act of stupidity. On Wednesday, the SNP voted along with the Tories to permit, under certain circumstances, the docking of the tails of a couple of breeds of dogs in order to facilitate blood sports.

The argument was that the working dogs are frequently injured by the tasks that they're called on to perform, and that injury and trauma to the dogs can be avoided by allowing the dogs' tails to be docked when they're puppies. Young puppies heal far more quickly than older dogs and are, apparently, less likely to suffer from complications and trauma from the procedure. The SNP was persuaded by this argument, and so voted along with the lairds and landowners party, people whose idea of a fun time is blasting a wee bird out of the sky with a shotgun.

According to the hunting lobby, their working dogs are frequently injured, and removing the injured tail from an adult dog is painful, traumatic and often results in complications. There is no reason to dispute that. But it's disingenuous for them to claim that they want to dock their dogs' tails because they're concerned for the welfare of their animals and nothing else. The operation to remove the injured tail of an adult dog is expensive, and during the time the dog is recovering it can't be used for work. It's a lot cheaper to do it to puppies and a lot more efficient from a business sense. None of that is about the welfare of a dog, it's about the welfare of a business. Animal welfare charities agree. A dog's tail isn't just a spare body part. It's a vital organ for communication, and dogs are supremely social beings. Cutting off a dog's tail is not unlike amputating a human tongue.

The crux of the matter however is that if a task is dangerous for a dog and is likely to result in the injury of the animal, then the problem is with the task, not with the dog. The task should be changed to fit the dog, not the dog changed to fit the task. I'm sure there are many jobs performed by humans which could be made safer if the worker was surgically altered, but no one would propose that because it's mad. It's not any less mad when the worker is a dog. If your dog is likely to be injured by the things you want your dog to do, then stop demanding your dog does those things, or change the way they're done.

You might not be surprised to learn that someone whose writing is named after a dug is a dog lover. Ginger is a rescued dog. He was found abandoned beside an irrigation canal in Spain, where he was most likely dumped because he's really rubbish at hunting. Ginger's natural environment is lying on a sofa with his paws in the air, not chasing down rabbits or wildfowl. He was a casualty of hunters who treat dogs as commodities and tools of the trade.

Some argue – but what about neutering dogs, surely that's just as bad. I've always been of the view that if you need to cut bits off your dog in order to be able to control it properly, you probably shouldn't have a dog. Rescued dogs from Spain very often aren't neutered, and Ginger has all his bits. It's my responsibility as a dog owner to prevent unwanted breeding, and that's what I do.

But essentially the issue of neutering is whataboutery. In politics it's the optics which matter, it's how things look. And it looks bad for the SNP to be seen to be voting alongside the hunting lobby and the Tories to permit dogs to be mutilated, after voting against fox hunting. It's an unnecessary distraction, and an own goal. On a day when the SNP should have been focussing on the Queen's Speech and the shambling disaster that passes for British government, social media was full of people upset by its decision to allow tail docking. We are not helped by unforced errors from the SNP. They need to concentrate on the day job – and that's winning us independence.

24 June 2017

What counts for indy is the bigger picture... not simply a referendum

This has been an important week in the history of the Yes movement which will regain Scotland's independence. It marks the start of Indy 2.0, the new, improved and better campaign that's got rid of the bugs of the first campaign which was bogged down in process and party politics. What had happened was that the independence campaign was getting stuck in the question of holding another referendum, and not doing what its main task ought to be, which is to make the case for independence. Independence had become too closely identified with the SNP, and that was making it vulnerable to party political attacks.

The question of Scottish independence should be immune from attacks by Unionist parties on specific aspects of SNP policy or SNP management. The truth is that however important and vital the SNP might be for achieving the political goal of an independence referendum, the case for independence is not dependent on how a particular political party manages our NHS or our schools; it's a far bigger and more important question which was getting lost in the noise of day-to-day politicking.

Independence is about the big picture, the big idea, the big vision. Above all independence is about the radical notion that the people of a country are the sovereign body in that land, that Scottish independence is about empowerment and enabling Scotland to identify and to make the changes that Scotland needs in order to achieve the social justice, equality of opportunity, acceptance and fairness that characterise a decent country whose citizens live in dignity.

Now the cause of independence is back where it belongs, with the people of Scotland. We have a clear task over the course of the coming months, to build a solid case for independence, to build an active, enthused and engaged grass-roots movement, and to tell the story of the better Scotland that is ours for the taking. It's not enough just to sell independence to the people of Scotland, we need to make them want to buy it.

That means we've got a lot of work to do, a lot of learning, a lot of listening, a lot of educating. We need to identify those people who are open to the idea of independence but who are not quite there yet, and discover what is holding them back so that we can dispel their fears and clarify their doubts. We need to energise and enthuse those who already support independence, and turn them into campaigners and activists. We need to show that democracy is an exercise in mass participation, not a sterile debate between people in business suits in parliaments and council chambers. That's where the Unionists want to keep politics, and that's why they're so afraid of independence.

The Scottish independence movement shouldn't want independence for its own sake, but because it can be a transformative act that delivers power into the hands of ordinary Scottish people. Independence can equip all of us with the tools that we require in order to make the necessary changes to wrest Scotland away from the landowners, the established elites, the big business interests, and turn it over to the people. It's an obscenity that in a country with an embarrassment of energy resources elderly people die in cold winters because they're too afraid of their electric and gas bills. It's outrageous that in one of the richest countries in the world, working families struggle to put food on the table and keep a roof over their heads. It's a scandal that homeless people beg for handouts in the streets of our cities while housing is treated as an investment opportunity. Independence can, and must, address these questions. It must show that poverty, deprivation and marginalisation are the inevitable consequences of a land which doesn't govern itself. The independence movement must turn itself into a direct challenge to the disengagement and apathy which are the tools of Unionist rule.

When there is sufficient clamour for independence, and there will be, then a referendum will follow naturally, like an unstoppable force of nature. The political will of a nation in movement cannot be resisted, no matter how much Theresa May or her successors say that now is not the time. Now will never be the time for them, but that's not the issue, the issue is when is the time for Scotland. We need to make it the time for Scotland, that's our task as supporters, members and activists in the Scottish independence movement.

If there's anything we've learned over the past couple of years, it's that Scotland will win its independence in the teeth of most of the media. Yes, we have a vital and vibrant digital media, we have valuable outlets like *The National* and its stablemate the *Sunday Herald*, but the message of independence is only going to get out to the people of this country if we take it to them ourselves. The real work is just beginning, and I for one am eager to throw myself into the task. I know I won't be alone.

1 July 2017

Theresa May's Brexit tears cannot hide Tory incompetence

Theresa May has admitted that she shed a wee tear on election night when the exit poll was released and it became clear that she had thrown away her party's majority and sunk her career. Quite a lot of us watching shed tears too, laughing hysterically can do that to you. The revelation that Theresa is capable of a semblance of humanoid emotion has been hailed as the greatest breakthrough in artificial intelligence since Deep Blue beat Garry Kasparov at chess, although it's not entirely obvious why anyone is supposed to think more highly of Theresa May now that she's allowed the public to know that she's competent at self-pity. She's not competent with much else, certainly not empathy. Theresa studied human as a second language, but failed her GSCE. She really ought to do some soul-searching, but it's unlikely that she'd find one.

It would be a bit more impressive if Theresa May had shed a tear for the victims of the Grenfell tragedy, the families that her immigration policies have divided, or the disabled people living in isolation because her government has taken away their transport and slashed their finances. She's not sorry she tried to destroy a functioning Opposition and take supreme power for herself by the mindless repetition of meaningless sound bites while running roughshod over what passes for a constitution in this country, she's sorry the public didn't allow her to get away with it. However since the only thing that Theresa May displays emotion about is the destruction of her own career by her own arrogance and stupidity, it's likely that the public will remain resolutely unendeared to her. People will still follow her, but only out of morbid curiosity.

This week, Theresa's government unveiled another chapter in its arrogant stupidity with the publication of the Repeal Bill. It used to be called the Great Repeal Bill but then Theresa lost her majority and the government decided that it wasn't a good look to make a big show of acting like a despot. Instead they're acting like despots but released the news about Theresa's tear in the hope that no one would notice the power grab. The bill gives the government the power to make and enact laws without bothering to consult with the elected representatives of the people. Not that this is new, it's what they've been doing to Scotland for years. The only novelty is that now they're going to do it to England as well.

There's still no plan for Brexit, other than a power grab for the British government and a resolute refusal to face up to the reality that there's no such thing as a good Brexit deal. The EU is running out of patience with the UK government, having neither the time nor the crayons to explain the real consequences of Brexit to David Davis. David is like one of those idiot savants, only without the savant part.

Meanwhile Scotland Secretary David Mundell, the voice of the UK cabinet in Scotland, is trying to argue that Brexit will be great for Scotland, and that ripping Scotland out of the EU against its will while trashing the devolution settlement and ignoring the Scottish parliament is a Scottish process too. It's going to be a bonanza for Scottish powers, he said, confusing government with a 1960s TV Western. Which is an easy mistake to make considering the number of out-of-date cowboys there are in the British government.

Contrary to popular belief, Fluffy Mundell does have a purpose in government, it's to serve as a warning to others. David isn't the most clued-up politician on the planet, but he must be amongst the most invincible. After all, what you don't know can't hurt you, and he knows practically nothing. David Mundell thinks a friend with benefits means having a pal who's claiming jobseeker's allowance, and that's why he doesn't have any because Tories won't associate with poor people. But to be fair he does have a point about Brexit. Brexit belongs to Scotland too. It's every bit as Scottish as Mary Queen of Scots, both ended up being tragically executed.

The biggest threat to our society, our security and our stability is our own government in Westminster. Well, I say "our own government", it is in fact a government composed of a party Scotland didn't vote for, in alliance with a party Scotland can't vote for, implementing a policy that Scotland voted against, and giving itself the power to legislate without bothering to get parliamentary approval. Despite telling us that Scotland and the other devolved administrations were going to be fully involved and consulted in the Brexit process, it turns out that the Conservatives meant it in the exact same way that their friends in the DUP consult gay organisations when deciding to block equal marriage in Northern Ireland. The British government has set itself up as the all-powerful arbiter of what devolution means, and Scotland isn't going to be consulted.

The devolution settlement is quite clear, everything that is not specifically reserved to Westminster is a devolved power. When Westminster refuses to allow devolved powers to be transferred automatically from Brussels to the devolved administrations, that's a power grab, a power grab which is being undertaken without any consultation with Edinburgh or Cardiff. Scotland and Wales can't block or veto Brexit, but they can certainly make it difficult for the Tories. They wouldn't be serving the best interests of Scotland and Wales if they didn't. Holyrood will refuse to consent to the Repeal Bill. Theresa May can grab the powers, but she'll only be able to do so at the expense of provoking a constitutional crisis. For a minority government that's no joke. This Repeal Bill will only make the repeal of the Act of Union come about that bit sooner. And that is the only thing to come out of this entire sorry mess that is to be welcomed.

15 July 2017

Row over The National's space front page shows Unionists like to imagine everything is impossible

On Saturday, The National published a report from the pro-independence think tank Common Weal about proposals to develop Scotland's space industry. The National is the only newspaper that gives publicity to reports from Scotland's premier pro-independence think tank, the Unionist press only gives space to reports from pro-Unionist think tanks that threaten Scotland with penury. The Fraser of Allander Institute has a remarkable public influence for an organisation which sounds like a knitwear shop in Pitlochry. It only needs to harrumph and it's all over the miserabilist Unionist media – although to be honest the phrase "miserabilist Unionism" is a tautology. Flogging knitwear to tourists in Pitlochry is what Scotland's Unionists consider the height of aspiration for the Scottish economy. Independence supporters want to reach for the stars.

Predictably, *The National*'s story was greeted with scorn and derision from the massed ranks of Unionists on Scottish social media, led by Adam Tomkins, the Tory MSP for Low Expectations, which is somewhere in Milngavie. Adam decried the report as science fiction.

Actually in much of science fiction set in future times, Scotland is independent and prosperous. I've just finished a novel by American sci-fi author Kim Stanley Robinson called *2312*, the year in which the events of the novel are set. It mentions in passing that an independent Scotland is one of the world's most prosperous countries. In the *Doctor Who* universe, a future Scotland is also independent. In one episode the former companion the Scottish Amy Pond found herself on a spaceship full of British refugees from a dying Earth. The plot revolved around the fact that the British spaceship had no functioning engines, very like modern Britain, come to think of it. Amy was surprised when one of the ship's inhabitants asked what a person with a Scottish accent was doing on the ship. "Scotland's got its own ship," she was told. One with engines that worked.

Unionism is the opposite of science fiction. Whereas science fiction is the art of imagining the possible, Unionism is the art of imagining that everything is impossible. How ridiculous that Scotland should dream of developing its satellite industry, how deserving of mockery that Scotland should consider building a spaceport. The story gave the Cringe a rocket-fuelled boost, and all weekend Unionists were mocking the idea that a highly developed northern European country might do something highly developed. This is the real Cringe in Scotland. We're a country of rocket scientists which is being held back by a bunch of Unionist rockets.

Although the report was predictably dismissed out of hand as science fiction by Unionist politicians who lack the imagination to see any future for Scotland other than flogging off expensive knitwear to tourists in Pitlochry, the reality is that Scotland already has a thriving space industry. Glasgow builds more small satellites than any other city in Europe. Scotland has a disproportionate share of the UK's space industry. We could do far more. We could do much better.

According to the economic consultancy firm London Economics, Scotland has a 11.7-per-cent share of the total UK space economy, a figure well in excess of Scotland's 8.25-per-cent share of the UK population. The space industry generates £134 million annually for the Scottish economy and provides thousands of highly skilled and well-paid jobs. It could generate considerably more income for the economy and provide many more well-paid and highly skilled jobs, all it takes is a bit of investment, work and above all imagination. A spaceport would both provide a use for Prestwick Airport and give an enormous boost to an already established Scottish industry. That was the point of the report from Common Weal. Scotland can reach for the stars, because it's already within our capacity to reach for them.

None of this was recognised by the small-minded Unionists, the political wing of the Cringe. Unionism is the philosophy that prides itself on its realism, but it possesses the realism of a person who refuses to go on a highway because there are traffic accidents. It's the realism of a person who will never get on a plane because they're afraid of flying. It's the realism of someone who hides under the Westminster duvet in a ramshackle house and hopes that it will save them from the ceiling that is about to fall on their head.

Unionism is what happens when a lack of imagination combined with an unhealthy dose of self-loathing is elevated into a political philosophy. Unionism is a bunch of space cadets who laugh at those who aspire to reach for the stars. Unionism demands that Scotland can only gaze upon the stars when it's lying in the gutter. They're scared and threatened by anything that might shatter their stranglehold of fear and lack of ambition, that's why they laugh and scoff at proposals for a Scottish space industry. Unionism can only succeed by destroying hope, undermining ambition and keeping Scotland firmly in a box. A Scotland that dreams of outer space is a Scotland that's outside the box. No wonder Unionists are threatened by that vision. Unionism is a dead weight that drags Scotland back into the gutter. It's a set of blinkers on the possible, a hand that's tied behind our backs. It's the politicisation of the Cringe. The only orbit that Unionism can countenance is the orbit around the dying star of Westminster. We can do better when we fly our own course. Realising that isn't rocket science.

Some Tories already go into paroxysms of cringery if you paint the Gaelic for "Police Scotland" on the side of a police helicopter. Apparently you can't put Gaelic on a helicopter because Gaelic doesn't have a native word for helicopter. Unlike English, right? When Scotland does build its spaceport we ought to name it in Gaelic, just to annoy the cringers, *Port-Fànais Nàiseanta na h-Alba*, the National Spaceport of Scotland. It has a nice ring to it. Then we can save a fortune on rocket fuel if we can work out a way to harness all the outrage from the complaints of Tory rockets.

19 July 2017

Scotland must make do with the UK's scraps – again

The first of three new Royal Navy frigates is being built on the Clyde. Whoop, and indeed, dee-doo. The news was plastered all over the Reporting Scotland news and the Unionist papers, all of whom bigged it up as one of those Union benefits that we're always being promised but which all too often fail to materialise. The fact that they were giving lots of publicity to a development that could be used to argue for Scotland's continuing membership of the UK wasn't at all surprising.

Neither was it at all surprising that all of them neglected to mention that during the 2014 referendum campaign the Clyde shipyards were promised that they would build thirteen new frigates, a number which was reduced to eight not long after Westminster secured its No vote, and then which was reduced further to three. Scotland should be grateful for whatever scraps are tossed its way. But never mind, the new ship is to be named HMS Glasgow. Doesn't that make you feel proud to be British? Rumour has it that the original name chosen for the frigate by the Ministry of Defence was HMS Friggy McFrigface, but that was rejected as it sounded too much like a sexual activity. The second ship is going to be called HMS Vote No, and the third HMS Patronising BT Lady. The ship's mess will only serve cereal.

The ship might be called HMS Glasgow, but it's going to be based in Devonport. Scotland will continue to be woefully undefended by the Royal Navy. Late in 2013, a Russian warship was spotted in the Moray Firth. It took the Royal Navy over twenty-four hours to get one of its ships into the area because the only one available was off the south coast of

England. By the time it got to the Moray Firth, the Russian navy could have invaded Inverness and renamed the Black Isle Черный Остров. Scotland only interests the UK as a base for its nuclear warheads.

Perhaps if there was decent investment in Scotland's ship-building industry it could be like Norway's and build a large range of civilian vessels, then it wouldn't be so dependent on the whims of the MOD. As it is it suits Westminster to have a weak shipbuilding industry in Scotland, because then it can be held hostage to promises from the British defence establishment. If you deny a person the resources that enable them to fish for themselves, you can keep them dangling from a hook.

Scotland having to make do with crumbs from the table is normal for the UK. This week the British government announced the latest phase of the High Speed rail line, which is to be built at a cost of £55.7 billion, which works out at £400 million per mile. The entire electrification project between Glasgow and Edinburgh was originally forecast to cost £742 million. Even when expected cost overruns are taken into account, it's still only about two miles' worth of HS2.

What many consider a vanity project costing billions gets the go-ahead, despite a number of studies showing that it will mainly be of benefit to London, which already enjoys a disproportionate share of UK transport investment. Meanwhile other rail investment projects are scrapped. The line from Cardiff to Swansea will not be electrified after all, and neither will the Midland Main Line between Sheffield and Nottingham, or the branch line from Oxenholme to Windermere. There are currently no firm plans for High Speed rail to reach Scotland. The line isn't expected to reach northern England before the 2030s, by the time it gets to Scotland many of the readers of this article will be dead. Realistically there's more chance of David Mundell acting as the voice of Scotland in the UK cabinet rather than the voice of the UK cabinet in Scotland than there is of Britain's

High Speed railway ever reaching Scotland.

If we're exceptionally lucky, High Speed rail might struggle into Scotland around about the same time that some genius born in the distant future invents a matter transporter making planes, roads and railways obsolete. Mind you, since at least one UK cabinet minister – that would be Andrea Leadsom – thinks that Jane Austen is a living author, that would still allow the Tories to promise High Speed rail to Scotland within our lifetimes. We'll be several hundred years old, and we still won't be eligible for a state pension.

Angered at the fact that Scotland was being left behind, a couple of years ago the Scottish government announced plans to build a high-speed railway between Glasgow and Edinburgh, but in the absence of any firm plans to connect the line to the rest of the high-speed network, it's not financially viable. While countries all over the world are investing in high-speed rail, Scotland is being left at the end of a branch line. Whether it's ships or planes, Westminster condemns Scotland to a third-class service.

22 July 2017

We need to stop fighting with each other and focus on the real issue – Hard Brexit

Over the past couple of weeks, Scottish social media has been particularly obnoxious. That's quite an achievement, because even at the best of times Twitter is like wading through a sewer of syrup of stupid in wellies filled with the waste you put in the food-recycling bin after it's been left to ferment for a fortnight in the sun. There are some people who apparently devote their entire contribution to Scottish politics to finding things to be outraged by on Twitter. Entertaining as this might be, it's a distraction from the real issues facing us. It's time we focussed on the seriously noxious waste that's heading down the pipeline and is about to poison us all in a far worse and far more serious way than, "He said something nasty on Twitter."

This week, just as you thought that the UK's Brexit plans couldn't get any more confused and damaging, that's exactly what they did. Brexit is increasingly resembling that barrel that you scrape the bottom of, only when you're scraping away there you can hear the sound of a Brexiteer underneath preparing something even more gobsmackingly stupid. It's rather like Twitter in that respect come to think of it. The difference is that Brexit is going to cause damage way beyond some hurt feelings.

A report by the think tank the Centre for Cities, based at the London School of Economics, claims that out of all the cities in the UK, it's Scotland's cities which stand to do worst from Brexit. In particular, the economy of Aberdeen is going to take a serious hit. £500 million could be lost from the Aberdeen economy annually if the UK goes for the hard Brexit which seems to be the preference of the UK government and the Labour leadership. Even in the best-case scenario of a soft Brexit, the Aberdeen economy stands to lose £284 million a year. Aberdeen will be, by quite some margin, the worst affected city in the UK.

Glasgow and Edinburgh won't escape damage either. Every one of the twenty UK cities examined in the report stands to see its economy damaged by Brexit. However Scotland's cities will lose out by a greater extent than the economies of northern English cities which voted to leave. This is because, according to the report's authors, Scottish cities are more integrated into the European economy. The damage to Scotland from a decision to leave the EU will consequently be greater. All of Scotland's cities stand to lose out by greater than the UK average because of a decision which Scotland rejected by a considerably larger margin than the margin by which it decided to remain a part of the UK.

Despite what the Tories like to claim, there is no such thing as a good Brexit. There is no such thing as a Brexit which works for all parts of the country. It seems, according to the report from the Centre for Cities, there is not even a Brexit which works for any part of the UK. Brexit, even a soft Brexit, is going to be damaging for every part of the UK, but Scotland stands to lose out even more. So much for those broad shoulders of the UK that Scotland can rely on.

The early part of the week was dominated by chlorinated chickens, and whether Liam Fox would allow them into Britain as part of a trade deal with the USA. That would be a trade deal that the UK isn't allowed to negotiate until after we leave the EU. A mass outbreak of angry clucking ensued, as it was pointed out to Liam that the consequences of reducing food safety standards would mean that British food could no longer be exported to the EU, the country's major market.

After fending off the attack of the angry chlorinated chicken during the week, on Thursday the Tories announced their plans for post-Brexit immigration, only it turned out that no one had told the Foreign Secretary or half the cabinet. After Michael Gove and other senior Tories had confidently assured the press that the cabinet was united on allowing freedom of movement to continue for an interim period after 2019, up pops Home Secretary Amber Rudd to say it wouldn't be.

Incredibly, while all this is going on, while the Tories are wandering around in the Brexit maze blindfolded and guided by nothing more than Boris Johnson's wish for a magic unicorn, the Labour Party manages to be even more confused on what sort of Brexit it wants than the Tories are. Out-idioting Boris Johnson is possibly the most embarrassing political achievement since Tory Secretary of State John Redwood mistook the *Teletubbies* theme song for the Welsh national anthem. It would, at this juncture, be useful to give a summary of what Labour's position on Brexit is, but I haven't got the foggiest idea of what it is. But then, neither does the Labour Party.

Meanwhile the EU's chief negotiator is warning that it seems increasingly unlikely that talks between the EU and the UK will be able to progress on to the nature of the post-Brexit relationship because of a failure by the UK to deal with the issues around the divorce. The chances are growing that the UK could fall out of the EU without any deal at all, with all the chaos which would ensue. The promises made to Scotland by Westminster during that fevered summer of 2014 are revealed to be as meaningless and trite as a Twitter dispute.

29 July 2017

Gay or straight, we must all be proud of progressive Scotland

There has been a lot of celebration in the media of late to mark the fiftieth anniversary of the decriminalisation of male homosexuality with the passing of the Sexual Offences Act on 27 July 1967. However that act only had effect in England and Wales. The original 1967 act wasn't extended to Scotland due to the opposition of Scottish MPs, both Labour and Conservative. Scotland, they claimed, needed to be protected from the evils of homosexuality. Gay men in Scotland had to wait another thirteen years for the Criminal Justice (Scotland) Act of 1980 to extend the same provisions to Scotland.

Sodomy, legally defined as anal intercourse, had been illegal in England and Scotland since at least the sixteenth century, and for much of that time it was a capital offence. The law was harsh, sentences were exercises in sadistic cruelty. One of the earliest attested Scottish cases was in 1570 when John Swan and John Litster were convicted by the High Court of the Justiciary in Edinburgh of "the wilde, filthie, execrabill, detestabill, and unnatural sin of sodomy, otherwise named bougarie, abusand of their bodies with utheris, in contrare the lawes of God, and all other human lawes". They were sentenced to be strangled at the stake, their bodies burned and their ashes scattered, depriving them of a Christian burial in a society which believed that only a burial in consecrated ground allowed the dead to rest in peace for eternity. It was a law which not only sentenced gay men to death, but sentenced them to eternal torment.

Laws against homosexuality were often conflated with

laws against witchcraft. On 2 April 1630 a certain Michael Erskine was convicted for "diverse points of witchcraft and filthy sodomy" and was burnt at the stake. In Scotland sodomy remained a capital offence until 1889, making ours the last country in Europe to retain the death penalty for homosexuality.

In the late nineteenth century Victorian morality demanded that all forms of homosexuality should be outlawed, even those where sodomy could not be proven or did not take place. The result was the so-called Labouchere Amendment of 1885 which introduced the crime of gross indecency. Only male homosexuality was outlawed by the law of 1885

. According to a persistent but unreliable legend, when the act criminalising homosexual behaviour was presented to Queen Victoria for her signature, she struck out all references to lesbianism because she refused to believe such a thing existed. In reality lesbianism wasn't outlawed because Victorian male lawmakers thought it was best not to draw any attention to it, and because they were incapable of conceptualising any form of sexuality that didn't involve a phallus.

In 1967 in England and Wales homosexuality was decriminalised under certain very specific circumstances. Whereas the heterosexual age of consent was sixteen, for gay men the age of consent was set at twenty-one. Whereas the underage partner in heterosexual sex was not committing an offence, an underage gay man was. If a twenty-one-year-old man had sex with his nineteen-year-old boyfriend, both faced criminal action. The lawmakers hypocritically set the age of consent at twenty-one in order to, they claimed, protect young men. Then they protected young gay men by criminalising them.

The other restriction was that sex between men was only decriminalised when it took place in private, and "private" was very narrowly defined. Gay sex was not to be subject to prosecution if it took place in a private residence in which no one but the two (and only two) participants were present on the premises. Threesomes were most definitely illegal. It was even technically illegal for a gay couple to have an overnight guest. If a gay act did not comply with this strict definition of privacy, it was still considered to be the offence of gross indecency.

Even the narrow window of legality introduced in England and Wales did not exist for gay men in Scotland. Gay sex remained illegal and being gay was highly stigmatised. I can remember when I was young being confidently told that we didn't have any gay people in Scotland. There was a modicum of truth in that, for many gay Scots the way that they dealt with their sexuality was to take the train south to the bright lights of London at the earliest opportunity.

It wasn't until 1980 that the law in Scotland was brought into line with the law in England and Wales. Ironically it took Margaret Thatcher's first government to impose it on the social dinosaurs of the Scottish Labour Party. But it wasn't the change in the law which brought about a change in Scottish social attitudes. It was the AIDS crisis of the 1980s.

As the magnitude of the epidemic revealed itself, thousands of gay men and lesbians all across the Western world, and Scotland, realised that we were staring death in the face. Our choices were stark. Die in silence, or die fighting for our rights. By the thousands, we chose the latter. The 1980s were characterised by closet doors popping open all over the place, mine amongst them. As Scottish lesbians and gay men came out of the closet, heterosexual Scots realised that Scotland did have gay and lesbian people, and they weren't the monsters of the tabloid gutter press, they were friends, family, colleagues and acquaintances. That's what started the sea change in Scottish social attitudes. Not the Labour Party. Not any political party. Not even a non-party campaign. It was thousands of ordinary LGBTQ Scots and their heterosexual families and friends.

It wasn't all plain sailing. There was the bitter campaign

supported by the *Daily Record* in the noughties to prevent the repeal of Thatcher's law preventing schools from mentioning homosexuality and thus preventing them from campaigning against homophobic bullying. But we won, and progress continued. In 2015 and 2016

the Rainbow Europe Index voted Scotland the best country in Europe for lesbian, gay, bisexual, transgender and intersex equality and human rights.

There might not be any significant anniversary for LGBTQ rights in Scotland this year, but we still have reason to celebrate. From being one of the last countries to remove the death penalty for gay sex, one of the last to decriminalise homosexuality, and from being one of the most repressive countries in Europe for LGBTQ people, Scotland has transformed itself into the country with the most progressive rights in the world. That's something we can all, gay or straight, be very proud of. As we celebrate, we must never forget the thousands who died in the epidemic. Our equality and social acceptance today is a testament to their suffering, and a testament to the good sense and respect for human rights of the people of Scotland.

2 August 2017

Another big orange man has just come out against independence

This week, the Scottish independence movement got its best news for months. It was so good that even Reporting Scotland was forced to give it the very briefest of mentions, though still without mentioning the best bits. We discovered that Donald Trump hates the idea of Scottish independence. He hates it almost as much as he hates CNN. That's bigly bad. Huge. He hates it so much that he'll use "bad" three times in a single sentence, and that's the official exchange rate for "terrible". There's three bads to the terrible, and four terribles to whatever it is that Anthony Scaramucci is calling Donald's new chief of staff after getting fired.

Trump's remarks on independence were revealed in the transcript of an interview with the *Wall Street Journal* which the paper didn't publish because the interview was an exercise in chummy sycophancy which made Nicholas Witchell's witterings on Prince Philip's last public engagement seem like a pack of pit bulls savaging Bambi's mammy. Despite the paper hoping that the interview's contents could be kept as secret as Donald Trump's tax returns, the full toe-curling transcript was leaked to a politics website.

Amongst other notable highlights, Donald asserted that the speech he'd given to the American Boy Scout Jamboree was the best speech the scouts had ever received, and that the head of the organisation had called him afterwards to say so. This was after the American Scouts had issued an official apology for the controversial and political nature of Trump's speech at what was meant to be an apolitical event. Managing to enrage the Scouts takes a special kind of political tone-deafness.

Apropos of nothing in particular, Trump asked his interviewer, Gerard Baker, about whether Scotland was going to have another independence referendum. It's unclear why he thought that the American reporter would be an expert on Scottish politics. Gerald had hitherto been far more interested in exchanging pleasantries with Ivanka about who they'd met while at a party for rich people in Southampton. That's a very posh bit of Long Island, and not the town in the south of England. Southampton England is nowhere near as posh, even if it does have a kebab shop with a soap dispenser in the toilet. Trump wouldn't be seen dead in a kebab shop in the other Southampton. Besides, it might be full of Muslims.

Trump was incredulous that Scotland might want another independence referendum. Apparently we've just been through hell. Had you noticed? No, neither had I. Donald didn't specify the nature of the hell, so we're left to speculate. Since the President's views are formed by whatever it was he last saw on *Fox News* or heard from some conspiracy theorist, the chances are that the hell he was referring to was a spate of alien abductions in Bonnybridge that he learned all about in the latest episode of *Nazi Alien Bigfoot Ghost Hunters* on the History Channel. Although to be fair, it has approximately the same grounding in reality as the Scottish Conservatives. Bigly divisive!

The main objection that the US President has to Scottish independence is that he's unsure what would happen to the British Open. That's the Open golf championship which is administered by the Royal and Ancient Golf Club of St Andrews. Despite the fact that the competition is run and managed by a golf club which is in Scotland, Donald Trump is worried about whether the Open can continue to be held in Scotland, or more exactly, his golf courses in Scotland, after Scottish independence. That's the kind of firm grasp on the details that we've come to expect from a fan of Brexit. Of course the chances are that Donald's courses might not host the Open after independence, but that will only be because the Scottish government has allowed Mexico to build a wall around them.

However since most of Scotland has hated the Donald long before it was fashionable, the revelation that another big orange man has come out firmly in support of the Union can only boost the chances of independence, in order to annoy Trump if for no other reason. Hence the grudging mentions of the story in yer usual Unionesque outlets, which glossed over the news as quickly as possible. It got all of ten seconds on the *BBC News* where we are, and none at all on the national news.

Compare and contrast with when the last US President made a far less equivocal statement in opposition to Scottish independence. When Obama hinted that he'd prefer it if the United Kingdom remained united, it dominated the headlines for days, was the lead story on the BBC, and was analysed and discussed in depth. Meanwhile Trump's outright condemnation of Scottish independence is being glossed over like a report from a pro-independence think tank that maybe Scotland isn't so poor and helpless after all. Good news for Scottish independence is never as newsworthy as bad news for Scottish independence. Funny that.

5 August 2017

We can imagine a better Scotland –
and Unionists hate that

Imagine a burn as it rises in the rain-lashed hills looming above a Scottish moor, and in your mind follow its path to the sea. There are waterfalls where it covers the vertical distance almost in an instant. It passes by the ruined cottages of an abandoned village. It pools in the stretches of calm water that appear still and tranquil in a boggy landscape that captures centuries sodden with pain and loss. There are meanderings. There are eddies. There is turbulence as the stream crashes into the rocks and leaps and sprays and gurgles and cries. As it approaches the end of its journey the tide sometimes creates a backflow as the stream broadens, deepens, becomes mature. But the current goes only one way, always onwards, always flowing. A Scottish burn always reaches the sea where the waters are freed from the confines of their banks to dance their way across the great world ocean. That's the path to independence. It's a journey of the imagination.

British nationalists don't like it when supporters of Scottish independence wax poetic. They don't like it when we talk of the spirit, the soul, the imagination. That's because there is no poetry in the Scottish rendition of British nationalism. There is no song and the only music they possess is the music of a marching band that beats the drum of pursed lips, of short-sightedness, of meanness of spirit. British nationalism in Scotland is founded in telling us what we can't do, who we can't be, what we can't afford, what we mustn't aspire to. It's not a dream, it's a fearscape. It's the chains on our imagination that drag us down and stop us soaring. It's the spitefulness of caging a wild bird. It is as poetic as a till receipt for a broken plastic flower.

This week the noted Scottish author Andrew O'Hagan delivered a lyrical speech to the Edinburgh Book Festival in which he spoke about his conversion to the cause of independence, his belief in the inevitability that Scotland will one day, one day soon, retake its place amongst the independent states of this world. He spoke about how the British state has been destroyed by those who claim to love and cherish it. He spoke about the searing betrayal of Scotland's distinctiveness by series of British nationalist politicians who put Scotland's interests behind those of their parties. He spoke about sitting in the Supreme Court as Scotland's voice was traduced by a British establishment that openly boasted that the Sewel Convention was meaningless cant designed to keep Scotland in its place. He spoke about the poetry of Scotland, and a land that finds itself in its lyrics and its verse.

It didn't go down well with British nationalists. One wrote in the *Guardian* to condemn it as beautifully expressed nonsense in a piece which was ugly and sneeringly expressed nonsense which resorted to legalism and lacked the ability to distinguish between what is legal and what is right. It may be legal for Westminster to claim that the Sewel Convention is meaningless in law, it doesn't make it right, it doesn't make it moral.

The British nationalists who don't have the insight to recognise their own nationalism were upset and angry that Andrew chose to speak about the value and worth of a Scotland that plugs itself directly into the rest of the world and which isn't mediated by Westminster, and not about the price of oil or taxes or budgets. They were outraged that he chose to speak of the limitless and boundless Scotland of his own imagination, and not the poor and helpless Scotland of a British nationalist imagining. They were furious that he spoke about the infinite possibilities of a land that's free to define itself instead of the bean-counting negativity of a budget deficit of Westminster's creation. They were contemptuous that he was no longer cooperating in their mission to squash Scotland's spirit with a spreadsheet, which to be fair to them is the only thing they've got that counts as creative writing. But above all they were angry because he refused to speak within the bounds of their narrow vision. How dare a creative writer create a vision of a Scotland that isn't a British one.

A country discovers itself in the voices of its creative writers. It sees itself in the mirror that literature and poetry hold up to it. The path to independence is a path that is hacked out by poets, made firm by novelists, given foundations by playwrights. The path to independence is a path that is made from dreams, from spirit, from imagination, not from spreadsheets and graphs. That's why the Union is over and the British nationalists have already lost. If you have no imagination of your own, you can't speak for the imagination of a nation.

Scotland is swimming in the sweet water of the independence stream. And we can smell the sea.

19 August 2017

Devolution improved Scotland but Westminster's as bad as ever

This week it's twenty years since the people of Scotland voted by a very large margin to re-establish a parliament in Edinburgh. Predictably, the British nationalist press has been full of miserable articles about how the Holyrood parliament has failed to live up to expectations. There's only one thing about Scottish culture that British nationalists will admit is distinctive and which isn't motivated by hatred of the English, and that's the belief that everything that ever happens in Scotland is substandard and something of a Krankie of light entertainment. For British nationalists to be Scottish is to live in the permanent condition of heading to iTunes to download the latest hit from Beyoncé and only ever hearing Fran and Anna. No wonder they always look so disappointed.

Naturally this doesn't apply to all those things which are graciously granted to us by the Westminster parliament. They're fab. Scotland in the Union exists purely in order for the Conservatives to have something to be altruistic about. If we are to believe British nationalists, Scotland is in fact the only thing on this planet that the Conservatives throw billions of pounds at out of sheer goodwill and human kindness.

The Scottish parliament was also granted to Scotland by the goodwill and human kindness of the Westminster parliament, but it's the exception that proves the rule. Westminster granted it to Scotland, but it has become the voice of Scotland, and in the view of British nationalists that's why it's rubbish.

Even at the best of times being a British nationalist in

Scotland means to bear the permanent expression of a person who sucks frozen lemons while needing root canal treatment. To be a supporter of the British state means promoting the view that everything about Scotland is a bit rubbish, except the SNP and independence which are extremely rubbish. That is after all the only argument that they've got left to support the Union. So it's not surprising that the anniversary of the rebirth of Scotland's parliament would leave British nationalists in Scotland feeling as positive and cheery as a serial philanderer who's just discovered that what he thought was a Viagra pill is in fact a stale soor plum with all the regenerative power of Anas Sarwar as the next leader of Labour's Scottish accounting unit.

However the miserable po-faced British nationalists do have, for once, reasons not to be cheerful. The establishment of the Scottish parliament at the end of the 1990s really didn't achieve what British nationalists wanted it to achieve. They wanted it to kill Scottish nationalism stone dead, and it has spectacularly failed to do so. Back in the 1990s there were certainly people who wanted independence, but the idea of independence was marginal in Scottish politics, kept firmly out of the mainstream. Twenty years on and the idea of Scottish independence is not merely slap bang in the middle of the mainstream, it is the pivot around which all of Scottish politics revolves.

The British nationalist parties have only got themselves to blame for this. When the Scottish parliament was re-established in the 1990s, the Labour Party treated it as an opportunity to indulge in some short-term game playing which it believed would advantage it against the Tories on one hand and the SNP on the other. The voting system for the new parliament was expressly designed in a deal between the Lib Dems and Labour to give those parties the best chance of forming a coalition administration in Holyrood in perpetuity. The much vaunted tax-raising powers promised to the new parliament were deliberately designed in such a way as to make them unusable. Powers which had been promised to the new parliament were stripped out of the final bill at the behest of Labour Party figures. That's why Holyrood does not have control of broadcasting as was originally envisaged. Tony Blair boasted that the new parliament would be little more than a parish council.

Although Holyrood was established amidst duplicity, opportunism and short-term party political politicking on the part of the Labour Party, Scotland took it and made it its own. The parliament was always Scotland's own. It was created in the first place due to massive pressure from ordinary Scottish people and a grass-roots campaign that couldn't be ignored. Labour was riding high in the polls in Scotland in the late 1990s, but the party knew that if it betrayed its promise to introduce a parliament, that popularity would evaporate. They gave Scotland the absolute minimum that they could get away with, they did their utmost to shape it in their own image, but once established the parliament was no longer a creature of the Labour Party.

Scotland is a different country as a result of the parliament. The sense of hopeless desperation which characterised the 1980s and 1990s is no longer the dominant theme in Scottish politics. Scotland can resist Westminster. Scotland has a voice to articulate a vision of something different. No wonder the British nationalists are unhappy with how the parliament has turned out.

Their unhappiness is now turning into a threat against the devolution settlement. Scotland didn't tug its forelock and settle into a quiet acceptance of whatever Westminster chose to give us. Instead Scotland used its parliament to do things differently. It used its parliament to explore the possibility of life without Westminster. And for that Scotland must be punished.

Westminster is using the Brexit legislation to undermine the devolution settlement and take powers back for itself. Brexit isn't just a threat to Scotland's economy, it's also a threat to the devolution settlement and the idea that underpins it that everything which is not expressly reserved to Westminster is devolved. Devolved powers which were exercised by the EU on Scotland's behalf are being seized by Westminster. The Tories even have the gall to argue that this Westminster power grab represents "extra powers for Holyrood".

Everything has changed, and nothing has changed. Twenty years on from devolution Scotland is a very different country, but Westminster remains as duplicitous, underhand and manipulative as before. It's that lack of good faith on the part of Westminster which has driven the demand for Scottish independence. It's what will result in the end of the devolution settlement and its replacement with independence.

13 September 2017

Jacob Rees-Mogg is a morally bankrupt Tory toff

Tory leadership hopeful Jacob Rees-Mogg, who bears a startlingly uncanny resemblance to posh Cuthbert from the Bash Street Kids comic strip, has yet again been demonstrating that his cartoon double is a more three-dimensional character than he is. You would almost think that Jacob had consciously based his entire persona on that of Cuthbert, if it wasn't for the fact that we can be sure that he's never read the Bash Street Kids, on account of the fact that The Beano was never published in Latin. Latin for Bash Street Kids is Gnati Viae Oppugnandī, in case Jacob was wondering.

This week, Jacob has decided to speak down to us from the lofty heights of his eighteenth-century affectations to say that the rise in the usage of food banks in the UK is a great thing. It's all "rather uplifting", said Jacob during an interview on LBC radio, or rather, "the LBC wireless telegraphy" as he doubtless prefers to call it. According to the food banks themselves, the rise in food bank usage over recent years is due to the increasing number of people who are sanctioned by the repressive changes made to the social security system by the Conservatives, and the rising number of people in low-paid employment who are unable to make ends meet.

Earlier this year, the largest provider of food banks, the Trussell Trust, reported record numbers of people approaching it for help, and firmly blamed the rise on the chaotic introduction of Universal Credit and the six-week delay in receiving benefits. The report from the Trussell Trust demanded that the government scrap the minimum six-week wait for payment of Universal Credit, which is causing debt and leading vulnerable people to seek short-term loans at excessive rates of interest. The trust reported that some of its clients had lost their homes as a result, adding to the numbers of homeless people, numbers which have soared under the Conservatives. For a Tory to call the rise in food bank usage "uplifting" is a bit like Dracula being pleased by the spread of blood banks. The fact that increasing numbers of people in one of the richest countries in the world are having to seek out a charity in order to have enough to eat isn't uplifting, it's shameful.

Jacob affects many things, like the entire put-on eighteenth-century gentleman schtick that even his schoolmates at Eton were able to recognise as an attention-seeking act. He's praised by his supporters for his honesty and his authenticity, which apparently means that as long as you cover your cruelty and lack of compassion behind a veneer of self-conscious Latin tags you're suddenly a man of the people. But with Jacob it's all pose. He thinks Bertie Wooster is a style guide. There's no real difference between him and someone who goes to a sci-fi convention dressed as a Klingon except that the Klingon isn't trying to persuade anyone that they really are from another planet. Mind you, Jacob isn't trying to persuade us that he's from another planet, even though he really is. He's opposed to abortion in all circumstances, even rape and incest. Jacob only cares about fertilised eggs, not real human beings. This is because once you develop a central nervous system even a foetus can see how ridiculous he is.

This is a man who's being touted by many Conservative activists as a serious prospect for party leader, once the walking wounded Theresa May has been deposed. There's a certain type of Tory who is attracted to a posh boy. Saying nasty and unacceptable things in a cut-glass accent apparently makes the unacceptable more acceptable. To be bereft of compassion, care and humanity, but to deliver it in Etonian vowels seemingly makes it plain-speaking. But cruelty is still cruelty, however you dress it up.

To affect to find it uplifting because other people are trying to remedy the wrongs that you and your own political party are responsible for creating takes moral bankruptcy to a whole new level. It means that you're no better than a thug who is happy to mug the poor and the vulnerable and deprive them of a dignified living and then have the hypocrisy to claim that it's a wonderful thing that other people are trying to right the evils that you have done. You're trying to claim that the fact that other people are trying to repair the damage you've done means it's fine for you to do damage.

You may be a very polite thug, an impeccably tailored thug, a thug with good manners who knows how to say "please" and "thank you". But you're still a thug who's excusing thuggish behaviour. The United Kingdom has become a nasty place where to be poor means to be punished and blamed for your poverty, and the Conservatives are the party of a thuggocracy that celebrates casual cruelty. No amount of expensive tailoring and an even more expensive education can mask the rotting smell of a party that's corrupting the soul of Britain.

16 September 2017

Here's why we're going to win the next referendum

Everything in Scottish politics changed three years ago. Well, everything except the Labour Party in Scotland's persistent search for a leader who can last longer than a gobstopper. On Monday it was the third anniversary of the first Scottish independence referendum. There will be another, and the next independence referendum will be the last Scottish independence referendum, because the independence movement is going to win it. Scotland is on a trajectory that leads only one way, and today, the twentieth of September, is the third anniversary of that journey. The eighteenth of September is the anniversary of a vote. The nineteenth of September is the anniversary of a hangover. The nineteenth of September 2014 was the day that we nursed our wounds, when we grieved for the hopes that were not to be realised immediately, we mourned for the dreams that were not about to come true.

The twentieth of September, today's anniversary, is a much more important date. The twentieth of September 2014 is the day that the independence movement picked itself up, dusted itself down, and said to Scotland and to the world, "This story isn't over. We've only just got started." The twentieth of September is when we realised that the dream of independence wasn't dead, it was still very much alive and it still danced and shone and lit the path to a better country. It was the day when we made a vow of our own, a vow to hold the British establishment to account for the promises and commitments it had made during the referendum campaign, a vow to keep the flame of hope burning bright.

Supporters of the British state constantly claim that Scotland has passed "peak Nat". It's a claim that's made even more regularly than the Labour Party in Scotland seeks a new leader. That would be the new leader who really is going to put the SNP back in their box this time. Honest. Pinkie promise. No really. It's a claim that's made more out of wishful thinking than anything factual. It's a claim that's based in a nostalgic longing for the days when the desire for Scottish independence was the preserve of big beardy men who put on kilts at weekends and ran about the hills pretending to be Pictish warriors. It's a claim that's based in denial of the reality that Scotland changed irrevocably in 2014, and the independence movement is here to stay. It's a claim that fervently hopes that any temporary reversal for the independence movement means it's going away for good. Sadly for them, but happily for Scotland, that's not going to happen. There is no country in the world where an independence movement has achieved the support of half the population and then just gone away.

In Quebec, the independence movement has only just been kept at bay by a federal Canada which has bent over backwards to accommodate the national aspirations of Quebec. The Quebec referendum of 1980 was followed by changes to the Canadian constitution which strengthened and enshrined the national rights of Canada's only majority French-speaking province. The Quebec independence movement remains strong and vital, even though Canada has gone a long way to answering many of the demands of the movement, and even though Quebec has considerably greater powers over its own affairs than Scotland does. There might not be any immediate prospect of a third independence referendum in Quebec, but only a fool would insist there could never be one, and only a bigger fool would be confident that the Quebec independence movement couldn't win it. The politics of independence are part of the Quebec mainstream.

In the UK on the other hand, the promises made to Scotland by the Westminster parliament during the independence campaign have turned out to be as empty as Jacob Rees-Mogg's *Big Book of Modernity* and as truthful as Boris Johnson's insistence that he puts the needs of the country before his career. The Scottish independence referendum has been followed by a series of vindictive and power-grabbing acts on the part of a Westminster which seems determined to punish Scotland for daring to be different. They told us that Scotland was a valued and equal member of a family of nations. The British parties competed with one another in the Smith Commission to give as little ground as possible and to strip the infamous Vow of any meaningful content. We got English Votes for English Laws, and the legal guarantees of the permanence of the Scottish parliament turned out to be meaningless window dressing. We were promised that the only way to be certain of our membership of the EU was to vote for the UK, and then we got Brexit.

The independence movement at large looked on the works of the not-so-mighty British state and didn't despair. Instead we all said, "I told you so," to our No-voting friends and colleagues. Every lie, every slight, every insult, it's only fuel for the independence cause. We don't need to go grievance hunting. Grievances are dished out by the British state like confetti at a wedding. It's the only thing they're generous with. Three years on and the independence movement is still active, still energised, still enthusiastic. We're going nowhere until we've achieved independence.

If you wanted a lesson in how not to deal with an independence movement, you couldn't do worse than to look at how the UK is riding roughshod over Scotland's vote to remain a part of the EU, and how it is using the Brexit vote as an excuse to weaken the devolution settlement and constrain Holyrood even further. Where Canada strengthened and empowered Quebec in the wake of its first independence referendum, the UK is weakening and trivialising Scotland.

It's because Westminster didn't take Scotland seriously that we had the first independence referendum. It seems that they've learned nothing. That's why, unlike in Quebec, Scotland's second independence referendum is going to produce a Yes vote.

20 September 2017

I voted SNP because they promised me indyref2 ... they must deliver it BEFORE 2021

Over the past couple of weeks, a number of senior figures within the SNP have aired the idea that the next independence referendum should be delayed until after the 2021 Scottish elections. The argument is that SNP should fight that election campaign on a renewed mandate for a referendum, and that the return of a pro-independence majority to Holyrood would therefore provide a solid response to the cries of the British nationalist parties that Scotland doesn't want another referendum. It's not an argument that some of us in the independence movement who are not in the SNP find very convincing.

The SNP already has a mandate for another independence referendum, a mandate which has been validated on no less than three occasions. Scotland voted for a pro-independence majority in Holyrood in the last Scottish elections. The mandate sought by the SNP in 2016 was for the right to hold another independence referendum should there be a change in material circumstances, and Scotland being taken out of the EU against the will of the people of Scotland was explicitly stated as an example of such a change in circumstances. The voters of Scotland agreed, and returned a pro-independence majority to Holyrood. That was the first validation.

The second validation came when the Scottish parliament voted through a bill giving the Scottish government the right to press ahead with an independence referendum and to negotiate with the Westminster government in order to bring that about. That's how democracy works. Ruth Davidson herself conceded as much when in 2014 she said that the way to get a referendum was for the pro-independence parties to get a majority in the Scottish parliament and to vote one through. She needs to be reminded of that. She needs to be reminded how democracy works. The Tories lost the election in 2016. The losers don't get to determine government policy.

The third validation came in the general election this year. Nicola Sturgeon said that should the SNP be returned as the largest party in terms of votes and the largest party in terms of seats, that would reinforce the existing mandate. The SNP didn't do as well as they wanted, but they still ended up as the largest Scottish party with more MPs than MPs from all the other parties combined. To concede that "Scotland doesn't want a referendum" because the parties which lost the election say so means to concede that the SNP didn't really win the election at all. It means to concede that a mandate for independence isn't as valid as a mandate for the Union. That's not how to win independence.

The SNP didn't do as well in the general election as they'd hoped, but the reason they didn't do as well as they might have done wasn't because they support another referendum. It was because they failed to explain to the people of Scotland why Scotland needs another referendum. It was because they failed to enthuse and engage with independence supporters and Yes voters and get them out to vote. It was because they tried to back off from the idea of independence, leaving the field clear to the vacuous naw-ness of Ruth Davidson and the Tories whose sole policy was "Scotland doesn't want another referendum". The SNP is always going to be attacked by the British nationalist parties on independence. It has to own the idea, not downplay it. You won't win independence by being afraid of mentioning independence.

The lessons that Scotland should learn from Catalonia and Kurdistan are that you don't surrender the cause of independence just because those who are opposed to it are predictably against it; you don't surrender the cause of independence just because you won an election but you failed to win it by a sufficiently crushing margin; you achieve independence because you believe in it, but no one is going to trust you if you don't act as though you believe in it. You don't win self-determination without being determined about it. You achieve independence by strength of will.

Many independence supporters don't vote SNP because we want to see Nicola Sturgeon lead a devolved administration. We don't vote SNP because we want to see SNP MPs in a Westminster parliament which we don't wish to have any control over Scottish affairs. We vote SNP because we want independence. We vote SNP because only a pro-independence majority in Holyrood can bring about the only legitimate route to independence – via an independence referendum in which the cause of independence is backed by a majority of Scottish voters.

If the SNP reneges on its existing mandate, many independence supporters will think twice before backing the party in 2021. Why vote for an independence party when it doesn't bring about an independence referendum even though it achieves a mandate for it? It's not a good look. Scotland needs an independence referendum before 2021, ideally towards the end of this parliamentary term. In 2012 a majority of Scots didn't want a referendum, yet once a date was set people became engaged and Scotland changed forever. Scotland can still achieve its historic destiny, but we won't achieve it if we lose our nerve.

30 September 2017

Biased Unionist media is the major obstacle to Scottish independence

Although there are interesting parallels and similarities between Scotland and Catalonia, there are also some very big differences. The biggest obstacle facing Catalonia as it attempts to achieve independence is the intransigence of the Spanish state, and the fact that the Spanish constitution explicitly rules out an independence referendum. The biggest obstacle Scotland faces is our truly lamentable media, a media which is grossly unrepresentative of the views of the country it purports to serve.

Opinion polls have been pretty consistent. A tad under half the population of Scotland support Scottish independence. The numbers who oppose independence and support independence are in the same ballpark, yet that's not the view you'd get if your sole source of information about Scotland was a Scottish print media which is overwhelmingly tilted against independence. For a print publication to support independence is seen as being "political" in a way that opposing it is not, even though both points of view are equally political. Out of all the many and various newspapers published in this country, just one daily and one Sunday support a view of the constitution which has the backing of almost half the population.

We have a print media in which frankly bigoted and ignorant assertions about aspects of Scottish culture are repeated as though they are fact and allowed to go unchallenged. It is not merely objectionable for a print journalist to assert in the pages of a newspaper that the Scots language is nothing more than English slang, or that Gaelic is a dead language, it is also factually incorrect. Gaelic is in fact amongst the top ten per cent of languages of the world in terms of its number of speakers. Most languages are spoken by very small populations. There is a legitimate argument to be had about the status of Scots, but what it's certainly not is "English slang". Far from challenging the infamous Scottish Cultural Cringe, all too often the anti-independence print media in Scotland sees its job as being the propagation and reinforcement of it.

Equally you'd find it difficult to discern in the Scottish media the reality that the much-touted GERS figures tell us very little about the finances of an independent Scotland. The GERS figures give us some very rough estimates of Scottish revenues, and tell us about UK spending priorities and UK taxation regulations. The entire point of independence is to do things differently. If the GERS figures are bad for Scotland all they tell us is that UK economic policies are not working for Scotland. You'd struggle to see that in a media which crows about Scotland being poorer than Greece as though this was some great argument in favour of continuing UK rule.

This is the same media which give huge prominence to statements from supporters of the Better Together campaign which assert that Scotland is a basket case, only all too often they neglect to tell us that the person concerned was a supporter of the Better Together campaign. Meanwhile comments from independence supporters are presented dripping with quote marks if they are presented at all. Think tanks which are opposed to independence receive huge publicity for their reports, even the Fraser of Allander Institute which sounds like a knitwear shop in Pitlochry. Reports from the pro-independence think tank Common Weal get reported in *The National* and the *Sunday Herald* and nowhere else.

The Scottish print media is overwhelmingly a British nationalist cartel in which opinion is dressed up as fact, but our broadcast media is every bit as bad. It is a sad and lamentable state of affairs that it is not widely realised in Scotland that the UK is the odd one out in not permitting its devolved and self-governing nations their own public service broadcasters. Catalonia has five TV channels. Even the tiny Faroe Islands and Gagauzia in Moldova have their own broadcasters. Catalonia even has its own twenty-four-hour, seven-day-a-week news channel, but in Scotland we were reduced to pathetically pleading with BBC management for an hour-long news programme on BBC1, a request that the BBC has seen fit to deny.

One anti-independence commentator referred to the campaign to get the so-called *Scottish Six* as the "holy grail" of the independence movement. There was us thinking that the holy grail of the independence movement was independence, but thanks to British nationalism we've now learned that it's really an extra half hour of Jackie Bird.

Instead the BBC sees fit to grant Scotland a few hours per evening on a poorly funded new ghetto channel. Then in a couple of years' time they'll turn round and claim that its low viewing figures prove that there's no demand for Scottish public service broadcasting. We're being set up for failure. What Scotland really deserves is Scottish control of the BBC in Scotland. British nationalists routinely decry this as "SNP TV" and assert that it's going to be biased and propaganda, while at the same time denying vehemently that the existing set-up is biased. The truth is that if the new Scottish broadcaster is set up according to the same charter that governs the BBC, then it will be neither more nor less biased than the BBC is. Opponents of Scottish public service broadcasting can't have it both ways. If they claim that a new Scottish public service broadcaster is going to biased, then it's a tacit admission that the BBC is biased in a pro-British nationalist direction, and that only makes the case for a Scottish public service broadcaster stronger.

Since the Scottish government isn't going to press ahead with the case for independence for the time being, it's incumbent upon them to highlight the inadequacies and shortcomings of the existing devolution settlement. One of those inadequacies is the lack of a Scottish public service broadcaster. The SNP needs to be more assertive in pressing the case for a Scottish media which is truly representative of the diversity of Scotland. Europe is full of examples of self-governing territories, nations and regions which are far smaller than Scotland, and often far poorer, yet they manage to have thriving national public service broadcasters of their own. The reason Scotland doesn't have one has very little to do with money, and a great deal to do with the politics of British rule.

The reality is that if Scotland had a media which was as diverse and as representative of public opinion as the Catalan media, we'd already be independent. That's precisely why the British nationalists are determined to ensure that we don't get one.

11 October 2017

Building the case for indy in Scotland is a DIY job, so let's get to work

The core of independence is independence of thought and action. If we want an independent Scotland in which citizens are empowered, in which ordinary people have voices that are heard, we need to put those principles into action in the campaign which achieves Scottish independence. Independence begins with independence of mind, and any independence movement worth its salt seeks to encourage and facilitate the independence of mind and action of the citizens of the country for which it's campaigning for self-determination. That means we don't sit back and wait for permission to campaign for another referendum and for an independent Scotland. We take matters into our own hands.

If we sit passively by and wait to be led, then we will find ourselves in a Scotland in which citizens are expected to be passive, in which decisions are made by elites. We would find ourselves in an independent Scotland where the only thing that had changed was the management. This is our movement, our Scotland, so it's up to all of us to speak up, to be involved, to lead ourselves. You don't achieve independence by being dependent. You achieve independence by listening to the advice of generations of Scottish mammies and grannies, who have always told us – if ye want something done, ye need tae dae it yersel. Scottish independence is us daein it wursels.

Over the past eighteen months I've been doing talks to local groups all over this country. Scotland is full of energetic, enthusiastic and talented people who are committed to winning the goal of an independent state in which they, their children, their grandchildren, can live dignified lives. However there's a perception amongst many local group members that there is a serious lack of direction and coordination on a national level, and that we risk the dissipation of all that energy and enthusiasm. So it's time for local groups to get together and decide upon a cohesive and coordinated approach, an approach that allows us all to feel as though we're a part of a truly national movement. And moreover a movement which belongs to us, rather than a movement which we're a subordinate part of. We need tae dae this wursels.

In a couple of weeks the Scottish Independence Convention is due to host a national Build conference in Edinburgh to discuss the future for the independence movement. This is the second such conference, and in my talks to local groups I've discovered that there's a widespread feeling that the great ideas and energies generated in the first Build conference went nowhere. There was a fantastic conference, but then nothing seemed to happen and local group members felt that they were left to their own devices, isolated and without any national direction or coordination. We need to avoid that happening again.

21 October 2017

Gaelic is a major part of Scotland's heritage – that's why Unionists have such a problem with it

The Tories really hate Gaelic. If you believe some of the guff that Conservative politicians and frothing Unionists with flegs in their social media avatars come out with, the Gaelic language possesses magical powers to cause potholes in the roads and to make police helicopters fall out of the sky. After Police Scotland unveiled their new logo, which has a Gaelic word on it, they've been at it again. Grìs de ghrìsean. That's "horror of horrors", in case you're a Tory MSP and you get upset by such things.

The new logo has a stylised thistle with a crown on top, underneath which are the words *Semper Vigilo*, which is Latin for "Always annoying Tory MSPs". Beneath that are the words POLICE in big letters, and underneath that POILEAS in slightly smaller letters. *Poileas* is of course Gaelic for "police", and it's pronounced "polis". Strangely, Conservative MSP Liam Kerr, who is the party's spokesmoaner for Justice Except Where Gaelic Is Concerned, decided that he was going to take exception to the single Gaelic word on the logo, and not the two Latin words. This is possibly because he doesn't want to offend Scotland's immense population of native Latin speakers.

Interestingly, Liam's own name is of Gaelic origin. Liam is the Gaelic short form for William, from Gaelic Uilliam, while Kerr comes from the Gaelic *ceàrr*, which means "wrong". A Tory MSP has a name that means "wrong". This is the clearest example of nominative determinism in reverse since Cardinal Sin was chosen as head of the Catholic Church in the Philippines.

I've been obsessed by language and linguistics since I was a wean. Scotland's linguistic history and heritage is rich and complex. This country has witnessed different languages dance across its landscape ever since written history began, and probably before that too. The Gaelic heritage of Scotland is written into our landscape in the form of countless place names, created by native Gaelic speakers and dating to a time when Gaelic was the dominant language locally. The place names trace the former extent of Gaelic and demonstrate that the language was once the dominant language of all of mainland Scotland north and west of a line drawn approximately from Dumfries to Musselburgh.

It's no exaggeration to claim that it was the use of Gaelic which formed the basis of Scotland as a nation, and many of the earliest historical sources for Scottish history were written in the classical form of the language. In the early Middle Ages, when a person was called a Scot it implied that they were a Gaelic speaker. Gaelic may no longer be the language of a majority of Scots, but it remains a vital and living part of Scotland's culture. It needs to be nourished and respected. That's why it appears on the Police Scotland logo.

Possibly the only thing that could have annoyed Liam and his fellow Conservative Gaelophobes even more than there being Gaelic on the police logo would have been if there was Scots on it. Personally I'd love to see POLIS written on the sides of Scottish police cars, or to use the technical term, "polis motors", just to witness the reaction from Tory MSPs and British nationalist commentators in the right-wing press.

The use of Gaelic and Scots in public signage isn't really about ensuring that Gaelic and Scots speakers understand something. After all, all of them are bilingual in English. It's about creating an atmosphere which tells speakers of Gaelic and Scots, languages which have been subject to oppression and ridicule in the past, that the languages are respected, are welcomed and can be used. But more than that, the use of Gaelic and Scots in public signage is about acknowledging

Scottish heritage and about making a public statement that Scotland is a country in its own right.

British nationalists respond with hysteria to attempts to protect and defend Scots and Gaelic, even though acknowledging the role of these languages in no way threatens or diminishes the place of English. English, Scots and Gaelic are all equally national languages of this country, however making that argument provokes the most ridiculous anger from British nationalists.

Some months ago I wrote a blog piece arguing that all three of Scotland's national languages deserve equal respect, only to find that a British nationalist blogger (who of course wasn't a nationalist at all because he favours the British state) claimed that what I was doing was exactly the same in principle as radio broadcasters during the Rwandan genocide calling on Hutu people to take machetes to their Tutsi neighbours. He was in all seriousness comparing English speakers in Scotland to victims of the Rwandan genocide because I was arguing that Gaelic and Scots are also national languages of Scotland.

The reason for the hysteria isn't because anyone is demanding that English speakers are forced to learn Gaelic or Scots, because no one is arguing that. What British nationalists really object to is that if Scotland has a culture and an identity of its own, then there must be more to the desire for Scottish independence than an atavistic hatred of the English.

4 November 2017

The EU's treatment of Catalans
is a betrayal of democracy

It's like being trapped in a heartless, loveless and controlling relationship, dreaming of escape and hoping that a good-looking and
glamorous European can whisk you away to a better life. Only
then you realise that the good-looking and glamorous European
isn't so good-looking and glamorous on closer inspection, and is
every bit as heartless, loveless and controlling as the domineering
partner in the relationship you yearn to escape from. Now you
find yourself reconsidering. That's a brief summary of the evolution of the attitude of the Scottish independence movement
towards the European Union. Because of the EU's shameful
treatment of Catalonia, Scotland's independence movement is
falling out of love with Europe.

If that's how you treat our sister, we know that we can't
expect anything better. If we do somehow get better treatment and greater understanding than Catalonia has received
from the EU, it will only be because the EU wants to use
us as a stick to beat up England. Scotland's independence
movement has spent decades fighting against the insulting
stereotype that everything we do is motivated by hatred for
England. We'll only be undoing all that hard work if we base
our independence campaign on being a proxy for someone
else's desire to do England down.

The EU's attitude towards Catalan attempts to achieve
independence peacefully and democratically has been
hypocritical and characterised by a disrespect for the rights
of Catalans – who are after all EU citizens – and a disrespect
for international law. The EU has shown that it's not a union
of nations, it's a club of states.

The EU has made it clear that it will only deal with Madrid, and that as far as it is concerned what's going on in Catalonia is for Madrid to deal with as it sees fit. According to a statement released by EU President Jean-Claude Juncker on 2 October, what is happening in Catalonia "is an internal matter for Spain that has to be dealt with in line with the constitutional order of Spain". However just because something is legal doesn't mean it's right. Apartheid was legal. Jailing gay people was legal. Colonialism was legal.

The fact is that the right to self-determination is a principle of international law, and as such it is a greater right than Spain's right to territorial integrity, and a greater right than anything enshrined in the constitution of any particular state. Madrid, and the EU, both argue that the Catalan referendum was illegal under Spanish law, and that's the end of the matter. However if that's the case then Spain and the EU have effectively abolished international law. It means that any state could pass a law or write a constitutional clause forbidding an independence referendum on part of its territory, and then no stateless nation anywhere would ever be able to achieve independence. The current borders of states would be pickled in aspic forever. It requires the international community to enforce international law, and as one of the world's most powerful and influential transnational organisations, by denying the right of Catalonia to self-determination the EU has betrayed us all, not just the Catalans. As Carles Puigdemont said on Monday in a statement from exile in Brussels, "This is not just about Catalonia. This is about democracy itself."

This takes us into the thorny question of nationhood. Spain insists that the Catalans do not constitute a nation. In fact one of the sparks for the push towards independence in Catalonia was the Spanish Supreme Court striking down Catalonia's statute of autonomy in 2010 because, amongst other things, it stated that Catalonia was a nation. The statute had been approved by a large majority in a referendum in Catalonia and passed by the Spanish parliament. However the court ruled that under Spanish law, Catalonia was not a nation and could never be recognised as such.

I lived in Spain at the time. I had numerous disagreements with Spanish friends and colleagues, some of whom were supporters of the Partido Popular (the party of Mariano Rajoy, the current Spanish prime minister). All of them supported Scotland's right to self-determination. All of them agreed that Scotland was a nation, because Scotland had a long history as an independent state and then voluntarily, or at least sort of voluntarily, entered into a union with the Kingdom of England. None of them, not even the most fervent right-wing supporter of the Partido Popular, had the slightest problem with the idea of Scottish independence, which is one of the reasons I was always confident that Spain would not block Scottish accession to the EU. But they denied that Catalonia was a nation. Catalonia has never been an independent state, they said. Catalonia was only ever one of the constituent territories of the Kingdom of Aragon before that kingdom united with Castile to form Spain in 1492. So, they claimed, Catalonia isn't a nation, and that means Catalonia has no right to self-determination.

It's a peculiar argument, that nationhood depends upon prior statehood, but it's an argument that's widespread and commonplace amongst those who oppose Catalan independence. In the history of the world it's generally been the other way about. A population which is culturally or linguistically distinctive comes to feel that it's a nation, and then they agitate for independence and create a state. However the real point here is that it's not for external parties to inform other people what their identity really is. The key part of self-determination is the self part of it. It's not for Greece to tell Macedonia that there's no such thing as a Macedonian nation. It's not for Turkey to tell the Kurds that there's no such thing as a Kurdish nation. And it's not for Spain to tell Catalonia that there's no such thing as a Catalan nation. People know for themselves what nation they belong to and to be told otherwise is as insulting as it is for supporters of Scottish independence to be told that the only reason we want independence is because we supposedly hate the English.

In turning a blind eye to Catalonia, in being silent as its leaders are imprisoned, in refusing to condemn the violence of the Spanish state on the day of the Catalan referendum, the EU has shown itself to be a union of elites, a union of the powerful and of existing state structures. It's not a union of European peoples. The EU has effectively agreed with Spain that there's no such thing as a Catalan nation and is not respecting the right of Catalans to define themselves. As Scotland is dragged into a disastrous Brexit by right-wing British nationalist ideologues, for Scotland's independence movement the lesson from Catalonia is that we need to rethink our attitude to the EU.

8 November 2017

Abuse from online trolls means I'm getting through

One of the joys of writing about Scottish politics is that you get your very own stalkers with a lovely line in hate mail. It's difficult to understand what they imagine that they're achieving, although truth be told I don't really mind as it's possibly some sort of therapy for them and they clearly lack more productive outlets. Amongst the more regular of my spittle-flecked correspondents there's the guy who frequently posts creepily overfamiliar comments on my blog, and there's the cranky old man who keeps sending hate-filled emails with all the obsessiveness of a stamp collector on crack.

There are a few reasons I don't mind too much about the slurs and insults. After all if you dish it out you can't complain about being dished in return. It would be nice though if some of them could display just a modicum of wit, or anything approaching a sense of humour, or indeed anything approaching the ability to spell. Sometimes it would be nice to be attacked for what I've actually said, instead of what the person thinks that I said.

Another reason for not minding too much is that thanks to the wonders of modern technology, it's remarkably easy to set up filters to catch all the hateful missives from my regular frenemies. Their communications go directly into the trash folder without me ever seeing them – unless I deliberately look in the trash like I did for the purposes of writing this article.

I wrote a blog article earlier this week which was about the topic of swearing and how it's permissible to say all sorts of cruel and hateful things, but if you use a sweary word that's beyond the pale. It was quite a sweary blog article as you might expect in an article about swearing, but amongst other things it included a translation into Ancient Greek of a pastiche of a well-known phrase. Then amazingly enough along comes some muppet to complain about how I was guilty of lowering educational standards because the article also contained the F-word. Well, several F-words. You can translate things into your actual Ancient Greek, but if the piece also contains a sweary word, then you're automatically an example of a shameful lack of educational standards and it's all the fault of the SNP. Cranky stamp-collecting guy got quite exercised about it too, and he's got problems spelling in English never mind Ancient Greek.

However what really gets the crankier members of the British nationalist brigade wound up, even more than when you write about Scottish politics from a pro-independence perspective, is when you write about Scottish culture. *The National* experiences this. The paper is a frequent target of outraged British nationalists on social media who are appalled that there should be one single Scottish daily newspaper that supports independence. Apparently this is terrible bias, and proper balance and neutrality can only be restored once there are no independence-supporting newspapers at all and Scotland returns to the days when all its print media choruses support for the Union. But what really gets the Better Togetherist goat is when *The National* publishes one of its regular pieces in Scots. How dare we have a culture. That's ethnic nationalism that is. And that's wrong. Writing things in Scots makes you a fascist. Etc. etc. *ad nauseam*.

Hate mail, insults, abuse and slurs directed at prominent supporters of the UK get plastered all over the media. It provokes anguished articles in the media about the cancer at the very heart of the independence movement and is cited as proof that independence supporters are all swivel-eyed loons with a discourse in hate. The same thing directed at supporters of independence passes unremarked, unless of course the abuse and insults are coming from other independence supporters in which case you can expect supportive noises from the usual Unionist suspects.

There's a very definite double standard at play. Independence supporters are to be judged by the actions of the tiny minority who are insulting and abusive, but opponents of independence who are insulting and abusive are a tiny fringe who are in no way to be considered representative of anyone but themselves.

This is deliberate. It's a tactic used by opponents of independence to depict the cause of independence as being supported only by cranks, nasty people and abusive zoomers. It's a way of trying to prevent people from engaging with the debate on Scotland's future, because once people do start to engage with the debate and to examine the arguments, more often than not they realise that the current constitutional settlement is not sustainable, and they become open to the idea of independence. The very last thing that the British establishment wants is a Scottish population which is politically aware, active and engaged.

The most important reason I don't mind too much about being the target of insults and abuse is that it means that we're getting through. Someone who obsessively spends their time writing to you to inform you in abusive terms that you're having no influence or effect is disproving their own argument by the mere fact of their obsessive interest in you. It's pretty clear that I'm having a strong effect on that person. And that makes me all the more determined to continue.

11 November 2017

How British nationalism fuels
Scottish sectarianism

Last week it was revealed that the amount of anti-Catholic sectarian graffiti in Glasgow had almost doubled in 2016 compared to the previous year. There were 188 instances of anti-Catholic graffiti that year, and a further fifty-six in just the three months beginning 2017. The bigots are out, and they're spreading their message of hatred with their spray cans, telling members of a community which has been established in Scotland for hundreds of years that they're not welcome here.

I'm the world's worst Catholic. I was dragged up in the Church by Catholic parents who were appalled that despite their best efforts it didn't take. Possibly because I was born without the shame gene. The "I'm not going to Mass any more" fight that I had with my parents back in the 1970s was way bigger than the "I'm gay" fight that came a few years later. I've not been to Mass for many years, and don't regard myself as a Catholic, but I'll always be a Catholic in the eyes of some.

I don't believe in transubstantiation or the apostolic succession. I certainly don't believe in the Virgin Birth and if Jesus did exist he wasn't the son of any god except in a metaphorical sense. We're born here on this planet in this life, and we all have a moral duty to try and leave it a wee bit better than how we found it. If a deity wants to condemn you to eternal torment because you decided not to believe in the truth of some religious text or other, or because you happened to have been born into the wrong religious tradition, then that's a deity with a lot less compassion than a mere frail mortal is capable of demonstrating. If you asked me what my religion was I'd tell you I was apatheistic. It's not that I don't believe in God exactly, although I tend to lean in that direction, it's just that I don't care enough in order to have a strong opinion. This is decidedly not Catholicism.

But according to some of the polyester-uniformed big-drum-banging brigade, I'm always going to be a Catholic. Being Catholic in Scotland isn't really about a person's private religious beliefs. It's about your family background and your ancestry. I'm of Irish Catholic descent, and therefore will forever be a Catholic in the eyes of some, even if I shaved my head, donned yellow robes, adopted a Tibetan name, and wandered up and down Duke Street in Glasgow chanting "Om" outside those bars that are festooned with Union flegs because the people who drink there hate nationalism. That means that when we talk about sectarianism in Scotland, we're not really talking about religion at all. How can it be when you can still be subject to it irrespective of your own religious beliefs? Religion is just one of the tags used to distinguish the out-group. We're really talking about anti-Irish racism.

There are those who argue that the way to tackle sectarianism is to abolish Catholic schools. I attended a Catholic school and am no great fan of them. However I'm not entirely clear how abolishing Catholic schools is going to prevent anti-Catholic bigotry amongst people who don't attend Catholic schools. That's like claiming that homophobia is caused by gay bars. Catholic schools were established by the Catholic community in the nineteenth century to protect themselves from the rampant sectarianism prevalent in Scotland at that time. Equally sectarianism is not about football. Football is just one of the ways in which underlying bigotries manifest themselves. These things are symptoms of sectarianism, not its cause.

Let's not bother with the false moral equivalences here. It's very easy to respond to the challenges of sectarianism with a plague on all their houses, but Scottish sectarianism does not affect everyone equally. Those who bear the brunt of it are Scottish people of Irish Catholic descent. Religious hate crime figures collated by the police show that although Catholics make up just sixteen per cent of the Scottish population, fifty-seven per cent of all religiously motivated hate crimes in Scotland target Catholics or Catholicism. There were 673 charges of religiously motivated hate crimes recorded by police in Scotland over the year 2016-17, which represents a rise of fourteen per cent on the previous year. This is the highest number for the past four years. If you are a member of Scotland's "Catholic" community, and the quotation marks are deliberate, then you are many times more likely to be a victim of a religiously motivated hate crime than a member of the majority community.

As someone who can remember the sectarianism of the 1960s, when your employment opportunities and life chances were heavily determined by whit fit ye kicked wi, I'd be the first to proclaim that the sectarianism of modern Scotland is but a shadow of its former self. That is an enormous testament to the goodwill and common sense of the great majority of the people of this country. But the recent rise in hate crime statistics proves that we can't rest on our laurels.

The rise in anti-Catholic sectarian graffiti in Glasgow is not unconnected to the 150 per cent rise in homophobic assaults recorded in England and Wales, and the rise in hate crimes against members of ethnic and racial minorities which was also recorded by police forces in England and Wales. All of these have come about because Brexit, with its message of xenophobia, of Britain going it alone, of isolationism, has emboldened the bigots.

The blame for the recent rise in public expressions of anti-Catholic bigotry lies squarely with those who have stoked the fires of sectarianism for political ends, and who have blown the dog whistle of bigotry in order to advance their own agendas. It's the fault of a political party which attracts individuals who have a history of expressing support for extreme right-wing organisations and the Orange Order and rewarding them with council candidacies. It's all very well claiming that these individuals have been sent on equality training, but most of us don't need equality training to know that bigotry is wrong.

Sectarianism in Scotland is a disease of British nationalism, and it's time that British nationalist politicians in this country looked to their own misdeeds instead of constantly blaming independence supporters for all this country's ills.

15 November 2017

Tories and the BBC up to their usual tricks over VAT bill for Scotland's emergency services

The Conservatives have always been the political version of Monty Python's Dennis Moore, who robbed from the poor to pay the rich. This week's budget has given them the opportunity to pretend that they're the saviours of Scotland, even though what's really happened is that they've decided to stop ripping us off in one particular way. Ruth Davidson and her not-so-merry band of thirteen are taking the credit for Philip Hammond's decision to stop charging the Scottish emergency services VAT despite the fact that the SNP have made no less than 139 representations to the government on the subject. They're a whole lot less noisy about the fact that the Chancellor also announced a funding increase for the NHS in England, but used an arcane funding method which ensured that Scotland's NHS won't benefit proportionately. They're not shouting from the rooftops that Phil is spending £3 billion to benefit homeowners in England, but not in Scotland. They're keen to trumpet a supposed £2 billion in funding for Scotland, but less keen to publicise all the many strings that come attached to it or the fact that day-to-day spending for Scotland will decrease as a result of this budget. So let's big up the VAT relief for the polis.

Asked to supply details of the representations that the Scottish Tories have made to the Chancellor about the VAT on the Scottish emergency services, which have apparently been successful where the 139 previous ones have not, Ruth Davidson has been doing what she usually does when faced with awkward questioning. She does her impression of a BBC

Scotland reporter doorstepping her over the Conservative councillors accused of racism and bigotry. Nowhere to be seen, in other words.

Since the Scottish emergency services were reformed into a single police force and fire service, they've been subject to VAT while the equivalent services elsewhere in the UK were VAT exempt. This was because of some fine print in the VAT regulations which only allowed VAT exemption for services controlled by local authorities. Once the police and fire services became Scottish national services and came under the direct authority of the Scottish parliament in 2013, they lost this exemption. At any time during the past four years, the Conservative government could have fixed this anomaly with a simple administrative procedure. They chose not to.

The Tories are now claiming that they've sorted a mess created by the SNP. However back in 2011 the SNP wasn't the only party which promised in its manifesto to create a single Scottish national police force. So did the Labour Party, and so did the Scottish Conservatives. There was only any need in the first place to rationalise the various Scottish police and fire services because of financial pressures on the Scottish budget caused by, you guessed it, the Conservative government in Westminster. So it was the Tories who created the mess, and they were proposing to tackle it in the exact same way that the SNP did.

Really what happened this week is that the Conservatives admitted that for the past four years they've been punishing Scotland for not being sufficiently Conservative. Over one hundred representations were made to the Conservative government, but the Conservative government wasn't minded to listen to them because they weren't made by Conservatives. Mind you, their forgiving mood doesn't extend as far as repaying Police Scotland the £130 million that they've already coughed up in VAT payments.

The BBC reported all this in its usual fair and balanced way. Political editor Laura Kuenssberg tweeted that the VAT relief came after interventions from Scottish Tories. It's strange that the BBC doesn't report everything in the same way that it reports politics, especially Scottish politics.

Can you imagine them reporting the weather the same way? Jackie Bird could thank Kawser Quamer for telling us that tomorrow it's going to be bucketing with rain, and then say, "And now over to Billy McHarrumpher, Conservative councillor for somewhere with loads of colourful historical parades, for a different view." Actually, given the BBC's definition of balance as far as the Scottish constitutional debate goes, we'd get weather reports from one meteorologist and three climate change deniers. This would then be followed by vox pops from the public in a snowstorm during which for every person who said it was a bit parky the BBC would show us someone wrapped up in scarf and hat and thick coat who was swearing blind that it was taps aff weather and they were looking forward to working on their tan. There's balance for you.

The Tories are now posing as the champions of Scottish interests. That's a bit like a rapacious laird during the Highland Clearances who had deported most of the crofters from his land but who decided to spare one small settlement after the tenants agreed to vote for him at the Laird of the Year Awards, and he's now posing as a champion of crofters' rights and land reform. Vote Tory, and we might rob you up slightly less than we have been robbing you. But don't expect us to pay you back anything that we've taken. It's not a great slogan, but it's a whole lot closer to the truth.

25 November 2017

Make sure you're royal or rich if your betrothed is foreign

I'm just back from spending a precious few days in Connecticut with my American fiancé, time which was devoted to planning a route through the tricky and hazardous immigration process so that we can set up home together here in Scotland. Well, that and marvelling at one of the traditional sights of a New England December – men bundled up in heavy winter coats, scarves, gloves and woollen hats, worn with shorts and training shoes with no socks. Apparently American winters only affect you from the waist up. And if you run into difficulties with the cold you can refuel at one of the donut shops sited every couple of hundred yards, seemingly always next door to a drugstore with a large range of antacids on sale.

Originally we had wanted to get married in Scotland, but thanks to changes that Theresa May made to the immigration rules when she was Home Secretary, that's not going to be possible. In order for us to wed here, my fiancé Peter would have to spend thirty days in the UK before the wedding, then would have to leave after the ceremony and apply to live here. Since he gets just fifteen days annual leave from his employer in the USA, that's not going to be possible. The only way we could get married here would be for him not to have a job to go home to. So we need to plan a wedding in the USA, which means that my elderly mother won't be able to be there, since she's got a phobia about flying. Thanks a bunch Theresa May, because you felt the need to suck up to the *Daily Mail*, my mother won't be at my wedding. Yes, I am taking it personally.

Prince Harry's bride doesn't seem to have all these problems. She swans in from across the Atlantic, sets up home with her betrothed, does a couple of photo ops, and there are reports that she's getting British citizenship, never mind permanent leave to remain. For the rest of us it takes at least five years residence before our foreign spouses would be allowed to apply for British citizenship and thus escape the malign clutches of the Home Office. Which only goes to show that you get special treatment when you have a queen in the family. We have one of those in my family too, but clearly I'm the wrong kind of queen. One of the pleasant side effects of a trip across the pond was escaping the interminable sycophantic guff about Meghanarry plastering the UK media. The only enjoyable aspect of the entire sorry proceedings was watching the *Daily Mail* pretend to be happy that an unemployed immigrant is getting a fast track to a British passport.

Frustrating and difficult as the process may be for those of us who are not multimillionaires and related to royalty, at least Peter and I know that we have a number of options and that although it will take a long time, eventually we will be able to live together. There are many British citizens who don't have even that much. They are permanently separated from their foreign spouses due to an immigration system which prioritises pandering to the right-wing press over the right of British citizens to a family life.

In order to bring a non-EU citizen into the UK as your spouse, the British partner needs to prove that they have an income over £18,600 annually. This figure increases by £3800 annually to £22,400 if the couple have a child, and further increases by £2400 for each subsequent child. According to the Joint Council for the Welfare of Immigrants, forty-two per cent of British people won't reach that financial threshold. If you are gainfully employed, but on a low wage or struggling to get by on a zero-hours contract, because of Theresa May's political need to score brownie points with the *Daily Mail* British immigration rules won't let you marry and live with a foreigner. Even if you do pass the threshold, you still have to negotiate the Byzantine complexities of an understaffed and under-resourced Home Office where documents are routinely lost or misplaced, and the onus is placed on the applicants to resolve the problem.

There's little compassion for those who are separated by the rules. Foreign partners who have expressed an intention to apply for a partner visa are prohibited from entering the country on a tourist visa. They're not even allowed to visit their loved ones. According to the Children's Commissioner for England, there are at least 15,000 children in England who are separated from a parent because of immigration rules. There is likely to be a proportionate number in Scotland – possibly as many as 1500 Scottish children are separated in the same way. They're called "Skype families", because the weans only get to see their mother or father in a video chat. That's better than nothing, but it's no substitute for a hug or a bedtime kiss.

Despite certain prominent Leave campaigners like Michael Gove promising that Scotland could control aspects of immigration policy, Westminster has denied it. Scotland thus has no chance of introducing a more compassionate and humane policy which prioritises the needs of Scottish families over the knee-jerk migrant phobia of the right-wing media. British immigration rules will continue to favour the rich and the well connected. Amongst all the hype about the royal nuptials, we should remember the thousands of British citizens and their spouses and children who don't have the benefit of Meghan and Harry's wealth and connections, and who don't have much prospect of a happy ever after.

9 December 2017

Scotland in Union letter plot isn't a conspiracy theory, it's a conspiracy FACT

Some of us who are active in the independence movement online are often accused – by supposedly respectable journalists no less – of being agents of the Kremlin, or agents of MI5. In the interests of full disclosure I should admit that I did indeed once have a meeting with a Russian handler, but that was a date some years ago with a guy from St Petersburg whom I had met on Grindr. I don't think that counts even though quite a bit of handling went on. Anyway, I'm not sure any more whether I'm an agent for MI5 trying to undermine independence, or an agent of the Kremlin trying to undermine the British state, since the same person has accused me of being both.

However it's not a crazy conspiracy theory when a supporter of the British state accuses an independence supporter of being a secret double agent, or a triple agent simultaneously working for Putin and the British state. Being a supporter of the British state gives you an automatic free pass from tinfoil hattery, just as waving a Union fleg while wearing a tee-shirt saying "God Save the Queen" means you're not a nationalist at all. Likewise it's only independence supporters who can be accused of being abusive online, just like it's only independence supporters who can be accused of being paranoid conspiracy theorists.

This even happened to the editor of the esteemed newspaper *The National*. When Callum Baird published a statement about the paper recently which mentioned that opponents of independence have been hiding copies of *The National* behind other papers, he was scoffed at by anti-independence journalists. This was despite the fact that readers of *The National* whom Callum had met during National Roadshow events have been telling him that they've actually caught people in the act of hiding *The National*. I myself have a regular troll who contacts my blog to boast about how many copies of *The National* they've hidden. In terms of journalistic rigour, Callum's statement was considerably better founded than most of the contents of certain right-wing so-called newspapers. That didn't stop British nationalists claiming that a free tinfoil hat would be given away with the next issue of *The National*.

Over the Christmas holidays a new conspiracy came to light, this time organised by members of Scotland in Union. Well I say conspiracy, it's not exactly up there with Ernst Stavro Blofeld's nefarious plans concocted in a glamourous underground base filled with monorails and piranha tanks. The closest Scotland in Union get to an underground base is when one of them gets on the subway to Ibrox. Anyway, when they're not falling out with one another over Brexit, or organising fundraising "Robbie Burns" suppers, where presumably someone reads his famous poem *Tom of Shanter*, the stalwart defenders of all that is red white and blue because they're not nationalists at all have formed a secret letter-writing group.

The not-nationalists-we're-British formed a secret hush-hush invitation-only group on Facebook to organise a campaign of letter writing to Scottish newspapers. This is why the exact same letter from the same person has been appearing in a local paper in Fife and a local paper in Argyll. It does raise some interesting questions about why people who defend the British state believe that the best way to do so is with an act of deception, attempting to pass themselves off as concerned locals when they are no such thing.

When this came to light, the independence supporters who had revealed it were once again accused by certain Scottish journalists of being conspiracy theorists. However plotting a particular course of action in secret in order to deceive people into thinking that you're something you're not is very much the definition of a conspiracy. It's not a conspiracy theory, it's a conspiracy fact. Admittedly it's not a very good conspiracy, but then these are British nationalists we're talking about here. They're not exactly noted for their competence.

What this latest episode tells us is that deception, misrepresentation and duplicity are all key elements in the British nationalist playbook. The Better Together campaign in 2014 was an act of deception, so it's not really surprising. Better Together based its entire campaign on the claim that Scotland is an equal and valued partner in a family of nations. How's that working out then? The British nationalist parties vied with one another to lie, deceive and short-change the people of Scotland. They don't call it Perfidious Albion for nothing.

The British nationalist campaign in 2014 was notable for supposedly grass-roots organisations like Vote No Borders, which bore as much relationship to real grass roots as a tinsel Christmas tree does to a conifer forest. Scotland in Union's Enid Blyton-inspired super secret letter-writing campaign is its bargain-basement brother.

If the only way you can make progress is through lies and deception, you've already admitted that you've lost the argument. No wonder they're so desperate to avoid another independence referendum.

30 December 2017

Unionism strives to protect
interests of the wealthy elite

Over the New Year holidays, someone closely involved with Scotland's supposedly grass-roots Unionist organisation Scotland in Union got so frustrated and fed up with the group that they revealed its most sensitive information to Vile Cybernat Prime, Stu Campbell of Wings Over Scotland. That information revealed that there's precious little grass roots in how Scotland in Union is funded. The group concentrates on seeking large donations from lords, ladies and lairds. It's not funded by ordinary people putting coins in a bucket at a public meeting. It's funded by cheques and bank transfers promised in elite London clubs and hunting shoots by the rich, the powerful and the well connected. Scotland in Union is far too posh for astroturfing. It's astrotoffing.

Some apologists for the British state have tried to pretend that there is nothing significant here. "Well of course the only people who can make large personal donations are people who have a lot of personal money. Mind. Blown, " say some. And you can hear the sound of the points they're missing whooshing far above their heads. Perhaps we should illustrate it with a graph. Others have tried to claim that this is yet more evidence of vile cybernats bullying those defenceless rich people with their small islands of lawyers. Apparently it's bullying to make it public that rich people try to influence politics by throwing large amounts of cash at the causes they support.

The obvious point is why do rich people support certain causes, because as a rule of thumb you don't get to be rich by giving money away. Typically rich people support those causes that protect their wealth and their privilege. That's why the kind of people who own vast acres of the Highlands tend to give their cash to conservative causes and not to parties like the Scottish Socialists. Scotland in Union's funding strategy lays bare the myth that opposing independence is about making a better Scotland for all of Scotland's citizens. Opposing independence is about defending the wealth and privilege of the rich and the powerful. They oppose independence because they fear that in an independent Scotland their power and influence might be diminished.

Another important point is that Scotland's supposedly leading anti-independence organisation is in such a state of dysfunction that someone closely involved with them was so angry and disillusioned with the group that they figured it was more productive to leak embarrassing information to Scotland's leading pro-independence blog than to try to address their issues internally with other Scotland in Union members. The leak comes not long after Scotland in Union had suffered not one but two fissures, as first the organisers of These Islands and then the people behind the pro-Brexit UK Unity group split off. The split leading to the formation of UK Unity appears to have been particularly rancorous and ill-tempered.

This leads directly to another issue. Whenever there's a Twitter dispute between independence supporters, Scotland's traditional media is all over it like a particularly irksome rash. We get days of commentary in the papers. Newspapers which usually avoid pro-independence commentators fall over themselves to offer an opinion column to any random independence supporter who is willing to criticise other independence supporters. Yet with the Scotland in Union debacle there is clear evidence of serious infighting and disputes at the very highest levels of an organisation which the Scottish media touted as the leading grass-roots Unionist organisation, and for the most part Scotland's media is remarkably lacking in interest. There's no real story here, they sniff.

The lack of interest in this important story in Scotland's overwhelmingly anti-independence press goes to the very heart of the problem with the media in Scotland. In Scotland we have almost forty newspapers, yet only two support independence. The independence issue is the most important issue in Scottish politics, it cuts across and informs all political debate in this country. It is a matter of existential importance to Scotland, to Scottish politics and to Scottish culture. It is a debate about what sort of country we want to be. Opinion poll after opinion poll demonstrates that almost half the population support independence, yet pro-independence voices struggle to make themselves heard in a traditional media which is overwhelmingly anti-independence.

That same overwhelmingly Unionist media consistently downplays and marginalises stories which aid or support independence, while simultaneously promoting anything which portrays independence in a negative light. The broadcast media tends to take its lead from the print media, with the result that the pro-independence half of the population in Scotland's constitutional debate feels systematically excluded and marginalised. No wonder trust in the media in Scotland is so low. The functioning of democracy is seriously impaired when one side's views and opinions are consistently hampered from getting an airing. Independence supporters feel beleaguered and besieged, constantly under attack from the media.

The media of any nation ought to hold up a mirror to the country. Our media ought to reflect the range of opinions and views found in the country. That's not what happens in Scotland. When Scotland looks in the media mirror we see Ruth Davidson saying, "Scotland doesn't want another referendum." We see Richard Leonard claiming that young people support Corbyn, even though opinion polls in Scotland consistently show that young people in Scotland support independence by a very large margin. The media mirror doesn't reflect the real Scotland. That's one reason why we must cherish and defend those few pro-independence outlets that we do have, like *The National*.

For the broader independence movement, the lesson is clear. Our primary task over the coming year must be to build and develop our own alternative grass-roots networks for spreading pro-independence information and news. With a few honourable exceptions, the traditional media isn't going to do it for us. We are the only real grass-roots movement in the Scottish constitutional debate. We can take the message of independence into every home, every street and every community. The British nationalists have the toffs, but we have the turf. That's why we're going to win.

3 January 2018

David Mundell had one job to do ... and he couldn't

There's a website called You Had One Job which is a compilation of videos and photos of spectacular job fails. There's a photo of a burger chain advertising its "new mighty anus burger", presumably because the old mighty anus burger wasn't a pass. There's the macaroni cheese being sold for seventy-nine cents a packet, but if you buy eight or more you can get each packet for the special bargain price of seventy-nine cents. There's the ecologically friendly car park, with a tree thoughtfully planted right in the middle of each parking space. There's the shop sign saying "All the best for your baby", above shelves of alcohol. And then there's a photograph of David Mundell, no caption necessary.

Despite an increasingly bloated budget, most of which is spent on spin doctors who can tell the media how wonderful the UK is for Scotland and how bad the SNP is, David Mundell doesn't have a great deal to do. Even if he were the most competent, capable and diligent member of the UK cabinet, and let's be honest here, the competition isn't up to a great deal because even a torch with a broken bulb and a flat battery could outshine David Davis, he'd still be one of the lowest-ranking members because his department doesn't have many responsibilities. There are pickpockets in nudist colonies who have more to do.

Being Scotland Secretary is the kind of job that even a sloth would find a bit slow paced. All you have to do is to turn up at Scottish Questions in the Commons once a month and blame the Scottish government for problems to do with matters that are reserved. It's not like the representatives of the British nationalist press are going to correct you for it. But that's just a side gig. The main justification for the existence of the Scotland Secretary is so that he or she can turn up for photos of cabinet meetings and then sit out of harm's way at the very back, partially obscured by an ornamental cabbage in a plant pot which has a higher visual priority. The purpose of this charade is so that apologists for British rule in Scotland can say that Scotland has a seat at the top table. Well I say an ornamental cabbage in a plant pot, it may be some other vegetable. With members of the Conservative cabinet it's not always easy to tell.

So you might think that when there is a real job to do that the Scotland Secretary would make busy-busy like a Jehovah's Witness in a door shop. If nothing else it must be a relief from the tedium. The Brexit Bill provided that very opportunity, it actually gave David something meaningful to achieve. This isn't the sort of thing that comes along very often. The last time he did something productive was when he grew a beard.

The EU Withdrawal Bill doesn't meet the requirements of the Scottish parliament because as it stands it turns the entire principle underlying devolution on its head. The bill gives the UK government the right to decide which of the devolved powers currently exercised by Brussels it's going to keep, and which it will allow Holyrood to retain. Worse, it proposes to do so without the need for parliamentary scrutiny. The Scottish parliament has made it clear that it's not going to approve the current draft of the bill. This could provoke a constitutional crisis, the sort of thing that a minority government would do well to avoid. It already has enough crises to deal with every time Boris Johnson opens his mouth.

Ensuring that the bill meets the requirements of the Scottish parliament was David's only job. Despite repeated assurances from the British government that the necessary amendments would be introduced which would meet the Scottish parliament's objections, the government failed to do so. To be fair, it is entirely possible that he did make representations to his cabinet colleagues to impress upon them the need to get their collective act together and to move ahead with the amendments, but if he did they confused him with the ornamental cabbage. The amendments were not introduced in time for the bill's final stage of scrutiny in the Commons, meaning that Scotland's elected representatives have no opportunity to examine them or suggest changes. The UK government deemed it far more important to reshuffle the cabinet after a minister resigned to spend more time with his computer.

Because David didn't do the only job he had, the UK government is now saying that the amendments will be introduced in the House of Lords. This means that Michelle Mone and Michael Forsyth will have more of an opportunity to scrutinise the bill than any of Scotland's elected representatives in Westminster. What was that about the point of Brexit being to bring back control to the House of Commons? But then even if it did, all this sorry episode proves is that Scotland has no effective voice in Westminster. There's only one way Scotland can make its voice heard, and it doesn't involve being a part of the so-called United Kingdom.

13 January 2018

Scottish media slam SNP for talking indy... and then for the opposite

On Monday, The National had an actual scoop of the kind that makes old-fashioned newspaper editors yell, "Hold the front page!" Or at least old-fashioned newspaper editors in most countries. In Scotland they're far more likely to yell "Hold the front page!" when Ruth Davidson has done a photo op with a farm animal again and they want to splash it all over the front page that neither Ruth nor the castrated pig she was posing with was in favour of another independence referendum. However The National's exclusive was genuine news. The National had managed to get a hold of the Scottish government's financial analysis of the cost of Brexit to Scotland. This is the analysis that the Scottish government did because the UK government had said that they were going to do one, only David Davis decided that he really would rather prefer to pretend that Brexit would give everyone in the country a free unicorn and some magic sparkly fairy dust.

The analysis shows that there is no such thing as a good Brexit for Scotland. Every possible Brexit scenario leaves the country worse off than remaining a part of the EU. When the Tories claim that they're seeking a good Brexit deal, what they really mean is that they're frantically hoping that the damage will be containable and that they can reduce the impact on places where Conservative voters live so it won't affect their chances of getting re-elected.

For Scotland, there's no positive outcome. The Scottish government's Brexit impact papers show that a hard Brexit is going to cost Scotland £2300 for every man, woman and child in the country. The total cost to Scotland's economy will be £12.7 billion every year. This is a considerably bigger hit than the £1400 per person which the UK Treasury claimed in 2014 that independence would cost Scotland. Even a Brexit with a favourable trade deal of the sort that Theresa May and Jeremy Corbyn claim to be seeking is forecast to cost each person in Scotland £1610 annually, still more than the worst forecasts for the cost of independence by the Better Together campaign and the British government. We're actually going to be quite a bit worse off by remaining in the UK than we would have been if we had opted for independence in 2014, even if the very worst economic forecasts for an independent Scotland had come true.

The least worst option for Brexit is to remain in the Customs Union and single market after Brexit, a scenario which both the Conservatives and Labour have ruled out. Even that is still forecast to cost each person in Scotland £688 annually.

You might just imagine that the revelation that the economic case for the Union had been blown out of the water – by the British government, no less – was news. The financial disaster facing Scotland isn't the fault of the Scottish government. Even the Scottish press would struggle to find a way of blaming the SNP for Brexit, although that won't stop them trying. The economic argument, the claim that independence would make Scotland far worse off, was the main argument that the Better Together campaign had back in 2014. Voting for independence, they told us, would make Scotland poorer, and it would bring about instability and create insecurity.

Now we discover that because Scotland chose to remain a part of the UK in 2014, it's going to be much worse off than it would have been if it had opted for independence, and we're facing political instability and economic insecurity which is far worse than anything independence would have caused. That's pretty earth-shattering news, or more exactly

Better-Together-shattering. It's news which demonstrates that Scotland was lied to in 2014. It's news which proves the moral and intellectual bankruptcy of the British establishment.

At the press conference on Monday to present the report, Nicola Sturgeon wanted to talk about the impact of Brexit on the Scottish economy. That was after all the entire purpose of the press conference. Instead certain representatives of the Scottish media wanted to ask her about a second independence referendum so that when she tried to steer the conference back to the topic at hand, they could attack her for avoiding talk of another independence referendum.

Still, it provided a headline or two, and naturally in its roundup of the Scottish press on Monday, BBC Scotland's online news pages chose to go with "FM faces indyref2 criticism". There's the Scottish Unionist media for you. The destruction of the economic justification for the Union by British political parties isn't news, instead it's news that Nicola Sturgeon doesn't want to talk about another independence referendum during a press conference that wasn't about another independence referendum.

The hypocrisy is jaw-dropping. After spending months, nay years, attacking the SNP for talking too much about independence and not concentrating on the day job, now they're attacking the SNP for not talking more about independence and for concentrating on the day job. It makes you wish that the British nationalist media in Scotland could make their minds up. Do they think that the SNP is damaging Brexit with talk of independence, or do they think that the SNP isn't talking enough about independence? They can't have it both ways.

There are some who say that independence supporters shouldn't criticise the media, that it undermines the cause of independence. That would be fine if Scotland had a media which was broadly representative of the range of views found in this country. But it doesn't. It's not a conspiracy theory or paranoia to say that Scotland's media is heavily biased against independence, it's a simple objective fact. Only two out of thirty-nine newspapers support a constitutional position backed by almost half of the people in Scotland, and our publicly funded public broadcaster follows the line set by that unrepresentative press.

Scotland's media grossly distorts events in pursuit of a British nationalist agenda. A genuine scoop from *The National* gets swamped in puffery and guff that criticises Nicola Sturgeon for not wishing to talk about another independence referendum on a day when she's trying to draw attention to the economic calamity being foisted on Scotland by a British government. If independence supporters don't continue to draw attention to the bias and shortcomings of the Scottish media, we'll never win independence at all.

17 January 2018

Until Scotland is independent our loss on aviation is Ireland's gain

We've already had the first casualty of the Scottish budget. Citing the failure of the Scottish government to introduce its planned cut in the rate of Air Passenger Duty, Norwegian Airlines this week announced that in March it would be axing its twice-weekly service between Edinburgh and Bradley International Airport in Hartford, Connecticut. The budget carrier is also reducing the number of flights on its route from Edinburgh to Providence, Rhode Island, from four a week to three. In a statement, the airline said:

"As of March 25, 2018, Norwegian Air will no longer operate its Edinburgh service out of Hartford's Bradley International Airport.

"The decision to pull the route, along with decreasing service to Edinburgh from other US airports, is due to the Scottish Government's postponement of a reduction to air passenger taxes."

However as services to Scotland are cut back, the airline is increasing the frequency of its service from Providence to Shannon Airport in Ireland. Meanwhile Ireland's national carrier Aer Lingus has said that when it introduces its summer schedule, flights between Dublin and Bradley International will increase from twice a week to daily. Scotland's loss is Ireland's gain.

My American partner lives in Hartford, and we've both flown on Norwegian Airlines' Edinburgh to Bradley International service a couple of times since it was introduced last summer. We were grateful for the service. It offered a relatively inexpensive and very convenient direct connection between Scotland and my partner's home city in the USA. Previously we'd had to make a connection in either Dublin or London in order to visit one another.

Last summer MSPs voted in Holyrood to replace Air Passenger Duty with a new devolved Air Departure Tax, which was due to be introduced in April this year. Although the rates for the new tax had not been set, it was widely expected that they would be lower than the existing rates for APD, which for economy-class flights is set at £13 for short-haul flights, and £75 for long-haul flights (over 2000 miles). It had been reported that the Scottish government would cut the tax by fifty per cent before eventually abolishing it altogether. Flights originating in Northern Ireland already have an exemption from the tax, allowing them to compete with airlines in the Irish Republic.

However the planned change has been postponed until next year. Currently flights to and from the Scottish islands are exempt from APD, but this exemption can only be maintained after an assessment is made by the European Commission. This requires the intervention of the UK government. In October last year Scottish Finance Secretary Derek Mackay claimed that Westminster had set "unacceptable conditions" on the process. More cynical observers might think that it suits the Scottish government to kick the issue into the long grass, as they need the support of the Greens in order to get the Scottish budget passed, and the Greens oppose any cut to APD.

But this isn't another SNPbad story. There are other reasons preventing Scotland from developing its airports and airline services to the level enjoyed by Ireland, reasons which have everything to do with Ireland being an independent state whereas Scotland is a part of the UK. Thanks to investment and tax breaks from the Irish government, Dublin is a major European hub airport, Edinburgh is not. Yet like Ireland, Scotland is geographically the nearest part of Europe for airline services originating in North America, and is ideally situated to act as a major hub airport for flights between European destinations and North America. Ireland is able to take advantage of its geographical position, Scotland is not.

Serving over twenty-nine million passengers annually, Dublin is the fourteenth busiest airport in Europe, offering direct flights to nineteen destinations in the USA and Canada. Many of the passengers on transatlantic flights to Dublin are catching connecting flights to elsewhere in Europe. Despite serving a catchment area with a similar population, Edinburgh, Scotland's busiest airport, is used by only 12.3 million passengers a year, and after the loss of the Hartford flights offers direct services to just seven destinations in the USA and Canada. Dublin also offers considerably more connecting flights to onward destinations, making transatlantic services to Dublin more attractive, especially to business users.

Speaking to the local press in Connecticut this week, Kevin Dillon, the executive director of the Connecticut Airport Authority, acknowledged that limited connections from Edinburgh were seen as a challenge to the Hartford-Edinburgh service from the start. On the other hand, he claimed that the Dublin to Hartford route continues to show promising growth.

Dublin enjoys an additional advantage for travellers, one which no airport in Scotland can compete with. Travellers to the USA pass through US customs and immigration in Dublin airport, meaning that when they arrive in the USA it's like arriving on a domestic flight, they only need to collect their bags and go. Passengers arriving from Scotland must queue up after a long and tiring flight, sometimes for over an hour, in order to be processed by US customs and immigration. Introducing this pre-clearance service in Dublin, and in Shannon Airport, required an international treaty between the Irish government and the USA. The Scottish government doesn't have the authority to do so, even though it would make Scottish airports a far more attractive prospect for travellers.

In November 2016, the US authorities included Edinburgh Airport in a list of European airports being considered for pre-clearance. Manchester and London Heathrow were already being considered. A final decision will have to be made by the Home Office and the British government. This is likely to take several years.

As things stand, travellers to and from Scotland have to put up with a second-class service compared to travellers to and from Ireland. Dublin picks up the extra jobs generated by the airlines, while Scotland loses out. The main reason for the difference is clear, it's because Ireland is an independent state but Scotland is not. The only way that Scotland will ever enjoy world-class connections to the rest of the world is when, like the Irish Republic, we compete with the rest of the world on a level playing field as an independent nation.

20 January 2018

Ireland-Scotland bridge is scuppered by the MoD

I've got a guilty secret. I'm a bit of a train anorak. It's not fashionable. Admitting that you like trains is, in the eyes of some, rather like admitting that you're middle-aged, you live with your mother, and the only meaningful relationships you've ever had are with your cat and an inflatable toy you bought on the Internet. Men, and it's usually men, who are able to glance at a passing train and confidently identify it as a Class 334 Electric Multiple Unit are seen as somehow less masculine than a Jeremy Clarkson clone who coos over a motor car and is able to discern the year of manufacture of a German sports car by the shape of its headlights.

Given my love of all things public transport related, it was fascinating to read in the press this week that there is a proposal to build a combined road and rail link across the North Channel between Scotland and Ireland, connecting Portpatrick in Galloway with Whitehead at the head of Belfast Lough. A fixed link between Scotland and Ireland would be a huge boost to the economies of both countries, opening up trade and putting the otherwise neglected far South West of Scotland in the centre of a major route. It would almost be worth the huge expense and the massive engineering challenges of constructing it just to call it the Sheuch Crossing.

It's a beautiful fantasy, but back in the real world it's highly unlikely that we'll ever see a bridge connecting Scotland and Ireland, and will never be able to catch a train from Glasgow Central or Edinburgh Waverley that offers a direct service to Dublin. It's not just that the construction of a bridge has been described as challenging. That's challenging in the same way that it would be challenging to build a bridge across the Firth of Clyde using nothing but papier mâché made from old copies of Scottish Unionist newspapers. It could be done. It's just not going to be easy, even though it would possibly be the first instance of something positive for Scotland coming out of the Unionist press.

One of the major difficulties is the geology. The North Channel might not be quite as wide as the English Channel, but it's considerably deeper. Facing the Rhinns of Galloway between Scotland and Ireland runs Beaufort's Dyke, a sea trench which reaches over 250 metres in depth. It's the immense depth of the channel that makes a tunnel impractical, and makes even a bridge exceptionally difficult.

There are additional problems. There would have to be massive investment in infrastructure to upgrade the road and rail connections, especially on the Scottish side. The main roads leading to Stranraer are narrow, twisting and unsuited for the amount of traffic that they currently have, never mind the increased traffic that would be generated by a fixed link. The single rail line from Ayr to Stranraer would have to be upgraded and electrified, and the rail link from Stranraer to Dumfries reinstated. Additionally there's the problem that Irish trains, uniquely in Europe, run on a broad gauge track which is incompatible with the standard gauge used in Britain and most of mainland Europe.

The biggest problem however, isn't the lack of infrastructure. It's not even the geology. It's the bombs and the chemical weapons. It's the legacy of Scotland being used for generations as a rubbish tip for the poisonous and lethal waste products of British militarism.

It's estimated that Beaufort's Dyke contains over a million tonnes of munitions, dumped there by the War Office and its successor the Ministry of Defence between the end of WWI and the mid-1970s. As well as conventional weaponry like artillery shells, the dyke was also used as a dumping ground for incendiary bombs containing phosphorus which ignite on contact with air, as well as chemical weapons, including mustard gas, tear gas, phosgene, and the nerve agents tabun and sarin. And that's just the stuff they'll admit to.

The dumping zone extends off the coast of the Rhinns of Galloway, along the full length of the peninsula. According to a report in *New Scientist* magazine in 1995 ("Danger from the Deep", by Rob Edwards), the sailors responsible for carrying out the dumping were not always too careful about ensuring that they were depositing the weaponry in the deepest part of the channel. Munitions litter the sea floor. Some of it was dumped just a few hundred metres offshore. Some of it ended up in unauthorised dumping sites to the north or south of Beaufort's Dyke, and some was even dumped in the shallow waters of the Solway Firth.

During the 1990s, British Gas dug a narrow trench sixty centimetres wide across the North Channel in order to build a gas pipeline connecting Scotland and Ireland. Although British Gas denied responsibility, according to the Scottish Office's Marine Laboratory in Aberdeen the works involved disturbed the weapons scattered on the sea floor, and an estimated 4500 WWII incendiary bombs were washed up on Scottish shores. For decades the MoD denied the existence of the weapons dumps. Even after the incendiary bombs were being washed up all along the coast as far as Saltcoats and Gigha, Islay and Arran, and all points in between, the MoD continued to deny any involvement. It was only after a meeting of Scottish MPs with the then Defence Secretary that the MoD owned up. Digging a trench sixty centimetres wide dislodged thousands of bombs, one of which injured a child near Campbeltown. The amount of work needed to construct the foundations for a bridge could potentially dislodge many more and release chemical agents and toxic waste into the waters of the channel.

There are other dumps of old bombs, radioactive waste from the UK's nuclear weapons programme, and banned chemical weapons around Scotland's coasts. One of Scotland's major roles in the UK is as a dumping ground for waste and as a host for nuclear weapons. The cost of cleaning up the seabed and removing Britain's military waste is likely to run into untold millions of pounds. The MoD claims that there is "no evidence" that the waste is harmful as long as it is left undisturbed. But there's only no evidence because no one has looked for it.

Britain's toxic legacy is preventing Scotland developing to its full potential. So instead of a bridge we should invest in some cutting-edge technology to link Scotland and Ireland. We could call it a "floating motorised short bridge" and have lots of them connecting the Scottish and Irish coasts at frequent and regular intervals. Or, if you want to be boring about it, call it "better ferry services".

24 January 2018

Can these flag-obsessed British nationalists please get on with the day job?

This week, the Scottish Conservatives got very exercised about a flag. The Scottish Conservatives care deeply about the Union flag, so deeply that it took them eight years to notice that the Scottish government had changed its policy about flying the Union flag on royal occasions. But when they did notice, after the guidance to Scottish civil servants was updated to reflect the practice and policy of the past decade, they got extremely upset about it. Those vile nationalists should be getting on with the day job and not obsessing about a flag, some nationalists screamed as they obsessed about a flag and didn't get on with the day job of ensuring that the EU exit bill complies with the devolution settlement.

Those vile nats, screeched the right-wing press, they want to destroy our flag! If Thatniclasturgeon and Thatessempee get their way there won't be any Union flags left in Scotland at all. Except those that are stamped on your new driving licence, fly at military parades, from Tory- and Labour-controlled council buildings, from Edinburgh castle, and are beamed 200 foot high on to the side of Castle Rock at the Tattoo, on Scottish produce in supermarkets, in the title sequence of every telly show called *Great British* something, at Rangers matches, Orange parades, fascist rallies, and on the social media avatars of all those people whose nationalism is better than other forms of nationalism by virtue of not being nationalist at all. But apart from that, totally eradicated.

The Conservatives, and their supporters in the right-wing press, are very quick to accuse supporters of independence of manufacturing grievances, and there they were blatantly manufacturing a grievance of their own. It provided a convenient distraction for the anti-independence press, allowing them to give space to Murdo Fraser to vent his fury instead of having to concentrate on the abject failure of the British government to respect the results of the 1997 and 2014 referendums and defend and protect the devolution settlement.

The stories in the right-wing press were followed by scores of racist comments directed at Scottish people. If the same comments were made by supporters of Scottish independence and directed at English people, there would be anguished articles all over the papers for weeks and special programmes on BBC Scotland about the cancer lurking at the heart of the independence movement. But when racism is directed at Scottish people, it's just a bit of banter and you're a humourless nat if you take it seriously. Anyway, it's only vile cybernats who poison debate and lower the tone. The outrageous and offensive comments of a single independence supporter on social media are used by the anti-independence media to characterise the independence movement as a whole, but don't you dare suggest that offensive comments from those opposed to independence should in any way be taken as characteristic of opponents of independence as a whole.

Absolutely nothing had changed between last week, indeed last year, and this, and yet there they were banging on about how the Scottish government wants to extinguish a symbol of the British state while the Conservative-run British state seeks to undermine and traduce the devolution settlement and destroy Scottish political distinctiveness. That's a whole lot more important than a flag.

In the very same week that the Conservatives got themselves all lathered up into an outrage over an entirely invented story, they say that they're bringing in measures to tackle the proliferation of fake news in the media. I'm shocked and surprised that the Conservatives are hypocrites, said absolutely no one ever. However the most fascinating thing about this week's episode is that it has illustrated all the many and varied ways in which the anti-independence project is founded in hypocrisy.

The harrumphing this week about the Union flag also exposes many of the hypocrisies lurking at the heart of the anti-independence project, not the least of which is the lie that it's not nationalist. Getting angry about a perceived slight to a nationalist symbol is one of the definitions of nationalism. This week the Conservatives stand exposed, the campaign to defeat Scottish independence is at its core a nationalist project.

It's one of the defining myths of British nationalism that somehow it's not really nationalist at all. It's not just the Tories who propagate this myth, Labour are pretty keen on it too. If Labour wasn't a nationalist party, their solidarity with working-class people would extend further than the borders of the UK. Their definition of solidarity includes workers in Dundee and Durham, but not those in Dublin. A Labour Party, like that of Jeremy Corbyn, which defends Brexit, is as British nationalist as the Conservatives.

So let's stop pandering to them. As independence supporters we pander to the delusions of British nationalists by describing opponents of independence as Unionists, when describing supporters of independence as Scottish nationalists. The Scottish constitutional debate is not a debate between nationalists and non-nationalists, it's a debate between two different visions of what the nation of Scotland can be. So let's not call opponents of independence Unionists any more. Let's call them what they really are – British nationalists.

27 January 2018

The photo didn't fit – but the UK
did send tanks into Glasgow

The heady days of Red Clydeside and the Battle of George Square have passed into the city's legend. The story goes that in late January 1919, striking workers in the city rioted in George Square, and fearful of a communist revolt, a frightened British government sent in English troops and tanks in order to quell the city. However according to recent reports in the press, research has debunked the myth of the 1919 tank which was sent into Glasgow by a worried British government to intimidate the rebellious workers of the incipient Glasgow Soviet.

The debunking in question referred to a photograph of a WWI tank rumbling down a Glasgow street, a photograph which has frequently been used to illustrate articles about the events of Red Clydeside. Cue the usual crowing from the usual suspects on social media that yet another Scottish nationalist grievance has been proven to be baseless. Only it hasn't.

What's not clear from the headlines is that the only thing that has been debunked is the photograph itself. The photo actually depicts a tank rolling down a street in Glasgow in 1918, during WWI, as part of a fundraiser for the war effort. This doesn't mean that tanks were not sent into Glasgow during the heady and rebellious days in 1919 when there was talk of a Glasgow Soviet. According to press reports from the time, the British government did indeed send in tanks. A headline from the *Aberdeen Daily Journal* in its issue of Tuesday, 4 February 1919, makes this clear: "Tanks Reinforce Troops in Glasgow." Likewise the deployment of tanks in the city was reported by the *Daily Herald* in its edition the same day. It is a matter of historical record that the tanks were based in the Glasgow cattle market in the Gallowgate in Glasgow, and trundled through the city after being unloaded from trains which arrived in Queen Street Station.

The tanks and troops were sent in following a meeting of the UK cabinet to discuss the unrest in the city. During the meeting the Scottish Secretary Robert Munro stated, "It is a misnomer to call the situation in Glasgow a strike – this is a Bolshevist uprising." It is estimated that 10,000 soldiers were sent into the city, in the biggest troop deployment against a civilian population ever seen in the UK.

To be fair, the recent piece in the *Herald* about the incorrect labelling of the tank photograph did make it clear within the body of the article that tanks were indeed deployed as a threat against the city's striking workers. The problem however is that most people don't read further than the headline.

Another myth which the recent press reports were keen to debunk is the myth that all the soldiers were English and that English soldiers were sent into the city because the authorities feared that Glaswegian soldiers based at the Maryhill barracks would be sympathetic with the workers. The authorities' fears were not unfounded. Willie Gallacher, one of the strike leaders, is later quoted as regretting that the strikers hadn't sought the support of the troops in Maryhill, saying, "The soldiers of Maryhill were confined to barracks and the barrack gates were kept tightly closed. If we had gone there we could easily have persuaded the soldiers to come out and Glasgow would have been in our hands."

There seem to be no contemporary records of English troops being deployed in Glasgow. There are records of thousands of soldiers being sent into Glasgow from other parts of Scotland. The existence of English soldiers being sent to crush rebellious socialist Scots has been decried as yet another myth nurtured by modern Scottish nationalists in search of a grievance. However no one has claimed that all the soldiers sent into the city were English, only that some of them were. At least one person who was an eyewitness to the military presence in Glasgow at the time is convinced that English soldiers really were present.

My grandmother Barbara Mosson (née McAdam), who died in 2010 a few weeks before her one hundredth birthday, was present during some of the events in George Square in that revolutionary winter of 1919. Her father (my great-grandfather) Tom McAdam was heavily involved in the socialist politics of the day. My great-grandfather was one of the striking workers, and he took his daughter to George Square to see the soldiers and the cannon there, to be a witness to the fact that the British authorities would not hesitate to put down ordinary working-class Scots with troops, bullets and tanks. She was eight years old and what she saw then stayed with her throughout her long life.

Many decades later she recounted her memories to me, saying that her father had told her to remember, to never forget that these soldiers and the explicit threat of violence that they represented were an illustration of what the British establishment really thought about ordinary working-class people. She told me my great-grandfather wanted us to remember that they were afraid of us and of the power of working-class people.

My grandmother remembered the howitzer which is recorded as having been sited in George Square. She also remarked that this was the first time she had ever heard English accents. In 1919 there was no television, movies were silent, and radio was in its very early days. A young girl from a working-class household in Glasgow would not have had much of an opportunity to hear English accents. My grandmother told me that she found the English accents of the troops difficult to understand, and was shocked by the coarse language that the soldiers used.

I have no idea whether the coarse language expressed in English accents which so shocked my grandmother issued from the mouths of troops from an English regiment, or from English soldiers who were part of Scottish regiments, or from members of the officer class who would have tended to have upper-class English accents. But to the end of her days my grandmother was convinced that English soldiers were sent into George Square to intimidate and threaten the people of Glasgow. She was equally convinced that those agents of the British establishment held ordinary working-class Scots in contempt.

One hundred years on, and it's clear that in that respect nothing much has changed. The British establishment still holds Scotland in contempt. That much at least is no myth.

31 January 2018

Boris Johnson is a laughing stock and Scotland isn't feeling the love

Are you feeling the love? Are you filled with a warm and fuzzy glow inside? I thought I did, but it turned out to be gas from the lamb bhoona that was for dinner. It's been a week for warm and fuzzy love-ins. Boris Johnson has delivered what was billed as a love letter for Valentine's Day to people who didn't believe his crap that was written on the side of a bus. Here in Scotland, Scotland in Union has asked people to write about their love for the "Union" on Valentine's Day, a project which they unveiled by having a go at almost half the Scottish population who'd rather have nothing to do with their so-called Union. Meanwhile, not to be outdone, the Labour Party branch office in Scotland released a new party political broadcast, one of those paeans to socialist jam that Labour is only interested in when it's in Opposition.

Boris Johnson's speech this week was billed in advance as a plea to Remain voters to get on board the Brexit bus. It was remarkably short of detailed information, such as the destination of the bus and any explanation of how it was going to avoid going over a cliff. In fact it was remarkably short of information of any sort. The Irish border issue didn't even rate a mention, but then issues affecting Ireland, just like Scotland and Wales, scarcely figure in the calculations of British nationalists like Boris. We are simply the colourful Celtic dressing which allows Boris to pretend that his British nationalism is really multinational non-nationalism and isn't just another word for Little-Englander nationalism.

Instead of providing any answers to the concerns of Remainers, Boris took the opportunity to attempt to show off his intellectual credentials and proceeded to slag off the EU in pseudo-intellectual terms. Boris Johnson being an intellectual is as plausible as your cat being altruistic, only not as cute and definitely not worth a wee video you'd want to share on YouTube. Boris called the EU a "teleological construction", by which he meant that it was an organisation bent on the purposeful development of a predetermined goal, which really describes any organisation. So for example the Conservative Party is a teleological construction with the goal of holding on to power by any means possible in order to preserve the privilege and wealth which allows the likes of Boris to have his overweening sense of entitlement, whereas the teleological construction that is the Labour Party has the purposeful goal of promising socialist jam while in Opposition and then doing the opposite once they get elected.

The teleological goal that Boris was referring to in his speech was the supposed federal European superstate which only exists in the imagination of *Daily Mail* leader writers. It would be lovely if Brexit was also a teleological construction and was actually being planned by a competent government which had a definite purposeful goal in mind, however the only predetermined goal in Brexit is the advancement of Boris Johnson's career. For the rest of us, Brexit is teleological in the exact same sense as a game of Jenga: it's going to end in pieces all over the floor and it won't be Boris Johnson who has to deal with the resultant mess.

In his speech, Boris referred to a "natural desire for self-government". To which every supporter of Scottish independence replied, "Really? You don't say, Boris." This is one to add alongside such gems as, "We don't currently have the full levers to make decisions in the interests of this country." That's courtesy of Chris Grayling. Or there's, "I'm tired of hearing that we're too little, too inconsequential." So said Iain Duncan Smith. Or perhaps you prefer, "Are we really too small, too weak, and too powerless to make a success of self-rule?" That would be Michael Gove. Or how about, "I believe that the decisions which govern all our lives, the laws we must all obey and the taxes we must all pay should be decided by people we choose and who we can throw out if we want change." That would be Michael Gove again. All of these are quotes which independence supporters have noted down and will be throwing back in the faces of Conservative politicians during the next Scottish independence referendum.

Boris Johnson is a laughing stock, widely derided in the UK as a clown. If people in the UK can't take our own Foreign Secretary seriously, it's probably better not to think about what kind of opinion foreign governments have about him. All Boris Johnson achieved with his self-serving speech was to reinforce the sense that the British government is hell-bent on the hardest possible Brexit and that it has no clue about how to deal with the consequences. Despite being billed as a speech for Remainers, there were no words of comfort for Remainers in Boris's words, and no comfort for Scotland either.

17 February 2018

Why should anyone trust the UK if it can't even take its own treaties seriously

This week there have been mutterings and grumblings from Brexiteers that the Good Friday Agreement isn't fit for purpose. How dare peace in Northern Ireland and the requirement of the Good Friday Agreement that there must be an invisible border on the island of Ireland get between Boris and Jacob and their Anglocentric Brexit fantasyland.

The Agreement isn't just an internal agreement between Northern Irish political parties, it's also an international treaty between the UK and an Irish state which has the backing of the other twenty-six EU member countries. Brexiteers would like to rip up an international treaty which guarantees peace in Ireland because it hinders them in their pursuit of an unrealistic dream which will cause huge damage to the economy of the UK. They want to unilaterally renege on the treaty with Ireland in order to chase the chimera of trade deals with countries outside the EU, never pausing to ask themselves what other countries will think of a state which unilaterally rips up treaties that it decides it no longer likes.

Why should the EU trust the UK to stick to the terms of an exit deal if it can't be trusted to respect its treaty with Ireland? Why should Australia or China or Brazil trust the UK to keep to the terms of a future trade treaty if the UK demonstrates that it's not prepared to respect the treaties that it already has in place? They'll just say to themselves, "They don't call it perfidious Albion for nothing," and impose even tougher and more onerous conditions on the UK and insist on stronger penalties for defaulting.

The Good Friday Agreement is more than just an international treaty. It was approved in referendums in 1998 in both Northern Ireland and the Republic. Seventy-one per cent of voters in Northern Ireland approved it, and ninety-four per cent in the Irish Republic, considerably larger majorities than Brexit achieved. Brexiteers want to rip it up because of the will of fifty-two per cent of the people in the EU referendum, because clearly some people's democratic will counts for a lot more than others'. The fact that Brexiteers are prepared to risk the peace in Northern Ireland illustrates their moral bankruptcy, and proves that their talk of respecting the will of the people is nothing more than self-serving cant.

Meanwhile here in Scotland the latest round of talks about the EU exit bill between the Scottish government and the UK government have got nowhere. The UK government is still refusing to allow Scotland any meaningful input into the Brexit negotiations, and is still preparing to use Brexit as an excuse to overturn the devolution settlement that was approved by the people of Scotland in the referendum of 1997. That would be the settlement which the winning side promised to strengthen and improve after the referendum of 2014. There's a definite theme here of some referendums being more worthy of respect than others. The Scottish government will now pursue its own EU Continuity Bill, and a constitutional crisis is looming.

The truth is that Brexiteers put their fetish of a hard Brexit above peace in Northern Ireland, and above the unity of the UK. They are happy to see Scotland becoming independent, and don't care if violence erupts again in Northern Ireland if that means that they can have their fantasy of a hard Brexit. According to the most recent Future of England Survey, carried out jointly by the Universities of Edinburgh and Cardiff last year, eighty-eight per cent of Leave voters in England were prepared to accept a Yes vote in another independence referendum in Scotland, and eighty-one per cent would accept risking the Irish peace process, in order to pursue Brexit. Those figures rise to ninety-two per cent and eighty-seven per cent respectively for Conservative Leave voters. Meanwhile seventy-eight per cent of Labour Leave voters in England are prepared to accept Scottish independence, while sixty-seven per cent are willing to endanger the Irish peace process in order to pursue Brexit. Those are crushing majorities and a stark illustration of just how little Leave voters in England value the interests of the other nations of the UK.

Remember how they told us during the 2014 referendum that if Scotland voted to stay a part of the UK we'd be leaders within the family of nations of Britain? Remember how they told us that they loved us and valued us, that Britain wouldn't be the same without us? The harsh reality for people in Scotland who voted No in 2014 is that Brexiteers in England, who now dominate and drive the British government, think so little about Scotland's concerns and needs that they would prefer us to be independent if Scotland's interests get in the way of their fantasy of a freebooting Britain making favourable trade deals with Burkina Faso. They're not going to fight too hard to keep us if we decide to vote again on our own future. I don't know about you, but I'd prefer Scotland to be governed by people who actually care about it, and it's increasingly clear that can only happen with independence.

24 February 2018

Westminster's attack on devolution is all the justification we need for indyref2

David Lidington thinks that the devolution settlement is a threat to the continuing existence of the UK. And all over Scotland, independence supporters were saying to themselves, "Meh. I'm fine with that." David is the Conservative cabinet minister for slapping down uppity Celtic types in Scotland, Wales and Northern Ireland. That's Celtic with a "k" sound, and not the fitba team, in case you were wondering. You could also spell it Keltyck, which is a whole lot more mystick, and that would be appropriate because our nations have magical powers to bring about the end of the Tories' fantasy of a hard Brexit. It's a Druid thing, like in Asterix the Gaul, with the Scottish government in the role of Realistix.

On Monday David was delivering a speech, which is what Conservative politicians call a patronising dismissal, to bored workers in a factory in North Wales. The purpose of the patronising dismissal was to lay the groundwork for making sure that it's the Scottish and Welsh governments which get the blame for the constitutional crisis that will erupt when Cardiff and Edinburgh reject the EU exit bill. Holyrood and Cardiff Bay have both stated that they're unable to accept the bill as it stands, because even with the recent small concessions from a Conservative government which is as trustworthy as an email from a Nigerian prince with a guarantee of millions of dollars, the Brexit bill still represents a fundamental undermining of the principles of the devolution settlement.

Despite the rumours of major concessions, Theresa May's government still insists that it's going to decide all by itself which of the devolved powers currently exercised by Brussels will be permitted to Edinburgh or Cardiff after Brexit. That alters the very basis of the devolution settlement, a basis which during the independence referendum campaign the Conservatives and their Better Together allies promised was going to be enshrined in law. Scotland was told in 2014 that no changes would be made to the powers of the Scottish parliament without the express consent of the Scottish parliament, and here comes David Lidington and the Tories proposing changes to the powers of the Scottish parliament without its consent.

David's speech was aimed at ensuring it was the Scottish and Welsh governments which get the blame for the ensuing debacle. They're just refusing his compromise out of spite, and there was him being reasonable for a change. The great compromise was that the Conservatives say that they're not going to blag all these powers, just some of them, and swore blind, pixie promise, that they'd only make use of the devolved powers for a short time and then they'd give them straight back. Honest. The Conservatives are totally principled and honourable. They upheld all the commitments they made to Scotland in the Vow didn't they? Oh. Right. Maybe that's a bad example. Naturally the Scottish and Welsh governments have reacted to this proposal with a certain lack of enthusiasm.

David's got the hump about this. It's terribly unfair of the Scots and Welsh to pour a bucket of cold Irish seawater on Conservative fantasising and self-interest. He supported Remain during the EU referendum but now he's got behind Brexit because his job depends on it, and it's jolly unreasonable of the Scottish government to keep on opposing it just because the evidence still says it's going to be a disaster. However his outrage is less than convincing. It's a bit like a burglar being upset with their victims for not accepting the generous offer of only stealing the jewellery and the credit cards, but leaving the householders with that juicer thing that lives in a cupboard under the kitchen sink, a broken exercise bike, and a TV set that can only receive the BBC. If the Scots and Welsh refuse to sign up to David's perfectly reasonable and conciliatory offer of only partial burglary instead of the full-scale house clearance, then he'll just legislate to do it anyway. You'll have had your devolution Scotland. Hello constitutional crisis.

Meanwhile, writing in *Holyrood* magazine, Theresa May argued that there was far greater common ground between her government and the Scottish government than most people realised. For example her cabinet also believes that David Mundell is a waste of space, which is why they didn't bother inviting him to the Brexit awayday. She was insistent that she'd not been ignoring Scotland and Wales during the Brexit process, and claimed that the Scottish and Welsh governments had had an influence on her thinking. For example she had personally intervened to ensure that during negotiations with Michel Barnier, Welsh rarebit and bridies would be on the snack menu.

Theresa May makes sacrifices for Scotland which she doesn't get credit for. She had even sat through David Mundell speaking about something for a whole three minutes without making it obvious that her eyes were glazing over because she was daydreaming about a walking holiday in Switzerland, where she doesn't have to be bothered by swivel-eyed Brexiteers as it's safely foreign and outside the EU. Admittedly the Fluffy one was talking about his collection of stuffed toys, but it was a valuable start to a listening exercise, and it was nice that he'd mentioned his fellow Scottish Conservative MPs. The Scottish government should be far more appreciative of her efforts, as after all expecting anyone to allow Ross Thomson to impinge on their consciousness for longer than ten seconds counts as a major concession.

The Conservatives are using Brexit as an excuse to weaken the devolved administrations and undermine the devolution settlement. They don't care that devolution only exists because it was chosen by the people of Scotland and Wales in democratic referendums. They don't care that they themselves promised Scotland that they would strengthen and entrench the devolution settlement if Scotland voted No to independence in 2014. The Conservatives are the ones responsible for the looming constitutional crisis. The Tories can have their hard Brexit, or they can have the Union. They can't have both. They are destroying the Union that they claim to hold dear, because if the British government doesn't feel it needs to respect the results of the 1997 and 2014 referendums, then they themselves have provided the justification for another Scottish independence referendum.

28 February 2018

We need to tell the Tories:
hands off our parliament!

Ruth Davidson has finally come out of hiding to release a statement. The other day she tweeted about the absolute state of things because Walker's Shortbread felt compelled to put out a statement about their wildly popular/unpopular (delete as appropriate) shortbreid tin plastered with a Union fleg and containing fleg-shaped pieces of shortbreid. The last time that she willingly got in touch with the media was to phone in to a radio show to talk about The Great British Bake Off. There's clearly something about UK-themed baked goods that is dear to Ruth Davidson's heart. If only she felt as passionately about protecting the powers of the parliament she was elected to, but when you try to track Ruth down and ask her about how her government in Westminster is traducing the Vow that they made to the people of Scotland in 2014, she's strangely and uncharacteristically silent.

Obviously the way to make sure that the Conservative government in Westminster doesn't use Brexit as an excuse for a power grab at the expense of Holyrood is to make sure that it's centred on bakery products, because then Ruth Davidson will have to make a public statement about it. Maybe Nicola Sturgeon should start talking about the yum-yums of democracy and the coconut buns of respect for the will of the people, and then perhaps Ruth Davidson would pay some attention. But probably not, because really Ruth represents the politics of an old Empire biscuit, stale, flavourless and well past its sell-by date.

Despite the promises of Ruth's own party that the powers and permanence of the Scottish parliament would be enshrined in law, and that no Westminster government would try to alter or reduce the powers of Holyrood without the express consent of the Scottish parliament, that's precisely what Ruth's party is attempting to do. The Conservatives are always demanding that everyone else respect the result of the 2014 referendum, but it seems that they themselves have not got the slightest intention of doing so. The result of that referendum wasn't just that Scotland voted against independence. In 2014 Scotland also voted in favour of a strengthened Scottish parliament which no Westminster government could meddle with without ensuring the consent of MSPs. If Ruth Davidson and the Conservatives refuse to respect the result of the 2014 referendum, they've got some nerve demanding that others do. But then self-awareness and respect for others were never noted characteristics of Conservatism.

The Scottish government has introduced a Continuity Bill which hopes to ensure that the Scottish parliament can continue to exercise the same powers post-Brexit as it currently does. The British government has announced its intention to take the matter to the Supreme Court. That's the final betrayal of the tattered Vow, a Westminster government using the courts as a mechanism to reduce the powers of Holyrood after promising that those same courts would protect Holyrood from a Westminster government which sought to reduce its powers without its consent. This is Scotland's parliament, it is not Westminster's toy.

Holyrood is a parliament that the people of Scotland campaigned long and hard for, for many decades, and its powers and authority are underpinned by the democratic result of not one but two referendums, the referendum of 1997, as well as the referendum of 2014. It is not for any Westminster government to take it upon itself to reduce or alter the powers of our parliament. Westminster cannot insist that it's only the result of the EU referendum which must be respected. They must respect the result of Scotland's referendums too, and they must respect the fact that Scotland voted against Brexit.

It's important that the people of Scotland demonstrate to Theresa May that we expect them to respect the result of the 2014 referendum and to respect the promises and commitments that they made to us to secure Scotland's place within the UK. Because if they do not respect them, then they have only secured Scotland's place within the UK for the time being.

On Friday, 23 March, there is an event in Edinburgh when the ordinary people of Scotland can show Theresa May and the Conservatives that we value our parliament, that we demand that the Westminster government keeps its promises to us, and that we will protect and defend Scottish democracy. The organisers of the event hope that enough people will attend to form a human chain, linking hands around the Holyrood parliament building in a symbolic gesture of protection. Hands Off Our Parliament, or HOOP for short, will take place outside Holyrood from 10 a.m. until 5 p.m. Everyone who values and respects Scottish democracy is welcome to attend, this is not specifically a pro-independence event. It is a pro-devolution event, a pro-Scottish democracy event. Bring your own yum-yums of democracy to Holyrood, and let's hold hands and show that we value our parliament, and won't give it up without a struggle.

10 March 2018

Sign the Indy Pledge – and help improve our movement

We hear a lot in the British nationalist media about vile cybernats. That same press is typically silent when it comes to abusive online behaviour committed by opponents of independence, even though the online activities of British nationalists is every bit as bad, if not worse. It's worth reminding them that the only people who have ever been imprisoned for their online abuse and death threats have been opponents of independence. However the vile cybernat meme is one which opponents of independence are determined to pursue, a convenient stick with which to beat the cause of independence in the absence of any substantive positive arguments for the UK.

The fact is that the British nationalist media in the UK is desperate to paint the independence movement as an evil and cruel bunch of social misfits. It's a deliberate tactic on their part designed to ensure that people who have not yet engaged with the cause of independence are put off from making contact with independence activists. The media seizes on the most trivial instances of less than ideal online behaviour and blows them up out of all proportion. We all recall the accusations of abuse and vandalism which turned out to be someone putting a Yes sticker on a Labour MP's office door. We all remember the unsubstantiated allegations of death threats against opponents of independence which were printed as fact, yet when pressed for evidence nothing was forthcoming.

The result is that the mainstream independence movement is subject to a trial by media in which it is judged by the actions of a tiny and unrepresentative minority who speak for no one but themselves. There are unbalanced individuals in all grass-roots movements, but that does not mean that the movement as a whole is characterised by the behaviour of the worst. There is a clear double standard at play in the British press. Mainstream opponents of independence would vehemently and angrily reject any suggestion that the views of the sectarian bigots, out-and-out racists, and the actual fascists on the fringes of British nationalism are at all reflective of the majority of those who campaign against Scottish independence. They are supported in their angry rejection by a press which is desperately seeking for anything that an independence supporter has said that can be portrayed as anti-English.

In order to demonstrate that the independence movement does care about its online image, and that the mainstream movement will have no truck with abuse, threats or hate speech, a group of local activists have developed the Indy Pledge. The Pledge is a voluntary code of conduct for both online and real-world campaigning activities. It is a statement of the core beliefs of the grass-roots independence movement.

The leading group in formulating the Pledge has been Yes Kelty, however Yes Dunfermline, Yes Kirkintilloch and the independence live-streaming group Independence Live have all had significant input in deciding on the wording. These groups have consulted with other individuals and groups in the independence movement in order to formulate the wording of the pledge.

This is a valuable initiative which demonstrates that those of us who form the backbone of the independence movement refuse to accept the characterisation of us painted by a hostile press. We are not swivel-eyed English-haters, we are ordinary people from all walks of life and all backgrounds and ethnic origins who just happen to be committed to the radical principle that a country is best governed by people who can be bothered enough about it to actually live in it. Abuse, hatred and threats play no part in our movement and do not represent the values that we stand for.

Unlike the Conservative Party, we will not silently tolerate sectarian organisations. Unlike UKIP we will not dog-whistle to racists. The independence movement holds itself to a higher standard, and we refuse to be judged by the online actions of individuals acting on their own who represent no one but themselves. The Scottish independence movement represents the best of Scotland.

The Indy Pledge

The Indy Pledge is an agreement of the YES movement's core values, offering simple positive principles, promoting our shared beliefs and actions as a force for positive change.

The intention is to encourage people to be mindful of how our actions, in person or online, can impact positively or negatively on the independence movement.

By signing this pledge, individuals, groups and organisations are agreeing to abide by the following core principles:

We are an inclusive movement that values all people equally and does not discriminate on the basis of race, colour, gender, religious beliefs or non-beliefs or sexual orientation. We will promote this inclusiveness in all our expressions and actions.

We work with respect for all people, regardless of our politics or differences of opinion.

We are a peaceful organisation and apply peaceful means of achieving independence.

We will promote a positive vision for independence.

We will work constructively towards the goal of independence: as individuals and as a movement.

We are an open grassroots movement and work with the utmost transparency in our ideas and actions.

We are a broad and diverse movement, and expect individuals to take responsibility for their own actions and contributions to the campaign for independence.

We are the grassroots of an independent Scotland. We believe that a dynamic and creative movement will bring a thriving Scotland, and we want all people to play a role. As we work towards independence, we will enable and encourage fellow members to develop their own skills and talents.

Independence starts with our movement and we must reflect the Scotland we want to be.

With this in mind, we ask that all people and all groups sign up to this pledge and make our contributions ever mindful of these principles.

The campaign we run in order to win independence will shape the kind of independent Scotland that we achieve. Let's win a Scotland which is kind, tolerant, open, and accepting of difference. Let's win a Scotland where we know how to disagree without being disagreeable. The Indy Pledge is a statement of that aspiration.

28 March 2018

Forget Twitter spats – the indy movement is as strong as ever

I'm just back from a trip to the USA to visit with my fiancé and to make plans for our wedding. We visited New York for a long weekend and coincidentally it was Tartan Week, where there was a parade of pipe bands, people in kilts, and a couple dressed up as the Loch Ness Monster, all the way along Sixth Avenue. It was a bit like the more famous St Patrick's Day Parade, only with morose drunk people instead. Because we're Scottish. For the first time ever the Parade Marshall was a woman, the singer KT Tunstall. Or as a wee guy standing beside me kept calling her, Katie Turnstyle. It was a strange experience to stand in the biggest city in the USA amidst a sea of Scottish flags.

I was standing in the crowd watching the parade go by, and was the only person in earshot with a Scottish accent. It meant that lots of people wanted to talk to me, and invariably they wanted to know if Scotland was going to become independent. Many of the Americans in the crowd either claimed Scottish ancestry, or had visited Scotland. There was one woman, a native New Yorker, who told me that she'd stuck a pin in a map at random in order to decide where to go on holiday and had ended up going to Kirkcaldy. She's loved Scotland ever since. Another woman told me that her grandparents had emigrated to the USA from Shettleston and was thrilled when I told her that I come from the East End of Glasgow myself. All of them were urging Scotland on to go for independence. "Getting independence from the English worked for us," said one American man to me.

To celebrate the event, the Empire State Building was lit up in the colours of the saltire, and there were as many saltires on display along Sixth Avenue as you'll see at an independence march. What you wouldn't see at an independence march however was the guy at the front of the parade. It was a certain Ken Wossisname, the eminently forgettable Presiding Officer of the Scottish parliament all dressed up in a kilt because he's a Proud-Scot-But – but not so proud that he doesn't put his British nationalism before the right of Holyrood to protect its powers from Theresa May's power grab. There were two Union flegs in evidence too, one at the front of the parade presumably to make Ken feel at home, and another carried by some organisation describing itself as a British heritage group. I took plenty of photies, although not of the Union flegs. I was going to take a pic of Ken too. But I forgot.

The trip to the USA meant that I was able to miss out on the latest arguments to have broken out on Scottish social media. Apparently in my absence, the independence movement has been torn in two. Again. Or possibly it's been torn in three, or maybe four. Or one of the pieces into which it was previously torn has torn itself into two. Or perhaps it's Jim Sillars, who is a piece all by himself. It's hard to tell really, but that's what comes from reading the British nationalist media in Scotland. Anyway, it seems we've all been falling out about the timing of another independence referendum.

This comes as news to me. I've only been visiting independence groups and organisations the length and breadth of Scotland for months and have dismally failed to find the evidence of the fallouts that so occupy the British nationalist press. The grass-roots movement is pretty determined that there needs to be a referendum within the term of this Scottish parliament. But what would I know? I don't do Twitter any more, just real life, but Twitter is far more important than real life for Scottish political reportage.

Mostly, what counts as reporting on the independence

movement in the British nationalist press comes from journalists trolling Twitter in the search of people falling out about stuff. Now admittedly it's true that when you put two Scottish people in a room you immediately have three arguments. Taking the humph is a vital part of our cultural heritage. However it has to be said that looking on Twitter for arguments is a bit like looking for cowpats in a field full of cattle and then getting all outraged because you keep standing in it.

To be frank, Twitter is really a just way for people who are too afraid to experiment with powerful illegal drugs to experience the brain damage, paranoia and addictive behaviours that drugs produce, but without the high or the temporary sense of well-being and being at one with the universe. The best you can hope for is being at one with a mildly amusing photo of a cat. But the biggest problem with Twitter is that however obvious it is that something someone tweeted is a stupid joke, someone else will have taken it seriously, and then at least three dozen other people will take it upon themselves to get outraged on their behalf. Then in turn this will be followed by the entire thing getting plastered all over the front page of a newspaper where a journalist will stoke up even more harrumphage because Nicola Sturgeon hasn't condemned it. This is what passes for the news cycle in the early twenty-first century.

Back in the real world, in the streets and in Scottish communities, away from the journalistic bubble of Twitter, the pride in Scotland and the confidence in this country's potential that was on display in New York is increasingly being felt in Scotland too. The topic of independence has been normalised. The question facing Scotland now is no longer "Should Scotland become an independent country?". The question is "When should Scotland become an independent country?". That question is going to be answered a lot sooner than Ken Wossisname might like, and within a few short years the Tartan Day Parade in New York will be celebrating an independent Scotland that has retaken its rightful place amongst the sovereign states of the world.

18 April 2018

Sold down the river by UK government 'promises'

Remember how during the independence referendum campaign in 2014 Scotland was told repeatedly that the only way that we could assure the jobs in the shipyards on the Clyde was to vote No? And remember how we were told with equal frequency that the UK never ever wouldn't possibly dream of building military ships in a foreign country? Well about that... It turns out that the Ministry of Defence is currently in talks with shipbuilders in a number of European countries, plus South Korea about contracts for building three new auxiliary vessels for the Royal Navy. But these are only supply vessels, not your actual warships, and apparently that makes it all OK.

Since the British government is allowing foreign shipyards to bid for the contracts for these auxiliary ships, then an independent Scotland could have bid for them too. Which means that when we were told back in 2014 that shipyards in an independent Scotland couldn't bid for Royal Navy contracts that wasn't entirely true. The British government, telling lies to Scotland! Imagine that. That is as unexpected as the sun coming up in the morning, as finding a midgie in the Highlands, or as *Reporting Scotland* devoting a huge chunk of the small and precious broadcast time available for Scottish news to a story about a cute kitten that can't play fitba and how it's all the fault of the SNP. What really would be unexpected would be if they allowed Hardeep Singh Kohli or some other prominent independence campaigner on the show to comment on it, but there's not much chance of that happening.

The predictable retort by apologists for British nationalism in Scotland is that Scotland was only ever told that warships wouldn't be built abroad. However to the rest of us a naval vessel is a naval vessel, and it doesn't really matter what its precise military role is. Contracts for the ships derive from defence procurement and therefore the British government is entitled to ensure that the ships are built within the UK, giving the Clyde a better chance of securing the order. But the British government hasn't done that. They might not have breached the letter of their promises to Scotland, but they've certainly breached their spirit.

This is all part of a very predictable pattern of behaviour from the British government when it comes to the promises and commitments that it has made to the people of Scotland, particularly those promises and commitments that were made in order to secure a No vote in the referendum of 2014. They all have get-out clauses as big as Ruth Davidson's ego. There are planetary gas giants which are smaller than that, and to be fair that's also a pretty good description of Ruth's ego.

Take for example the promise made by the British government that the permanence of Holyrood would be enshrined in law, a provision which would also enact that no change could be made to the powers of Holyrood by a Westminster government without the express consent of the Scottish parliament. The provision was duly written, and it was passed as part of the new Scotland Act. It was only later we discovered that the said provision has no legal standing and can be ignored by Westminster whenever it sees fit. You might think that the whole point of writing something into law was that it was, you know, the law. But that doesn't apply when it involves a promise made by Westminster to Scotland.

Westminster's promises to Scotland are a bit like a mobster promising that if you give him a large amount of money then he won't break your leg. So you give him a few grand in order that you can keep walking, but then he kneecaps you in both legs and smashes both your ankles. Technically he's not broken your leg, but his promise doesn't have a leg to stand on, and neither do you. Then he goes on a BBC Scotland news and current affairs programme that doesn't feature Hardeep Singh Kohli to tell you that the Vow has been delivered, so what are you complaining about? You're an ungrateful separatist who needs to learn to respect the fact that the promise has been kept. Your leg hasn't actually been broken. Just your kneecaps and your ankles.

Maybe I should retract that last paragraph. It's a bit unfair to compare the British government to mobsters. The Mafia does actually have a moral code of sorts, which is a lot more than you can say about the British government's promises to the people of Scotland.

But the British government has only made a hoist for its own petard. During the next independence referendum campaign, we will be able to point to all the promises and commitments made in 2014, and show how what was delivered fell very far short. Then whenever a new Vow or promise is made, all we'll have to do is to say, "But you said that the last time, and it turned out to be a lie." No wonder they're so desperate to avoid a second independence referendum.

21 April 2018

Royal baby? Let's focus on
the real news please

Earlier this week the Herald newspaper revealed the results of
a poll which showed that a significant majority of Scots would
prefer to remain a part of the EU. The story was published on
Monday, when there was no other news of note cos some royal
wummin had just had a wean. The royal wummin having a
wean was a cue for all sorts of people draped in Union flegs to
parade on the telly and gush about how excited they were and
how this was the best thing to happen since the last time that
the same royal wummin had had a wean. This is of course an
example of how British nationalism is so much better than
other nationalisms because it's not nationalist at all.

Displays of British nationalism are an unsettling combination of the weirdly comic and the deeply sinister, like a
villain from a Batman movie but without the special effects
budget. The Tories have spent the last few years destroying
hospitals, so they've got quite a lot in common with Heath
Ledger's Joker. British nationalism wants us to believe that
Prince Charles is deserving of his internship as leader of the
Commonwealth, the first time in seventy years that the self-
pitying privileged posho has got a job, and then only because
his maw had a wee word with the selection committee.

There was real potential for a news story about who would
expire first from paroxysms of royalist hysteria, the reporting
teams from *Sky News*, or the one from the BBC, although
personally my money was on Murdo Fraser. But sadly we were
spared that and instead were treated to assorted reporters
standing outside a hospital desperately filling in time because
nothing was actually happening. I was only watching in

the vain hope that one, just one, reporter would point a microphone at one of the Union fleg-bedecked people who'd been camping outside the hospital for the past fortnight and ask, "What in God's name is wrong with you?"

There was some real news happening elsewhere, but that didn't count because some royal wummin had just had a wean. And we've not even had that bloody wedding yet. Just kill me now.

But back to some of that real news. The EU poll in question was an online poll of readers of various publications across the whole of the UK. It showed that Scotland is, by a decent margin, the most pro-European part of the UK. The poll was an online poll, and although it wasn't statistically balanced in order to ensure that those answering the question were properly representative of the population as a whole, the results are probably rather more representative of Scottish opinion than anything that comes out of the mouths of Scottish Conservative politicians. Although to be fair, that wouldn't be hard, as most people in Scotland instinctively know that pretending to be Saddam Hussein for a joke isn't a good look for an MP, nor do they have to go on special diversity training to know that sectarianism is a bad thing.

Even though the poll wasn't statistically balanced, we can still learn a lot from it. Which again is rather more than you can say for a Scottish Conservative politician. Mind you, I did once learn something from Jackson Carlaw. I learned that Scottish Tories think that Gaelic road signs are magical incantations to get people to vote for independence. I also learned that Scottish Tories aren't the brightest bunch on the planet, but we all knew that already. But back to the poll, it's confirmation that Scotland remains strongly pro-European, and that public dissatisfaction with the British government's handling of the Brexit process is widespread in Scotland. Dissatisfaction with the amount of time that the media devotes to royals having weans is also widespread, and it would be nice to have a poll to confirm that too.

The poll confirms that Scotland's relationship with Europe is going to be key in the next Scottish independence referendum. Mind you, I strongly suspect that if an independent Scotland could give a cast iron categorical guarantee that we'd never have to see Nicholas Witchell on the telly ever again, that Yes vote in the next referendum would be a shoo-in.

Despite the strongly pro-European sentiment in Scotland, it would be a mistake to fight the next independence referendum campaign on the basis of seeking independence in order that Scotland can still be a member of the EU. Research carried out by the pro-independence think tank Common Weal has shown that there has been significant churn in support for independence. The Brexit issue has caused many former No voters to shift to supporting independence, but equally there's been a dropping off in support for independence amongst some "soft Yeses". This is why there's been no real change in support for independence in the polls since 2014.

What we need to focus on in the next independence referendum campaign is the right of Scotland to decide its own relationship with the EU and the rest of the world, instead of being stuck with a Tory Brexit. There's one thing we can be certain of, and that's that Boris Johnson, David Davis and Michael Gove aren't seeking to take the UK out of the EU in order to transform it into a paradise of workers' and human rights. Scotland needs its own relationship with Europe, whether that's EU membership, membership of EFTA, or some other relationship, that's for the Scottish people to decide after independence.

What the churn in support for independence tells us is that the biggest task ahead of us isn't to convert No voters to Yes, although it's certainly important that we continue to work on that. However what's going to win us the next Scottish independence referendum will be getting those soft Yeses who have drifted away back to Yes again. The people we will be targeting are people who have already voted Yes. They were already persuaded to vote for independence, and they can be persuaded to vote for independence again. That ought to be a much easier task than persuading someone who voted No last time to change their mind. If we combine everyone who voted Yes last time with those who have since come over to Yes because of Brexit, there's already a majority for independence. That's why I am so confident that Scotland is going to vote for independence next time.

Approximately 145 children are born in Scotland every day. If the independence movement can get back those people who once supported independence but have since drifted away, we can make sure that those babies will have a Scotland worth living in, an independent Scotland where their votes will count for something when they're adults. And then as well as deciding what sort of relationship that we want with Europe and the rest of the world, Scotland can also decide what sort of relationship it wants with the Windsors and the legions of gushing propagandists who fill our airwaves every time they reproduce or marry.

25 April 2018

It's the Unionists who are
politicising Scots – not us

Last week the Scottish government announced that it was giving £2.5 million in support of an initiative to produce a new Gaelic dictionary. The news was greeted with the usual opprobrium from sections of the Scottish media, and a howling barrage of derision from British nationalists on social media complaining about nationalism. Because, as we all know, British nationalism is better than any other nationalism because it's not nationalist at all.

The *Faclair na Gàidhlig* (Dictionary of Gaelic) project aims to produce a comprehensive dictionary of Gaelic, citing the etymology and origin of words, their history and development, as well as their usage and meaning. It will be far more complete than any existing dictionary of the language, and would give Gaelic a dictionary fit for the twenty-first century. It would provide a Gaelic equivalent to existing dictionaries of English such as the Oxford English Dictionary, which itself has recently been provided with some £34 million in funding in order to complete its third edition. The Oxford English Dictionary is not capable of supporting itself from profits from its sales. Those who complain about the funding given to Faclair na Gàidhlig don't complain about the much larger amount of money spent in support of an English dictionary. Gaelic for hypocrisy is *fuar-chràbhadh*, in case you were wondering.

Gaelic, and Scots, are every bit as much the heritage and cultural inheritance of those who mock them as nationalist hobby horses as they are of anyone else in Scotland. Gaelic and Scots belong, insofar as languages belong to anyone, to the whole of Scotland, to everyone in the country, irrespective of their political views on the constitution or independence. It's certainly the case that independence supporters tend to be more positive in their views about Gaelic and Scots than diehard opponents of independence, and are definitely more positive about the languages than those who wave Union flegs on social media while claiming that they hate nationalism, but the truth is that Scotland's languages do not play a significant role in the independence debate, and that is right and proper.

Unlike Catalonia or the Basque Country, where the politics of language play a central role in arguments about nationhood and independence, Scots and Gaelic are marginal in the debate about Scottish self-determination. Partly that's to do with the multilingual history of Scotland, with the fact that we have no less than three languages – Gaelic, Scots and Scottish Standard English – all of which have equal claim to the status of national languages. Partly it's to do with the historical fact that Scotland had a centuries-long existence as an independent state. Scottish identity is not closely associated with a single language in the way that, say, Catalan identity is.

When displaying support for Scotland's ancient languages, independence supporters are often accused by British nationalists of "politicising" Gaelic and Scots. However what is really politicising the languages is to deny them the resources and funding that they require to survive in the modern world because of a fear of stoking up pro-independence sentiment. If your terror of Scottish independence leads you to deny Gaelic the same resources that English gets then it's you who is politicising Gaelic.

British nationalists politicise Scottish languages in other ways. *The National* is unique in Scotland in offering space in its columns to the Scots language as well as to Gaelic. Articles in Scots frequently come in for abuse on social media for the supposed crime of using words which are not "proper Scots". Ironically people who don't themselves use Scots seem to regard themselves as the best judges of what is or is not Scots. These offending terms are older words or spellings which the writer has resuscitated, or are Scots neologisms. When Scots writers use such terms they are accused of creating a plastic or synthetic Scots.

Yet these processes of reviving words from older stages of the language, or using existing words in novel ways, are precisely how any language extends its vocabulary and range of expression. That's how modern standard literary languages come into being. Back in the nineteenth century, Catalan was in a similar situation to the one Scots is in now. It lacked an agreed spelling, and people who spoke it freely mixed Catalan and Spanish. Catalan authors devised a spelling based on the language of the Golden Age of Catalan literature in the Middle Ages, they revived obsolete words, and they began to use existing words in new and novel ways. In doing so they created the modern literary Catalan language.

The modern Finnish, Faroese and Frisian literary languages came into being in the exact same way. The Estonian literary language contains words which were originally complete inventions. All literary languages are by definition artificial in the sense that they are the deliberate creations of writers. However when Scots writers adopt the same tactics to produce a literary variety of Scots, they're accused of creating an artificial plastic Scots that isn't real. They're accused of politicising Scots. Yet what is really politicising Scots is to deny it the same means of enriching and developing itself which have been used by every other literary language. By denying Scots these avenues of enrichment, opponents of the language are seeking to diminish its use and confine it to a dialectal ghetto. Scots, they say, isn't a proper language, and they're going to do whatever it takes to ensure that it can't act or be used as a proper language.

There are a lot of myths and misconceptions about language. Perhaps the most common is that we should concentrate our efforts on "useful" languages like Spanish or

French. It's arguable just how much more useful it is to learn a language that you're only going to use a couple of weeks a year on holiday. But this is an argument made from the perspective of an adult English monoglot. The entire point of bilingual education for children, which is generally agreed to be the best way to ensure the continuing survival of Gaelic and Scots, is that it means that Gaelic or Scots can then be used as the medium of instruction for other subjects. There is no logical reason why a child can't learn Spanish through the medium of Gaelic, and it's certainly the case that the more languages you learn, the easier they become to acquire. Learning Gaelic or Scots makes it easier to acquire French, or German, or Swedish. It doesn't make it more difficult.

It's wrong to politicise Scotland's languages. Opponents of Scottish independence need to stop using them as footballs, and need to recognise that Scotland's languages have the same right to enrich themselves as any other language, and the same right to support that other languages receive. Gaelic and Scots belong to everyone in Scotland, not just independence supporters.

2 May 20185

May 2018

Recently, Ruth Davidson made the *Time* magazine list of the one hundred most influential people in the world. Not the real world, naturally. She's one of the one hundred most influential people in the fantasy world inhabited by arch-Thatcherite British nationalist Scottish expats living in America. This is also the same fantasy world in which people who bear British passports and who live abroad are expats and not immigrants, because immigrants are people who speak English with funny accents – like that special accent that Fraser Nelson invented all on his own.

Ruth joins some talented company, comedian Sacha Baron Cohen and star of Ugly Betty America Ferrera have featured on previous lists, and unlike Ruth they're funny on purpose. But then Osama bin Laden has also appeared on a previous list, so getting your name on it isn't always a recommendation. Being influential isn't necessarily a good thing. It's like compiling a list of things that have the greatest influence on the human body, like Novichok or cyanide, and then calling it a list of medicines. A lot of us would happily agree that the Scottish Conservatives with their dog whistles to sectarian bigotry and their serially offensive candidates are pretty toxic.

Ruth was chosen for this illustrious list by the historian Niall Ferguson, who has spent a significant portion of his academic career writing about how the British Empire and its rampant colonialism really wasn't such a bad thing after all. Some countries need to be conquered for their own good, and quite possibly Scotland is one of them. If it wasn't for the good graces of the Westminster parliament Scotland would revert to an atavistic wasteland where we fight to the death over a bridie from Greggs, so organising things like a currency or paying for pensions is way beyond our little Caledonian capacities.

Niall was obviously influenced in his choice by the hagiographies that appear about Ruth in the Scottish press, and he's clearly come to see her as the long heralded and much awaited Messiah of the Union, the spiritual heir to Jim Murphy, Kezia Dugdale and all the other saviours of the UK who were supposed to kill Scottish nationalism stone dead but who failed miserably. The fact that he chose her was based upon what the British nationalist media in Scotland have written about her, and this was then used by the British nationalist media in Scotland to justify what they'd previously written about her. It's a cosmic circle jerk of Conservative self-congratulation which they then use as a halo around Ruth's heid.

Back on our planet, and despite the panegyrics which regularly appear about her in the fawning British nationalist media in Scotland, Ruth isn't even remotely close to being the most influential person in the Scottish parliament. She's a long long way short of being the most influential person in the Conservative Party, for whom she's at best a sort of cheery pet Jocko who engages the public with her cheesy photo ops and cheeky *Bake Off* appearances but who is kept at arm's length from any actual policy decisions. And now it turns out that she's not even the most influential person in the Scottish Tories. That would be Jacob Rees-Mogg.

A gang of four Scottish Tory MPs, Ross Thomson, Stephen Kerr, Colin Clark and Alister Jack, pay considerably more attention to what Jacob Rees-Mogg says than they do to what Ruth tells them. They're hell-bent on pursuing Jacob's fantasies of a revived Ukania, leading a Commonwealth that doesn't want to be led. They want to create a red white and blue dreamland of royalism as a colourful pageant to distract from the destruction of our employment and civil rights. The fact that every single economic assessment proves it will be bad for Scotland, and bad for their own constituents, makes not the slightest bit of difference.

During the general election last year, all Scottish Tories stood as candidates for "Ruth Davidson's Scottish Conservatives". Ruth insisted that she was the leader of the Conservatives in Scotland, and that Scottish Tory MPs sent to Westminster were going to be responsible to her and answerable to her. We now know that isn't true. Actually, many of us knew it during the general election campaign, but were drowned out by the tidal wave of enRuthiasm gushing out of the British nationalist media. They weren't listening to us then, and for the most part they're not listening now. Ruth does indeed have a highly influential superpower, and that's the power to get her pals in the Scottish media to protect her.

We shouldn't be too churlish though. Ruth Davidson does after all deserve her place on the list of the one hundred most influential people. She's highly influential amongst the reasons why Scotland needs independence, and she's highly influential amongst the reasons why she and her party are going to cause Scotland to vote for independence in the next independence referendum.

A message to those who can't see a buzz without wanting to kill it ...

Last Saturday Glasgow hosted the largest pro-independence demonstration in Scottish history. For those who participated, it was a massive affirmation of our belief that the only way to achieve a better Scotland is with independence. The day created a buzz and an excitement, a strength of purpose and a resolve to double our efforts to bring about the better Scotland that we dream of.

But it didn't go down well with everyone. Some people are incapable of seeing a buzz without wanting to kill it. The event was criticised by some independence supporters who believe, reasonably enough, that no one is converted from No to Yes because a bunch of people walk down a street in Glasgow waving Scottish flags and pushing a big model unicorn. They tell us that we should concentrate our energies on persuading people to vote Yes. It's a fair point, but it's also the case that unless we have a body of energetic and enthused campaigners, we won't have anyone to do the persuading. A successful campaign needs to look in both directions. It needs to look outwards to attract undecideds to its cause, to persuade those who formerly were opposed. But it also needs to look inwards, to nourish and support its existing base.

Saturday's rally wasn't predominantly aimed at attracting No voters. Let's face it, you're not going to get up early on a Saturday morning and schlepp into Glasgow from the furthest parts of Scotland unless you are already pretty strong in your belief that Scotland needs to become an independent country. This wasn't an event about convincing anyone who wasn't already convinced. The point of the march and rally was precisely so that people who already believe in independence, the foot soldiers of the coming campaign, could be energised and enthused by the company of others who feel the same way.

However there is also an argument that a successful march and rally can help to persuade undecideds. Scotland is a country where the media narrative is overwhelmingly opposed to independence and is British nationalist in sentiment. That means that people who support independence, and there are many of us, or people who are undecided, and there are many of those too, feel inhibited about speaking our minds in a way that opponents of independence don't.

A march of tens of thousands through the streets of Glasgow is a very public display that the independence movement is large, vital and will not be ignored. A march tells people that we are many. We fill the streets of Glasgow saying that the only thing we're shopping for is a better Scotland. It's empowering, and by being so it encourages those who are sitting on the fence, who are uncertain that they will be supported, that there are thousands of us who are here to welcome them.

The rally was also criticised by those who oppose independence but who apparently want to give us some constructive advice. Because the way to achieve independence is to listen to campaign advice from people who want you to lose. Well who knew? The gist of their criticism is that reaffirmation and morale boosting for the committed Yes supporters who took part in the march and rally is nothing more than confirmation bias. All that independence supporters are achieving by congregating together is reinforcing our own existing beliefs. Well, that, and annoying Tory MSPs. And the appropriate response to that is, "Yes? And your point is, caller?"

People who oppose independence don't need rallies in order to reinforce their existing beliefs, they have the overwhelming majority of the media in Scotland for that sort of thing. They have Ruth Davidson snarking on social media about how drivers were inconvenienced. Although it's funny how she never says the same about Orange marches. They have the snide remarks and comments of the apologists for the British state who dominate the press narratives and preside over the airwaves and who write articles for the papers decrying the confirmation bias of Yes supporters.

Every time you turn on the TV or pick up a newspaper in Scotland, with the honourable exception of *The National*, you will have your anti-independence confirmation bias reaffirmed. Yet Scotland is a country which is more or less split right down the middle on the topic of the constitution. We live in country where the independence movement is consistently marginalised and where it's not a conspiracy to state that the vast majority of the media is against a view of the constitution which is backed by almost half the population. It's a simple fact. And then that part of Scotland whose bias is constantly reaffirmed in the media snarks about the other half of Scotland building its own affirmation for itself.

Pro-independence voices struggle to be heard. That half of Scotland which supports independence has far less opportunity to see its views reflected in the media than that half of Scotland which opposes it. The arguments in favour of independence are drowned out in a barrage of opposing arguments, if they are ever aired at all. There is an entire industry in Scotland devoted to reaffirming the confirmation bias of opponents of independence. That half of Scotland which does believe in independence needs to find its affirmation in other ways. We do it for ourselves.

The fact that we build our own affirmation from marches and rallies, community events and grass-roots organisations doesn't make our self-validation any less meaningful, or indeed valid, than that of a person who gets theirs from reading an editorial or opinion piece in Scotland's legion of anti-independence press. You could argue the opposite. It means that the affirmation and validation of the Yes movement is organic in a way that British nationalism in Scotland never can be. The affirmation of the independence movement is based in the grass roots. It grows upwards. It reaches up for a prize worth marching for, worth chapping on doors for, worth making leaflets and organising town hall events for. The prize is a better Scotland, a Scotland where all of us are equally validated and affirmed, and not just those who support the British state.

9 May 2018

Faslane nuclear submarines: the price we pay for living in a 'remote' land

Fifty years ago this week, the first nuclear submarines armed with nuclear missiles arrived at the naval base in Faslane, cutting the district off from the rest of Scotland with barbed wire and warnings. There was a time, not so long ago, when holidaymakers from Glasgow came to the shores of the Gareloch to enjoy the peace and tranquility. Now the landscape is scarred by machines of death and weapons of mass destruction. A once beautiful bay is defaced and deformed by military equipment and armaments that threaten devastation.

Perhaps it was fate. According to one interpretation the name Faslane derives from the Gaelic *Fàs-Lann*, the barren place, the land laid waste, the land of desolation. There is little that is more desolate than the grey concrete of the military base, occupying the green hillside like a malevolent beast that lays waste to the landscape. It's a creature with the power to make the world barren and bare.

On the site of the base, now buried underneath metres of concrete and steel and the tramping boots of servicepeople who know nothing about the significance of the site in Scottish myth and legend, there used to be a stream which flowed into the Gareloch. At the site where the stream entered the loch there was a low hill called Cnoc a' Chullaich, the hillock of the cockerel. According to an ancient story there was once an oak tree there underneath which lived a cockrell, and when the Faslane cockrell crowed it was a warning of death.

Scotland wasn't consulted when the British government decided to host nuclear weapons and nuclear submarines on the banks of the Gareloch, just twenty-five miles from the largest city in the country. The decision was made on the banks of the Thames, by people for whom the Clyde was a remote and distant province, far from power, far from anywhere important. Ever since, Scotland has lived under a nuclear shadow, fearful of the crowing of the cockrell of Cnoc a' Chullaich. It's the price we pay for living in a land which its government considers to be remote. Scotland as a part of the UK is remote from power, remote from influence, its voice drowned out by the crowing of the nuclear cockrell.

We do not know what damage the MoD base has caused to the environment, yet it is likely to be significant. We do know that between 2013 and 2014 alone there were ninety-nine reported "radioactive incidents". We do know that during the 1980s the MoD refused to allow the exploitation of oil reserves in the Clyde because it would interfere with its precious submarines. Instead of enjoying an oil boom in the 1980s, Scotland enjoyed Thatcher's deindustrialisation. We know that the base isn't creating jobs, but rather preventing real economic development and creating environmental damage.

The Polaris missiles and warheads based on the Clyde, and the Trident missiles and warheads which succeeded them, exist to perpetuate the myth that the UK is still a major power, even though their guidance systems are built and determined by the Americans and no British government could ever countenance their use without the Pentagon's approval. They're as much a myth as the cockrell of Cnoc a' Chullaich, only infinitely more harmful. There are few things in modern Scotland more delusional than those politicians who claim that Trident is a glorified job creation scheme, as though the sole purpose of hosting obscene weapons of mass destruction on the Clyde was to keep open a medium-sized Tesco Express in the greater Helensburgh area. If a job creation scheme was the primary consideration, we could spend a fraction of the cost of Trident on creating jobs on the Clyde, and still have billions to spare.

For as long as those weapons have been next to Scotland's largest city, Scotland has protested against them. We have marched. We have demonstrated. We have set up peace camps. Yet all these decades later we are still no closer to ridding Scotland of a blight on all humanity. It's clear now that there is only one way to rid Scotland of nukes, and that's with independence. Then the base can be converted into the base for a new Scottish conventional navy, preserving and creating jobs, and removing the threat of nuclear mass destruction from our soil.

For half a century, Scotland has lived in fear of the death warning of the Cullach of Fàs-Lann, the whining howl of sirens that signal impending destruction. One day, when Scotland takes back control of its own destiny, the weapons of mass destruction will be removed from this country. The cockrell will be silenced and will vanish into the pages of history books. The site of the barren wasteland will be restored to the people of Scotland, and we will no longer fear the siren scream of the Cullach of Fàs-Lann.

12 May 2018

Written constitution is the recipe for indy Scotland

There's been some discussion this week of the importance of starting now on preparing a draft constitution for an independent Scotland. It's an excellent idea. One of the greatest problems with the British state, and so one of the reasons Scotland needs independence, is the lack of a written constitution. The British establishment loves the UK's unwritten constitution, because it effectively gives British governments carte blanche to do exactly as they please. If the UK had a written constitution, the powers of different parts of government would be explicitly described and circumscribed, which means that Theresa May wouldn't be able to use the Brexit vote to undermine the devolution settlement in the way that she's doing.

A written constitution is at the core of how we go about making an independent Scotland a better country than the Scotland of the UK. A written constitution pins our political class down, it gives them a precise legal framework within which to operate, it spells out the limits to their power. A written constitution specifies where sovereignty lies, that it belongs to the people. A written constitution is the recipe for a better country. It's up to us to bring the ingredients.

Fundamentally this is about accountability. So many of Scotland's problems have come about because the lack of a written constitution means that British politicians are not held accountable. It doesn't matter what we vote for in Scotland, there are never any consequences for failure for a British politician. The man who most clearly represents that is Michael Forsyth, Thatcher's man in Scotland.

Michael was leader of the Scottish Tories during the 1997 general election. He presented Scotland with a distinctively Scottish Conservative manifesto that year. The people of this country looked at Michael, they looked at his manifesto, they looked at his party, and they voted every single Tory out of power. Democratic rejections do not come more forceful or definitive.

Yet here we are, twenty-one years on, and Michael sits in the House of Lords, making our laws and influencing government policy. During the EU referendum, Brexiteer Michael even had the unmitigated gall to appear in a debate and complain about the injustice of our laws being made by unelected and unaccountable people whom we can't vote out of office. You don't say Mikey, you don't say. With a written constitution, Scotland could specify that politicians can only have power because they're elected.

I want independence because I don't trust politicians. We need to keep them close to us so that their backsides are within kicking distance of our feet. When we kick them out of office they will stay out of office until the people vote them back in again and they will not keep influencing our laws because their pals give them power. A written constitution spells out the limits to the powers of politicians. It shackles them and constrains them. That's got to be a good thing.

By starting the conversation now about the shape of a future written constitution, we are already putting into effect one of the key principles of Scottish independence, that this is a country where the people are sovereign, not the parliament. The creation of a constitution becomes an exercise in participatory democracy, which is exactly what an independent Scotland should be. This is our country, and we all have a right to a voice in shaping its future and determining the path it takes. That's the singular difference between an independent Scotland and a UK which regards Westminster as the only sovereign body, because in practice that means that the UK is an elective dictatorship without effective constraints on the power of the government of the day.

There are at least three separate projects at the moment working on draft constitutions for an independent Scotland. All of them are exciting initiatives, and each has a slightly different focus. As well as Elliot Bulmer's *Foundations for Freedom* discussion paper which was highlighted in *The National* this week, there is the Centre for Scottish Constitutional Studies (CSCS), which is an independent think tank founded several years before the independence referendum of 2014. The CSCS has also been working on its own proposals for a draft Scottish constitution and will be inviting comments and discussion. The CSCS is shortly due to unveil its new website, which promises an exciting and fully interactive process on creating a new Scottish constitution. The site will contain a full copy of the group's provision draft constitution for discussion and comment, all twelve articles and 179 sections of it. The CSCS is quite explicit that this is a provisional draft of a constitution, and recognises that the constitution of an independent Scotland can only be drafted properly with the collaboration and input of all groups in Scottish society.

Last, but by no means least, constitutional scholar Dr Mark McNaught has also been working on draft proposals for a constitution for a Scottish state. Mark is an American academic of Scots descent who teaches constitutional law at Rennes University in France. Mark brings to the task years of experience in studying constitutional law, and seeks to incorporate best practice from other nations into the creation of a new Scottish constitution.

All three of these projects are immensely valuable contributions to the independent Scotland that is already starting to come into being. The fundamental reason for independence is that it should be up to the people of Scotland, and no one else, to decide the path that this country takes. That means that questions like whether Scotland is a republic or a monarchy, or whether Scotland becomes a member of the EU or not, are questions that can only be decided by a sovereign and independent Scotland. But we can't expect people to take a leap into the complete unknown, and the more certainty that can be provided before Scotland becomes independent, the more likely it is that more people will be comfortable voting for independence.

One way we can do that is to start discussions now on the shape of a future constitution. If nothing else that will help lay to rest the idiotic myth so commonly propagated by the anti-independence parties that independence is purely an SNP project and that an independent Scotland would be a one-party SNP state. Let's get started now, and we will be able to see a better Scotland taking shape before our eyes.

16 May 2018

Get ready for a terrifying day
of British nationalism

If you're reading this you've been brave enough to pop your head out from underneath the duvet. Whatever you do, just don't turn on the TV, not unless you want to have your brains sucked out and replaced by royal wedding candyfloss. The Kay Burleys and the Nicholas Witchells have been unleashed. You have been warned.

Watching British telly today means being beaten up with a rolled-up copy of *Monarchy* magazine, and then being drowned in a vat of red white and blue treacle by some vacuously smiling people who keep telling you how lovely it all is. It's like that Japanese horror video, the one that if you watch it you're guaranteed to die in a screaming fit of insanity, only this time with bunting and plummy accented interviewees talking about the etiquette of Meghan's dad not attending. It's fair enough that Meghan's dad isn't going. A lot of people think that Harry's isn't going either.

There are few things more quintessentially British than political and media commentators sycophantically gushing about the royals while surrounded by Union flegs, and then they will pop up some time later during a Scottish independence referendum to tell us how much they despise nationalism. As we all know, British nationalism is distinguished from the nationalisms of lesser breeds, like that of hairy-legged Caledonians, by virtue of not being nationalist at all. In the press and on the telly today, it's wall-to-wall non-nationalism. The sea of saltires at the recent march and rally for independence in Glasgow – an off-putting and narrow-minded display of parochial nationalism. The sea of Union flegs during the royal wedding – a joyful expression of patriotism and happiness for the royal couple which envelops us all in a cosy bath of inclusivity. Got that? Good, now you can write a comment article for the British nationalist press in Scotland.

In Scotland, the overwhelming reaction to the royal wedding is indifference. For the majority of Scots, the sole reaction to the news that Harry was going to marry was "whatevs" and a shoulder shrug, followed immediately by "Does that mean we get a day off work?" However since it quickly transpired that the wedding was going to be on a Saturday, any vestigial interest quickly drained away. The only enjoyable thing for most of us has been laughing at the reactions of the deeply conflicted royalist racists in the *Mail*'s comment section. All of a sudden they have to pretend to be happy about an unemployed immigrant coming into the country and sponging off the state.

For the majority of people in Scotland, they have at best the same amount of interest in the royal wedding as they would have in a wedding on a reality TV show. Although to be honest there is less interest for most as the only real difference between those two things is that we can't vote anyone out of the Buckingham Palace Big Brother House. While *Big Brother* is every bit as pointless and irritating as the royal family, at least it doesn't cost us anything and you can actually avoid it fairly easily. You can't say the same for the royal soap opera.

Scotland is once again proving that it's the least royalist part of this so-called United Kingdom. The BBC had planned to install massive outdoor video screens in public places so that interested and enthused loyal subjects could enjoy the proceedings – the royal wedding and not *Big Brother* that is – as they had street parties. However the BBC cancelled its plans to erect outdoor screens in Scotland, as it seemed like an awful lot of bother to go to just for Murdo Fraser. They just bought him a life-sized cardboard cut-out of the happy couple instead. He's still not noticed the difference, but then most

Tory MSPs are cardboard cut-outs so that's understandable. Just install one with a recording saying "Scotland doesn't want another referendum" and they're indistinguishable from the real thing.

It has been noticed amongst certain sections of the British media that Scotland is the only part of the UK where there are no street parties to celebrate the event, apart from one on an RAF base in Morayshire, and that probably doesn't count. But it's not true that Scotland never has royal-themed street parties. We have royalist street parties every June in Scotland, usually accompanied by copious amounts of tonic wine, songs about killing Catholics, and attacks on people who dare to try and cross the street while the event is going on. There's that joyful inclusivity of non-nationalist British nationalism for you.

There are a lot of people in the rest of the UK who have zero interest in the royal wedding, it's not just Scotland, but on the whole the different reactions between Scotland and the rest of the UK whenever there is a royal event show that Scotland really is a different country. A country that is increasingly drifting away from the rest of Britain.

19 May 2018

Labour must take blame for the failings of BBC Scotland

Back in the 1990s when Scotland was still campaigning for a devolved Scottish parliament, the Labour Party assured us that once they got into power and ushered in a new era of light and goodness the powers of the new parliament would be far-ranging. That era of light and goodness turned out to be Tony Blair and Gordie Broon and we all know how that turned out, so it's not surprising in retrospect that Labour also fell far short on the promises it had made regarding Scottish devolution.

The original proposals included the devolution of broadcasting, but Labour reneged on that commitment and removed Scottish broadcasting from the remit of the new devolved parliament. The result was that when Scotland achieved self-government, it became the only self-governing country in Europe without a public service broadcaster of its own. Instead, we have BBC Scotland, a branch office of a decidedly British Broadcasting Corporation. The BBC is British, and it's not going to let us forget it. The mendacity of Labour back in the 1990s has set the tone for the media coverage of Scottish politics ever since.

Scotland is short-changed by its public service broadcaster. Scotland contributes more than £320 million annually to the BBC in licence fee payments, but only 54.6 per cent of that is returned to Scotland in the form of Scottish-produced programming. Scotland is very much the unfavoured child amongst the devolved nations of the UK. Ninety-five per cent of the BBC licence fee raised in Wales is spent on Welsh programming. Seventy-five per cent of the BBC licence fee raised in Northern Ireland is spent on Northern Irish programming. Scotland is the largest devolved nation, and as British nationalists are very fond of telling us, the one with the most powerful parliament. Yet it's the one which is the most deprived in terms of broadcasting.

That poverty of resources and poverty of ambition is in stark contrast to what happens in other self-governing but non-independent countries. Whereas Catalonia has a rich and diverse set of TV channels of its own, including a twenty-four-hour seven-day-a-week news channel, Scottish news is covered by our national broadcaster in a half-hour segment after the main evening news. Two decades on from devolution, and *Reporting Scotland* still isn't anything remotely close to a national news programme for a self-governing country. It's still a regional news segment, telling those of us outside London about the news where we are. It's an uncomfortable couthy mixture of cute kittens, murders and far too much sport.

BBC Scotland has decided that its focus in the coverage of Scottish politics lies in finding new ways of telling us how bad the SNP is and how rubbish Scotland is. If the news agenda in England is focussing on problems in its Conservative-run health service, the BBC in Scotland will likewise focus on the health service, even though Scotland's health service is performing considerably better than its English counterpart.

Reports from economic think tanks which can be spun as damaging to the cause of independence receive wall-to-wall coverage, but reports from pro-independence think tanks like Common Weal, or reports which show how the economic priorities of the UK are damaging to Scotland scarcely get a look-in. The Fraser of Allander Institute recently published a study demonstrating that the Scottish economy exports over £9 billion annually in Scottish-generated wealth to the rest of the UK and abroad. It never got a look-in on a BBC Scotland which is fixated on SNPbaddery, and because the BBC chose to gloss over it, the rest of the media in Scotland could ignore it too.

There remains widespread suspicion amongst the independence movement that pro-independence voices are being excluded from the BBC. Hardeep Singh Kohli has claimed that his name was on a blacklist. Another respected broadcaster told me in a private conversation that since coming out as a supporter of independence, invites to appear on BBC current affairs programmes had all but stopped. I'm active in the independence movement, doing public speaking events the length and breadth of the country, but it was only last week that I received an invite to appear on a BBC current affairs programme – one which I was unable to accept due to other commitments. And that invitation was to speak during a segment attacking a pro-independence newspaper.

Scotland is being systematically let down by its public service broadcaster. That would be bad enough in a country with a diverse and representative privately owned media, but in Scotland the press is overwhelmingly biased against independence. Out of some thirty-eight daily and Sunday newspapers just two support independence, despite the fact that almost half the people in Scotland back it. That in turn means that the BBC in Scotland ought to be bending over backwards to ensure that that part of Scottish public opinion which isn't represented in the print media gets a fair representation in the broadcast media. But that's not what BBC Scotland does. Far from it. BBC Scotland acts as a sounding board and amplifier for the bias that already exists in the Scottish print media. The media in a democracy ought to act as a mirror to that country. Scotland's media doesn't present Scotland with an image of Scotland, it presents us with an image of Ukania.

None of this is going to get any better with the introduction of the new Scottish digital channel promised by the BBC, a channel which is provisionally titled BBC Scottish Ghetto. The new channel will be tucked away in the distant reaches of the EPG, broadcasting only for a few hours in the evening, and working on a shoestring budget. It's almost as though it is being set up for failure, and then the BBC bosses in London can claim there's no demand for Scottish broadcasting.

It's right and proper that the Scottish government should be making submissions to Ofcom about the shortcomings of broadcasting in Scotland, as Ofcom consults on the licencing of the new Scottish Ghetto channel. However the problem with broadcasting in Scotland is essentially a political issue, not a regulatory one. The Scottish government shouldn't just be making submissions to Ofcom, it should also be making a political demand to Westminster for the devolution of broadcasting. It's only when Scotland has control over Scottish broadcasting that this country will get a broadcast media that is truly representative of all of Scottish opinion.

23 May 2018

A 'material change' for indyref2? Take your pick

It's been quite a week. Theresa May's government poisoned the soil of the devolution settlement and refused to allow a meaningful debate in the Commons on how the EU exit bill would affect Scotland despite repeated promises that they would make time for a debate. They were hoping that they could hide behind some procedural sleight of hand and no one would notice that they were undermining the entire basis of the Scottish devolution settlement. It was an act of naked contempt, one which was exacerbated by the jeering derision with which Tory MPs reacted to SNP interventions.

The following day the SNP stormed out of the Commons after the Speaker first said there could be a debate but then changed his mind, seemingly unsure of what the correct procedures were. All over Scotland, thousands of independence supporters who had been getting irked at the seeming caution of the SNP rose with them and cheered. Over 5000 new members have joined the party, and the independence movement is reinvigorated and re-energised. The actions of the SNP in Westminster succeeded in forcing the Westminster power grab to the top of the media agenda, when that media had like the Tories been hoping that any fuss could be contained then would quietly go away. It is now a racing certainty that there will be another independence referendum sooner rather than later.

In their unbridled arrogance the Tories thought that they could do as they pleased with Scotland, and there would be no consequences. That's what you get when you take your advice on the Scottish political scene from Ruth Davidson.

However the high-handed manner in which Theresa May's government has treated Scotland has come at a heavy price. The episode prompted a prominent opponent of independence to come out as an independence supporter.

Murray Foote might not be a household name, but everyone in Scotland understands who the editor of the *Daily Record* is. Murray wasn't just editor of the *Daily Record* during the independence referendum campaign, he was the architect of the Vow that the anti-independence parties hastily cobbled together in the final weeks of the campaign. The Vow promised all sorts of goodness would befall Scotland if only it voted No. It promised a Scotland that would be treated with respect. It promised a stronger and more entrenched devolution. Ever since the No vote in 2014, the anti-independence parties have claimed that the Vow has been fulfilled. Now whenever they make that claim all we need to say is that the man who wrote it disagrees with them. The Foote is on the other boot.

As if this wasn't a bad enough week for this so-called Union, it was capped off by the Ewok Mundell twittering in the Commons that Scotland isn't a partner, it's a part of the UK. So it's not just the Vow and the foundations of the devolution settlement that have been killed off this week, it's also the solemn commitment made to the people of Scotland in 2014 by the anti-independence parties that Scotland was a valued and equal partner in a family of nations.

Worse than even that, he took it upon himself to redefine the tattered remnants of the Sewel Convention. He insisted that Westminster has the right to act unilaterally when no agreement has been reached with the Scottish parliament. In other words, instead of consent "normally" being *required* from the Scottish parliament before its powers can be changed by Westminster, according to Mundell consent must merely be *sought*. He has just admitted that Westminster regards itself as having the right to change the powers of Holyrood whenever it chooses. Home rule as we know it is dead and buried. Holyrood's foundations are built on the quicksand of Conservative goodwill, and we saw this week how treacherous that is.

You wait for ages for a material change in circumstances to appear, and then several come along at once. At this rate we won't have to do any campaigning in order to win the argument for independence, the Tories and their pals will have done it all for us with their special combination of evil and incompetence.

During Furst Meenister's Questions, the anti-independence parties were naturally keen not to draw attention to the shame of their Westminster colleagues' contemptuous treatment of Scotland this week. Ruth Davidson decided to pose as tough on crime – her party's treatment of Scotland has been verging on the criminal, so she must have felt she was on familiar ground. Daylight robbery and deception are Tory strong points after all.

Richard Leonard launched his foray into Furst Meenister's Questions with a bizarre request, asking whether Nicola Sturgeon knew of alternative words for a hummingbird's beak. Well Richard, there's wee neb, toothless gob and tiny little pecker. All of which are words which could also be used with reference to Richard Leonard, funnily enough. Now I will never be able to look at Richard again without seeing the image of Woody Woodpecker futilely banging his head off a Holyrood desk. Still, at least when Richard is flapping about uselessly it does mean he's not sitting on his hands, which is what Labour usually does. That must count as progress of sorts.

What none of them wanted to talk about was the destruction of the devolution settlement by a Westminster government, in the face of the objections of the Scottish parliament. Devolution isn't just any old government act, it was introduced following a referendum in Scotland during which it was approved by a large majority of voters. Yet here we are with a Tory government citing a referendum which

Scotland rejected as justification for destroying something that Scotland approved in a referendum. Shamefully, Labour, the so-called party of devolution, did absolutely nothing to prevent it.

What we learned this week is that those parties which oppose independence are unwilling or incapable of standing up for Scotland. They cannot or will not protect Scotland and speak up for Scottish interests even within the context of the UK. Devolution was sold to Scotland as the great British alternative to independence, and now it has been destroyed by the very parties which promoted it. If there is no longer any meaningful devolution, if Scottish Home Rule can't do what it was set up to do – to protect Scotland from the depredations of a Conservative government that it didn't vote for – there is no alternative left except independence. When even prominent opponents of independence can see that, the writing is on the wall for British rule in Scotland.

16 June 2018

Drug policy in Scotland is
trapped in the 1980s

It's about time that this country had a grown-up discussion about drug policy. Back in the 1980s when I was living in Easterhouse, I had many friends who self-medicated on drugs and alcohol as a coping mechanism, dealing with the lack of jobs and opportunities, with poverty and deprivation, by getting out of their faces so that they didn't have to think about how their lives were beyond their own control. They were ground down by hopelessness, destroyed by despair. Drugs were the symptom of that disease, not the cause of it.

Far too many of my friends didn't survive the 1980s. They were killed by overdoses, by bad drugs, felled by the health complications created by constant drug use, or by attempting to come off drugs too quickly with weakened bodies which couldn't deal with the strain of detox. Others had their lives blighted by convictions and criminalisation, caught up in the nightmare world of the violence of drug dealing and the gang fighting that came with it.

I know what drugs can do. I've walked friends through the night, pacing up and down a room in order to stop them passing out until the drugs worked their way through their systems. I've cleaned up the puke and the vomit and worse. I sat with them through the tremors and the nightmares, the sweats and the visions. The tragedy is that all these decades later the nightmare is still going on.

Scotland has radically changed in many ways since the 1980s, but discussion of drug use in this country has remained stuck in the same Just-Say-No rut that characterised public policy all those decades ago. It didn't work then, and it's not working now. Criminalising people who already have a problem doesn't help them deal with their issues. It just gives them an additional problem. We've tried criminalising drugs for a century, yet we still have a big problem as a society with drugs. It should be obvious to everyone by now that criminalising drug use is not an effective means of reducing drug use and the harm it causes. If drug policy isn't working, if the so-called war on drugs isn't working, then it's time to change drug policy. The simple use of drugs, as opposed to dealing in drugs, needs to be treated as a public health issue, not as a criminal one.

Recently a project in Glasgow designed to give IV drug users a safe space to shoot up was closed down by the Home Office. The project aimed to remove drug use from the streets and to help ensure that drug users had access to clean needles and so were less at risk of HIV or other disease. Although the project had the support of the Scottish government, the UK government keeps a firm control over drug policy and insisted on the closure of the project, claiming that it encouraged drug use. Glasgow's drug users are back on the streets leaving dirty and used needles in public places where children can find them.

We need as a society to approach drug use as responsible adults and not as hand-wringing hysterics. It is adult to recognise that not everyone who uses drugs develops a problem with them, and that not all drug use is problematic. In the same way that not everyone who drinks alcohol ends up as an alcoholic, not everyone who uses drugs ends up with a drug problem. That doesn't mean that we should encourage alcohol use or drug use. It doesn't mean that drugs should be freely available to everyone. It means that the goal of an effective drug policy should be to teach people how to use alcohol or drugs in a responsible manner that minimises health risks and social harm. It means that our drug policy ought to seek to undermine organised crime rather than give it a ready market.

One of the ways to start a grown-up debate is to recognise that there are different drugs, different reasons for using drugs, and to treat these different categories appropriately. The recent discussion about the medical use of cannabis is a case in point. Our current drug policy lumps the medical use of cannabis in along with shooting up heroin in a dingy close or smoking crack. That's nonsensical. When the law is so clearly nonsensical, we only encourage people not to respect the law.

When my late partner Andy was diagnosed with cancer in the early 2000s, he found that smoking cannabis helped alleviate some of his symptoms. Treatment for cancer is gruelling, but Andy believed that cannabis helped him to get through the process. It helped him to control his pain, and it helped him to get to sleep at night. He also used it to help promote his appetite, and that in turn helped him to maintain his weight at a healthy level. We were living in Spain at the time, where the personal possession of small amounts of the drug had been decriminalised. In Scotland, he'd have been at risk of prosecution.

A different issue again is the use of medical products derived from cannabis. These are also illegal, despite the fact that the psychoactive ingredients have been removed from them. Our drug laws are so terrified that someone might be using a form of cannabis that they don't consider the circumstances of the use or any therapeutic benefit from that usage. It's this type of drug use that the British government says it is planning to review, although the government has firmly ruled out changing the law on other aspects of cannabis use.

Many of the problems around cannabis use are created by the status of cannabis as an illegal drug. Cannabis use can lead to the use of other drugs because cannabis is an illegal drug and that makes it convenient for it to be sold by the same people who sell other illegal drugs. The link is the illegality. Equally since cannabis is illegal, growers and dealers compete with one another to produce ever stronger strains of the drug since the only motive is profit maximisation. That means that if we were to compare cannabis to alcohol, there is no cannabis equivalent of a low-alcohol beer, only to spirits high in alcohol. It also means that consumers have no idea what they're getting, how strong the product is that they're consuming.

Several US states, Canada, Portugal and Uruguay have taken steps to decriminalise cannabis, both for medical and recreational use. Civilisation has not collapsed in those places. Here in Scotland we're still trapped in the 1980s.

But then drug policy, along with abortion rights and broadcasting, is amongst those things that Westminster doesn't trust Scotland with. We are trapped in a puritan time warp, governed by the fear that someone somewhere might be enjoying themselves. That's no way to run a public policy. Time is long overdue that all drug use was treated as a medical and public health issue, and not as a criminal one.

20 June 2018

Twitter is a platform for bullies
– that's why I quit

About nine months ago, I stopped being an active user of Twitter. I didn't do what certain Scottish journalists have done. There's a pattern to leaving Twitter if you're in the Scottish media: announce loudly on the social media platform that you are leaving, flounce off in a huff, then write an anguished article for the anti-independence press about how dreadful it is to be abused by vile cybernats. This is frequently accompanied by a photie of the writer looking wan. Then a few days later you come back to Twitter after getting some useful publicity and a fee for the article.

Maybe I was missing a trick, but I just left. There are very limited outlets in the Scottish media for anguished articles about how you're being abused on social media by vile British nationalists. I certainly came in for more than my fair share of personal abuse on social media from opponents of independence. Some of the biggest and nastiest bullies on Twitter are prominent opponents of independence. But that's not why I left.

I didn't leave Twitter because I found myself the subject of some wild-eyed and frothy conspiracy theories put about by certain people on the fringes of the independence movement. Neither was it because I was fed up with constantly being asked to take sides in disputes between independence supporters. When you have a degree of prominence in a grass-roots movement, that sort of thing comes with the territory.

The real reason for leaving the platform is because it turns everyone who uses it into a bully. The more followers you have on Twitter, the bigger the bully you become. That happens even when you strenuously attempt to avoid it, even when you strongly disavow it. It's inherent in the way that Twitter is designed.

On Twitter when you disagree with someone, your disagreement can then be seen by people who follow you on the platform. The more followers you have, the more people are likely to see the exchange. The more people who see the exchange, the more likely it is that someone else will join in, which means that the exchange can now be seen by everyone who follows that person too, which in turn makes it more likely that yet more people will join in. Before you know it there are dozens, if not hundreds, of people piling in to share your displeasure. It's called dogpiling. It's exponential shaming, and when you're the subject of it it feels like abuse.

We are quick to see ourselves as victims, and people in the British nationalist media in Scotland are expert at claiming victimhood, but we are very slow to recognise how our actions might lead to others being victimised. By virtue of having prominence in the media, Scottish media people tend to have followers who number in the thousands. The more followers you have, the greater the power you have on the platform.

When someone in the Scottish media disagrees with someone else on Twitter, there is enormous potential for dogpiling. That's even more the case because Scottish people in general can be sharp-tongued and not inclined to take prisoners. Twitter favours instant reactions, not all disagreements are going to be polite and measured. That sets the tone and encourages even sharper responses from those piling in. The more responses there are, the more likely it is that some of them will cross the line between criticism and personal abuse. The more responses there are, the more people feel enabled to join in. It's a vicious circle, in this case a circle of viciousness.

Insults and hurtful comments posted on the Internet never go away. Weeks and months later, the hurt and upset can still be posted at the person who was its target. It's a constant reminder, like a leper's bell. There's no escape and no forgetting.

Simply by having thousands of followers, you enable bullying, even if that was the furthest thing from your mind, even if you had not the slightest intention of doing so. Far too many prominent Twitter users, people with thousands of followers, don't pause to consider the hurt and upset that they unleash. No side in Scotland's constitutional debate is innocent, but some of the worst offenders are prominent opponents of independence. The real reason that I left Twitter was because I don't wish to be a party to bullying, even unintentional bullying.

We're very good as a species at taking note of slights and insults. We obsess about perceived slurs, but we take compliments for granted. It's hardwired into us as human beings. Threats are significant for our very survival, so over millions of years of evolution we have been primed to pay attention to them. Praise doesn't threaten our survival, so we pay it less heed. That means that it's not the ninety-five per cent of positive and supportive comments that we obsess over, it's the small minority of negative ones.

Twitter magnifies negativity until it can seem overwhelming. When you have thousands of Twitter followers, you sit at the top of a chain of negativity without necessarily being aware of how it cascades down from you. The more Twitter followers you have, the greater the emotional havoc you can unwittingly wreak. Then someone pushes back at you, and you flounce off and write a newspaper column about how you're the real victim here. But most people don't have the opportunity to flounce off and write newspaper columns. They're just left with the feeling of victimisation, the horrible disempowering sensation of being at the bottom of the dogpile.

The next time, and there will be a next time, that some prominent opponent of independence takes to the press to complain about Twitter abuse, remember that this isn't something peculiar to the independence debate. Twitter abuse isn't a bug in the system that can be cured. It's a feature. I don't want to be a part of it.

27 June 2018

Ugly ideas of a minority fringe do
not define the Yes movement

Who's a Scot? Some claim that it's to do with where your
ancestors came from. On a trip across the pond I once
encountered an American with a thick Southern yeehaw
y'all accent who asserted that he was more Scottish than me,
because all of his great-grandparents were Scottish, but many
of mine were Irish. "Gaun dook fur chips ya choob," I replied.

He didn't understand me, which kind of proved my point.
Then he got quite annoyed when I pointed out that there
are people all of whose great-grandparents were Asian who
are more Scottish than he was.

There is no one in Scotland who doesn't have at least some
ancestors who originally came from somewhere else. We are
not all entirely descended from the first humans to set foot
on this land after the glaciers retreated at the end of the last
Ice Age.

Scottishness has nothing to do with where your ancestors
came from. This nation was created by people who came
from elsewhere. Scotland is the original mongrel nation,
formed from the fusion of Picts, Irish Gaels, Cumbric
Britons, Old English-speaking Angles, and Vikings. Over
the centuries many other people from all over the world have
migrated into this beautiful and infuriating country on the
edge of a continent. English, Irish, Welsh, Flemings, Dutch,
Danes, French, Roma, Jews, Germans, Poles, Lithuanians,
Italians, Pakistanis, Chinese and many more have come
to live in Scotland and added their threads to the glorious
multicoloured tartan that defines Scotland.

Scottishness is not about where your ancestors were from,

and it's not even about where you were born. Everyone born in Scotland is Scottish, but not everyone who is Scottish was born in Scotland. Scottishness is a state of mind. Scotland is honoured by the presence of people who trace their roots to England, to Pakistan, to Syria, to Angola or to any other part of the globe, who come to live in this country and choose to throw their lot in with us.

The Scottish independence movement is not about Scotland's past, it's about Scotland's future, and that future is enriched by people from all over the world coming to Scotland to live here, to make their lives here, and to help create a future for Scotland.

There is a tiny fringe minority, reviled and rejected by the overwhelming bulk of the independence movement, whose concept of Scottish is defined by genetics and by ancestry. They represent a miniscule fraction, and have zero influence on the shape and direction of our movement. However because they choose to march in All Under One Banner rallies with a large and conspicuous banner, opponents of independence latch on to their presence and call on Nicola Sturgeon to ban SNP members from participating in these rallies, rallies which are not organised by the SNP.

We all know the reason why opponents of independence don't organise rallies of their own. Whereas only a tiny and ridiculed minority of independence supporters are attracted to the far right and xenophobia, such people make up a considerable proportion of those opponents of independence who'd be likely to turn up for an anti-independence rally. The Orange Order, Britain First, the BNP, anti-Muslim fans of Tommy Robinson, they would all be present in significant numbers to show us the ugly face of British nationalism in Scotland. A rally opposing independence would be all but indistinguishable from a far-right march.

It is of course wrong and distasteful to associate ordinary mainstream opponents of independence with the far-right genetic essentialists of Britain First or the atavistic sectarian bigotry of the Orange Order. The vast majority of people who oppose independence are not racists or sectarian bigots. Yet the British nationalist media in Scotland constantly tries to associate the mainstream independence movement with the actions and activities of tiny groups who have far less numerical impact on the independence movement than their British nationalist equivalents have on the opposing side.

No one invites groups like Siol nan Gaidheal, who have some ugly views about the English in Scotland, to participate in All Under One Banner rallies. They just turn up. Nicola Sturgeon is no more responsible for them than Ruth Davidson is responsible for the Orange Order or Britain First.

However we've yet to see an opinion piece in the British nationalist media in Scotland calling on Ruth Davidson to condemn the support of such groups for Scotland remaining a part of the UK. That's an even more startling omission given the repeated outing of Scottish Conservative councillors as having links to far-right or sectarian groups. I've yet to see a single SNP councillor being identified as a supporter of the likes of Siol nan Gaidheal. I've lost count of the Conservative councillors identified as supporters of the Orange Order, or who have propagated far-right propaganda on social media.

If the British nationalists in Scotland want to taint the SNP with association with far-right ethnic nationalists, perhaps their cries would have a lot more credibility if they tackled the actual fascists and racists who infest their own ranks. There are a lot more of them. Get your own British nationalist house in order first, and then the independence movement might be prepared to listen.

30 June 2018

Cheating Brexiteers must be
stripped of EU referendum win

Being Scottish within the UK is the experience of being had, of being taken for granted, taken as a fool. Despite being assured in 2014 that the only way Scotland could remain a part of the European Union was to vote against independence, those same Conservatives who made the assurances are now dragging Scotland out of the EU. They're dragging Scotland out despite the fact that in 2016 Scotland voted to remain in the EU by a considerably larger margin than it voted to remain in the UK. That's all bad enough, but now it transpires that the Electoral Commission has ruled that the Vote Leave campaign systematically broke electoral law. Scotland is not just being hauled out of the EU against its will, this is happening on the basis of cheating, lying, and a sham of democracy.

During the EU referendum, the Vote Leave campaign fronted by Michael Gove and Boris Johnson broke electoral law by channelling large sums of money to third parties in order to circumvent campaign spending limits. Campaign spending limits exist in law for a reason, they are meant to ensure a level playing field and to prevent one side using larger resources or wealth in order to flood the public with its information and propaganda, and drowning out the other side. The Vote Leave campaign treated that law as though it were a serving suggestion on the side of a packet of cereal.

If there were any justice, or indeed democratic responsibility in the UK, the Westminster government and parliament would now be pressing for a rerun of the EU referendum. That's not going to happen. Instead the Vote Leave campaign will be slapped on the wrist with a fine which represents a mere small percentage of the amount of money that it spent illegally, and those at the head of the campaign will continue in their jobs protesting that they've done nothing wrong. Anyway, they will argue, whatever oversights or errors that took place didn't affect the result.

In any other field of life, when people cheat they are deprived of whatever it was that they won through cheating. Olympic athletes caught taking performance-enhancing drugs are stripped of any medals that they won. It's perfectly possible that they would have won those medals even without taking the drugs, but that's not the point. They cheated, and cheaters shouldn't be allowed to enjoy the fruits of their deception.

What Vote Leave did during the EU referendum was an exact electoral analogue of an athlete taking performance-enhancing drugs. The campaign secretly and covertly employed extra funding that it should not have used in order to boost its performance. It did so in order to gain an unfair advantage over its competitor. Yes of course it's possible that the Vote Leave campaign might have won anyway, we don't know. We will never know, that will forever remain in the realms of the hypothetical. But that's not the point. What we do know is that in the real world, the Vote Leave campaign cheated and its winning result was based upon a contempt for the rules. If the result of a cheat is allowed to stand, then the entire campaign is a lie.

The consequences of Vote Leave's cheating are immense. Thousands of jobs are at risk. The economy looks likely to take a major hit. The lives of EU citizens in the UK and UK citizens in the EU will be disrupted. The Irish peace process is threatened. The international reputation of the UK has suffered a serious blow. This is all considerably more serious than being allowed to keep a sporting medal, and yet the result will be allowed to stand. Boris Johnson and Michael Gove's careers will continue unimpeded in their self-serving smug paths and they will continue to assert that they did nothing wrong and knew nothing about the machinations of a campaign that they fronted.

The revelation that the Vote Leave campaign cheated comes on top of the news that the Scottish Conservatives have been funding themselves with dark money. Our democracy is drowning in a pigswill of dodgy donations and contempt for the rules of fair play which underpin any fair and open society. The Westminster parliament which feeds at the trough of dark money and illegal donations will do nothing to clean itself up, and nothing to ensure that democracy is respected.

There has been a lot of discussion within the independence movement about the best time for a referendum. The recent revelations demonstrate that we shouldn't be talking about the best time, we should instead be talking about the necessity of another referendum. Westminster doesn't want a popular vote on the dodgy dealings of British political parties and organisation, but that's all the more reason why it's imperative that Scotland has one. This next independence referendum will be a vote on the very fundamentals of democracy itself. Does Scotland want to be a country where democratic rules and laws are respected, a country where there are consequences for breaking them, or are we content to allow decisions to be made for us by cheats and liars that Scotland cannot hold to account?

7 July 2018

End the annual shame of
Orange Order marches

It's that time of the year again, when the streets of Scotland's towns and cities, or at least those in the Central Belt, are filled with the cacophony of sectarianism. I had planned to go into the centre of Glasgow last weekend to do some shopping, but decided against it because listening to people singing that they would like to be up to their knees in blood, and specifically your blood, isn't exactly conducive to a pleasant retail experience. This isn't made any easier by the knowledge that the DUP and other extreme Ulster Loyalist organisations supported by the Orange Order are also deeply and implacably homophobic.

Every year it's the same. We have to avoid our town centres and public parks because a band of drunken bigots want to dress up as toy soldiers and sing about their hatred for Catholics. Every year we cannot cross public streets because a shower of vindictive and hate-driven reactionaries act as though they own our public places. Every year a band of drunken louts attack someone, cause disturbances in our streets and make the rest of us feel unsafe in our own communities, all in the name of expressing atavistic hatred.

This year a group of Orange supporters spat on and attacked a Glasgow priest who was outside his church greeting his parishioners. The incident happened because the police who had been guarding the church had been called away to deal with another incident caused by the marchers. In Glasgow in 2018 a house of worship requires police protection, and on social media there were people blaming the priest for daring to appear in the open air when an Orange walk was taking place nearby. Just pause and think about that for a second.

But it's not really Catholics that the Orange marchers hate. Their hatred extends equally to atheists and agnostics who happen to have been brought up in Catholic households. The real targets of Orangeism in Scotland are Scottish people of Irish Catholic descent. Sectarianism is just anti-Irish racism to the tune of a flute band. When you protest or complain about it, they tell you that you're the one who's bigoted. It seems that it's not offensive to express your hatred. What's really offensive is to object to it.

In recent years the targets of Orange hatred have also extended to Scots from any religion or none who happen to support Scottish independence. It's an easy extension for them to make. They hated "Catholics" because of the supposed threat of Catholicism to the British state. And now they hate independence supporters for the same reason. Orange parades are a sickness of British nationalism in Scotland and Ireland. Let's be very clear here, this isn't a Scottish shame. It's not an Irish shame. It's a shame created and caused by British nationalism.

Supporters of the British state in this country must own up to sectarianism and condemn it. Instead they prefer to take to social media in order to search out a small number of accounts where some clown expresses anti-English sentiment, ignoring the bigotry that is openly expressed against their fellow Scots in the streets of our towns and cities. Over the past years and months we have seen dozens of newspaper articles and opinion pieces decrying the Anglophobia that supposedly characterises the Yes movement. How many have we seen decrying the Orange bigotry and drawing an explicit link between Orangeism and British nationalism in Scotland? About as many as there are Catholic priests marching behind a Lambeg.

What's almost as bad as the entirely predictable violence is the equally predictable calls for something to be done from politicians who campaigned for an end of the Offensive

Behaviour at Football Act and empowered the bigots who now think that they can sing their hate songs freely.

But these parades are our heritage and our culture, is the usual squeal. That's no defence. Apartheid was a part of the heritage and culture of white South Africans, that didn't make it moral. Female genital mutilation is part of the heritage and culture of several cultures, that doesn't stop it being an offence against the rights of women. Discrimination against certain social groups is ingrained in many cultures. That doesn't make it right. Just because yer maw and da were bigots doesn't give you the right to be a bigot too.

Before any British nationalist indulges in whataboutery, a Yes rally is not remotely comparable to an Orange walk. There may be a tiny fringe of bigots who associate themselves with a Yes rally, but Yes rallies are all about inclusivity. No one gets beaten up or threatened for trying to cross the road in the middle of a Yes march. On the other hand bigotry and the exclusion of large segments of Scottish society are the entire point and purpose of an Orange walk. Trying to draw an equivalence between the two is like refusing to see a difference between a happy and cheerful birthday party with an obnoxious drunk sitting ignored in a corner, and a gang of intoxicated yobs on the rampage.

Ruth Davidson and her minions are very quick to protest against entirely peaceful Yes marches and the disruption that they cause, but faced with the much greater disruption and outright violence associated with the annual Orange parade season, Ruth and her pals say nothing at all. They're all too ready to condemn the supposed divisiveness of the Yes movement, but when it comes to the very real and visceral divisiveness created and fomented by their own Orange supporters they say nothing at all. If you look up the word "ruth" in a dictionary of Scots, it's defined as "Tory hypocrite".

It's all very well complaining about Orange walks on social media, or indeed through the medium of columns in Scottish newspapers, but councils can't take action on that sort of protest. There has to be a specific communication with your councillor or a complaint to the police. This has nothing to do with the views of any individual political party or councillor, and everything to do with the recognised procedures which are required in order for councillors to take action. If you want Orange walks banned, restricted or curtailed, you can't do so by complaining about it anonymously on social media. Let's get writing to our local councils. That's the only way we can bring about an end to this annual shame of British nationalism polluting our streets. The walk has had its day, and that day was in 1690. This is the twenty-first century, not the seventeenth.

11 July 2018

BBC Scotland's problem? It's a branch office of a London company

As someone fluent in Spanish, who also reads and understands Catalan, the most striking difference between the Catalan and Scottish constitutional debates is that the Catalans have a media which is far more representative of the range of opinion in Catalonia than the Scottish media is of Scottish opinion. Scotland's print media is overwhelmingly biased against independence. The broadcast media goes hand in hand with the print media and follows its agenda. It's not a conspiracy theory to point this out. It's a simple observation of fact.

I've believed for a very long time that if Scotland was fortunate enough to have a media that was as diverse and representative as Catalonia's, we'd be independent already. Just one single daily and one Sunday newspaper in a country with around thirty-eight daily and Sunday newspapers support a constitutional position backed by almost half the population. *The National*, the single daily newspaper which supports independence, is reviled and hated by British nationalists who feel that it's tantamount to censorship that they no longer have total control of Scotland's traditional media space. Only *The National* is accused of political bias, whereas the visceral British nationalism of the Scottish *Daily Mail*, the *Express* or the *Scotsman* is somehow regarded as balanced.

Scotland's digital media, its bloggers and digital platforms, represent the majority of pro-independence media output. This output is sidelined and ignored by the traditional media. It is invisible to that large section of the Scottish public which doesn't go online much. It's no coincidence that those demographics which are less likely to consume news online are also those who are least likely to support independence. The leading figures in the Scottish pro-indy digital media are rarely to be seen in the broadcast media. In all the many years I've been blogging and writing about Scottish independence, single-handedly producing the most-read politics site in Scotland after Wings Over Scotland and the multi-author Common Space site, I've only once been asked on a BBC political programme to comment on Scottish current affairs. That was when they wanted me to criticise another pro-independence newspaper. I politely declined the invitation.

It's this background which makes the recent BBC shut-down of Wings Over Scotland and Moridura's YouTube channels such an alarming development. As has been reported, there has been no equivalent BBC action taken against opponents of Scottish independence who continue to host thousands of BBC clips on their YouTube channels. There was silence from the majority of the anti-independence print media which went to town on the alleged "silencing" of anti-independence opinion writer Stephen Daisley and the supposed "intimidation" of David Torrance. It now transpires that the BBC claims that the person behind the complaint resulting in the shutdown was a Labour councillor, although he denies it. This merely raises another question – if true, why did the BBC act on what was clearly a politically motivated complaint? On the face of it, it's clear evidence of an anti-independence bias in the national broadcaster.

The Wings Over Scotland YouTube channel was restored on Thursday morning, with the exception of thirteen clips to which the BBC had objected, but it took a mass campaign and the publicity generated by the intervention of a former first minister in order to achieve this. There has still been no explanation from the BBC about why it has seemingly only gone after pro-independence YouTube channels but left anti-independence ones alone. The corporation's London bosses refused to explain themselves when the issue was aired on the BBC Scotland *Good Morning Scotland* radio programme. And to be fair, BBC Radio Scotland has covered this issue well.

Trust between the BBC and a large section of the Scottish public has now irretrievably broken down. When a public service broadcaster loses the trust of its public, it's not the public which is to blame. It's not the public which needs to change. It's not the public which needs to rebuild bridges.

When Donalda MacKinnon was appointed as the new controller of BBC Scotland late in 2016 she spoke about the need for BBC Scotland to rebuild trust with its audience. She wrote, "There is a feeling among a significant percentage of the population, that trust might need to be rebuilt." That statement remains true today, only you can remove the "might". If anything, the breakdown of trust is now worse than it was in the aftermath of the BBC's shameful performance during the independence referendum.

The takedown of Wings Over Scotland and Moridura occurred because the BBC is managed in London by people who know little about Scottish politics or sensitivities and who are instinctively British nationalist. It matters very little what Donalda MacKinnon or anyone at Pacific Quay does as long as BBC Scotland continues to be a branch office of a London-based organisation which is deeply antithetical to Scottish independence, and which has the support and maintenance of Britishness written into its charter. This recent debacle would not have occurred with a public service broadcaster run and managed from within Scotland.

It bears repeating, the Scottish government must be far more active in making the devolution of broadcasting an issue. It is the normal state of affairs for self-governing countries and territories to have their own public service broadcasters. Its shouldn't be up to Scotland to make the case for having its own public service broadcaster, it's the British state which ought to be explaining why Scotland doesn't have one already.

4 August 2018

This is why there's no story which can kill off independence

When there are serious allegations against a former first minister, and that first minister is taking the government he used to lead to court because he claims that he is being denied due process, that's a big news story. However the unseemly glee with which sections of the Scottish media have rushed to hang, draw and quarter Alex Salmond means that whatever the outcome of the investigations into the allegations against the former first minister, the Scottish press will have a lot of questions to answer.

I sincerely hope that the allegations against Alex Salmond prove to be unfounded. It is always distressing to discover that a person you have looked up to and trusted is subject to allegations of this nature, and there is an instinctive reaction to circle round the wagons and adopt a defensive position. That's all the more true in Scotland, where the media is overwhelmingly opposed to independence and actively seeks accusations to hurl at the independence movement and its leaders, and very often those accusations turn out to be baseless. But we cannot prejudge the matter. Otherwise we are guilty of the same rush to judgement that we as an independence movement accuse the media of.

There is a serious problem in Scotland, as there is in all societies, of powerful men using their positions to abuse, harass and mistreat women. It is a testament to the maturity of Scotland that we are now in a position where even the most powerful amongst us can be called upon to answer for allegations made against them by those who do not enjoy the same power and influence. That is a sign of progress.

It is certainly true that the victims of sexual offences have a right to put their case forward and to have their allegations fully investigated in a way which is respectful to victims. It is true that victims should feel that if they come forward that they have a guarantee that they will be listened to, no matter how powerful or prominent the person against whom they are making allegations. We need that guarantee, otherwise we'd be campaigning for an independent Scotland which is no better for victims of abuse and which doesn't listen to women or the weak and powerless. That's not a Scotland anyone should want.

But it is also true that those who are the subject of those allegations have the right to the presumption of innocence until such time as the investigation has been completed, and for the matter not to be prejudged by the media. When we have a prominent commentator in the Scottish media announcing that it's all over for Alex Salmond irrespective of the truth or otherwise of the allegations against him, it's clear that the media has taken it upon itself to act as judge, jury and executioner. Making that statement was bad enough, but when it comes from the same person who urged everyone to give Alistair Carmichael a second chance after a court had ruled he lied, it's clear that double standards are at play.

The eagerness of the overwhelmingly anti-independence Scottish press to condemn Alex Salmond is based in its desperation to find something, anything, to kill off the independence movement for once and all. That remains its overriding consideration and the media treatment of the allegations against Alex Salmond is a perfect illustration of it. The Scottish media hasn't come to terms with the new political reality of a Scotland where talk of independence is mainstream and normal, and still longs for the days when dreams of independence were the preserve of hairy men who put on kilts at weekends and ran about the hillsides pretending to be Pictish warriors.

The Scottish media is still in denial, still hoping that talk of independence is just a phase that Scotland is going through, and all they have to do is to find an SNPbad story that's big enough to kill it all off forever. Then they can get back to the cosy consensus of the 1990s when Scottish newspaper editors lunched with the leaders of the British political parties in Scotland and between them the boys club determined the Scottish political agenda. The boys, and they are largely boys, of the Scottish media have no great burning interest in furthering the rights of women, this is just one more stick for them to use against the cause of independence, one more hope that this might be the magic bullet to kill off talk of independence for good.

The sad truth for Scotland's anti-independence media is that this latest SNPbad story isn't going to dent the cause of independence, because the reality that our anti-independence press still hasn't grasped after all these years is that independence isn't about the SNP. It's about much deeper issues going to the very heart of the British state and the changing nature of Scotland.

Independence is about the democratic deficit that sees a Scotland which regards itself as a partner and founder in a Union being treated as little better than an English county. It's about Scotland's increasing confidence as a nation, and the growing political chasm that has opened up between Scotland and the rest of the UK over the past few decades. It's about the British state's destruction of the post-war consensus and its rush to adopt right-wing neo-liberalism as an article of faith. It's about the cavalier dismissal of the devolution settlement by a British political establishment which always prioritises the political concerns of England. It's about the way Scotland's interests and concerns have been completely sidelined and ignored by a British state that's only interested in placating the Tory right and the right-wing press. And it's about an anti-independence media in Scotland so terrified of anything that might rock the British boat that it will not stand up for Scotland even within the UK.

None of these deeper issues is addressed by a media which revels in mud-slinging about the alleged personal behaviour of an individual SNP politician. They will still be with us irrespective of the outcome of investigations into Alex Salmond. The reasons for the rise of the Scottish independence movement are not predicated on the personal behaviour of any single prominent individual, and will not be affected by screaming SNPbad headlines about that person.

The grass-roots independence movement is continuing to organise. The British state is continuing to career towards its own self-destruction. Sorry Scottish media, but no amount of SNPbad stories is going to make the independence movement go away. We're here until we win.

29 August 2018

Scotland's independence movement is an inspiration to Welsh Yes groups

Over the past couple of years, the dug and I have been travelling the length and breadth of Scotland, talking to local Yes groups and SNP groups about Scottish independence. But on Wednesday, we had a new and different experience. We were invited to come along by Aled Job of Yes Cymru to give a talk to Yes Cymru's local group in the picturesque town of Caernarfon, deep in the heart of Welsh-speaking Wales.

Yes Cymru is one of the newest and fastest-growing organisations in the Welsh political scene. Directly inspired by the network of Yes groups across Scotland, Yes Cymru was founded in 2016 by Iestyn ap Rhobert, who wanted a national grass-roots organisation to promote the cause of Welsh independence in a nation where Plaid Cymru seems to many to blow hot and cold on the topic. Like the Yes groups in Scotland, Yes Cymru consists of a network of autonomous local groups. At the last count there were some thirty-six of them, to be found in every corner of Wales.

Independence supporters in Wales look enviously on the Scottish scene. Within Scotland we all too often concentrate on our weak points, exacerbated by an overwhelmingly anti-independence media which revels in perceived divisions or disagreements within our movement. Seen from the outside however, observers of Scottish politics are struck by a large, diverse and powerful grass-roots movement which has branches in every part of the country and which is independent of any single political party. They are impressed that the Scottish independence movement has been able to ensure that the topic of Scottish independence isn't merely normalised in political discourse, it is the most important topic around which the rest of Scottish politics revolves.

There are important similarities between Scotland and Wales. We are both devolved nations within the UK. We both have a long history of trying to assert our identities and political independence in the face of our much larger and more powerful English neighbour. We both were scourged by Thatcherism and struggle to make our voices heard within the political structures of the UK.

However there are also some very important differences. On my trip to Caernarfon it was heartening to hear the Welsh language spoken all around. The language appears everywhere, in shop signs and on commercial premises as much as on official signage. People in the street speak the language to one another, and to strangers. On mistakenly entering a shop which didn't allow dogs, I was politely informed in Welsh that dogs were not permitted. That wouldn't have happened in Gaelic-speaking districts in Scotland, where in my experience Gaelic speakers only use Gaelic to address those they are familiar with.

The prominence of the Welsh language means that language issues play an equally prominent role in Welsh independence politics. That's very different from Scotland, where even those of us who are passionate about Gaelic and Scots recognise that language issues are minor in the independence campaign. Welsh is the everyday language of some twenty per cent of the Welsh population, and those Welsh-speaking districts are the heartland of both Plaid Cymru and pro-independence sentiment.

One of the key aims of Yes Cymru was to bridge the divisions within Wales. Wales can, according to some observers, be categorised into three broad regions. There's Wales Cymraeg, the Welsh-speaking areas in the north and west, there's Welsh Wales, the largely English-speaking industrial districts which still have a strong sense of a Welsh identity, and then there's British Wales, the English-speaking regions in the north-east and south-east which have close ties to their neighbouring regions across the border in England and where the sense of a Welsh identity is weaker.

Traditionally, Welsh politics have been dominated by the Labour Party, which allied British Wales and Welsh Wales against Wales Cymraeg. Yes Cymru seeks to change that, and to ally Wales Cymraeg with Welsh Wales in order to form a majority which is receptive to the idea of greater self-government, and indeed full independence, for Wales. Their goal is to do what Yes Scotland has done, and to normalise the idea of independence in Welsh political discourse. The rapidly expanding network of Yes Cymru branches is proof that this idea is falling on fertile ground.

Wednesday night's talk in the meeting room of a hotel in Caernarfon was packed out, with standing room only. It's yet more proof that it's not just in Scotland that there's a widespread dissatisfaction with the British state, and a sense that if the smaller nations of the UK seek something better, we're going to have to do it for ourselves. The enthusiastic attendance at the meeting certainly demonstrated that the energy and willingness are there. People in Wales have been watching Scotland's experience closely and are determined to apply the lessons of the Yes Scotland movement to their own circumstances. For me personally, that was the most heartening aspect of my trip to Wales, the discovery that Scotland is a model that others are learning from.

1 September 2018

Claims of civil war within the Yes community will not stop the movement

This is a despatch from the front line of the SNP civil war, delivered to the HQ of The National tied to the leg of a doo that was radicalised during an indy rally at George's Square. There it was, pecking away aimlessly at a bit of haggis pakora, when all of a sudden it realised that it was a more useful member of Scottish society than your average Tory MP. The doo spends its life clearing up garbage, whereas Tory MPs spend theirs creating it. The doo had discovered that it was welcome in Scotland even though it had originally flown in from England, following a coach trip returning from Blackpool in the hope of some discarded chips soaked in curry sauce. Now it has carved out a useful niche for itself, working in communications for a Scottish independence movement that is tearing itself apart in a vicious SNP civil war which mostly seems to consist of people in anti-independence newspapers writing articles about how vicious the SNP civil war is.

You can witness it for yourself if only you look hard enough. This is why we need media professionals to tell us what's going on. Signs of the civil war were everywhere at the independence rally in Dunfermline on Saturday, which the dug addressed while I interpreted into human for him.

There was a kid of about ten who gave his maw a really dirty look after she took some chips from him. There was a man in his late sixties who noticeably failed to guffaw when his pal told him a joke about how he was full of the cold, congested, a head full of cotton wool and finding it difficult to be coherent, with dreck pouring from every orifice, so now he knew what it felt like to be Ross Thomson. There was the young couple having a mild disagreement about whether to go to the pub afterwards or to go for a bite to eat. There were some weans engrossed in digging trenches. Admittedly they were playing in a sandpit, but still. It was pure carnage out there.

Thankfully, the horrors of the SNP civil war have had as much effect on Scotland's prospects for independence as the last *Star Trek* movie, which like the SNP civil war is entirely fictional. Although with better special effects, even though the independence movement does have its very own tribbles in the shape of Scottish Tory MSPs. An opinion poll published late on Sunday was greeted with howls of derision and outrage from British nationalists on social media who'd suddenly forgotten how polling works, because this poll showed that a majority of voters in Scotland will opt for independence if the UK presses ahead with Brexit.

All those previous polls which had shown a majority against independence had been received with smugness and glee from British nationalists. This one was different. Because *The National* was the first of the papers to report it, it was immediately denounced as a biased poll from Thatessempee. Then they discovered that the poll had actually been commissioned by Better for Britain, an organisation opposed to Scottish independence. Ooops.

Even worse for opponents of independence, and for the overwhelmingly anti-independence Scottish press that revels in SNPbadness, the fieldwork for this poll was conducted while the newspapers were screaming at the top of their lungs about the allegations facing Alex Salmond. Last week in this newspaper, I wrote that no amount of SNPbad stories would dent the campaign for independence, because the desire for Scottish independence is not motivated by the SNP. It is not driven by the personalities of individual politicians. By far the biggest and most important driver of Scottish independence is the failure of the British establishment and the British political parties to listen to Scotland and to fulfil the needs and desires of Scotland within the framework of the UK.

No matter how loudly Scotland's media, implacably opposed as it is to independence, screams allegations against an SNP figure as though they were proven fact, it doesn't alter the fact that Scotland is still being taken out of the EU against its will. It doesn't alter the fact that Scotland is not being consulted in the process and has no voice in it. It doesn't alter the fact that the promises and commitments made by Better Together lie broken and shattered, crushed by the Brexit bus.

On Monday we received the news that SNP membership now stands at a record 125,000, making the party the second largest in the UK, larger in terms of membership than the Conservatives. And with a considerably younger average age. There are indeed parties in the UK which are mired in civil wars, but the SNP is not amongst them. Compared to the divisions within a Conservative Party which is destroying itself over Brexit, compared to a Labour Party whose politicians hate one another far more than they hate the Tories, the SNP is a paragon of unity of purpose.

Meanwhile Ruth Davidson tweets at Nicola Sturgeon telling her to end the uncertainty and cancel any plans for an independence referendum, which is rather like an arsonist telling a building manager to stop talking about fire escapes.

What the events of the last week tell us is that the UK can have Scotland or it can have Brexit. It can't have both. If the People's Vote campaign really want Scotland to cooperate with their campaign for a second EU referendum, if they want Scottish independence supporters to support their efforts, then they are going to have to change their views on a Scottish vote. They're going to have to explicitly come out in support of a second Scottish independence referendum should Brexit go ahead.

What the events of the last week tell us is that the independence movement is on the right track, that our efforts are paying off. It means we need to keep campaigning, to keep organising our meetings and rallies. It means we need to keep up our persuasion and maintain our resolve to keep our eye on the prize and not to allow ourselves to be distracted by the agenda of the anti-independence press. Even the doos in George Square know that a change is in the air. Independence is coming.

5 September 2018

Brits don't want to listen to Scottish voices anymore? You don't say

There was an article in the Spectator magazine this week entitled "The Myth of the 'Trustworthy' Scottish Accent", complete with scare quotes. The article announced the death of another Scottish export industry, providing voice-overs for advertisements broadcast throughout the UK. Only this being a Conservative publication, naturally it didn't blame the loss of this particular export industry on Brexit. It's all the fault of Scottish people for being ungrateful.

According to the author of the piece, Scottish accents were favoured by advertisers, particularly companies advertising financial products, because Scots had, allegedly, a reputation for financial probity. Clearly these people had never met anyone in my family. However what he really meant was that there was and is a widespread racist stereotype in England that Scots are tight-fisted and reluctant to part with cash. That stereotype can be used positively by an advertiser trying to flog a financial product.

Naturally the writer couldn't say that in a piece in a Conservative magazine slagging off Scottish people, because when the English are racist about the Scots that's just friendly banter and if you object to it you're just being dour. Oh look, there's another friendly banter racist stereotype. So the myth that Scottish accents are trustworthy can be added to everything else about Scottishness that's mythical. And there's yet another friendly banter racist stereotype, because as every British nationalist knows the entirety of Scottish culture is invented. It's only Scottish stereotypes about English people that represent a deep and dark evil lurking at the very heart of the national psyche.

The anti-Scottish tropes were trotted out one after another. Apparently Scottish people no longer have a reputation for financial probity because of Gordie Broon, who proved Scottish politicians can't be trusted. No mention of Liam Fox, or Michael Gove, or Ruth Davidson there then. Advertisers in England have fallen out of love with Scottish accents because ungrateful Scottish people used them to say such nasty things about England during the independence referendum, a political event which as everyone who reads the *Spectator* knows was really entirely about England. They're falling out of love with Scottish accents because Nicola Sturgeon is "sour" and wilfully refuses to get behind Great British projects. But the icing that finally made advertisers choke on the Scottish accent cake was the World Cup, and the refusal of Scotland fans to get behind the England team. Like that was a new thing and hadn't happened in every single World Cup ever.

However the real reason that Scottish accents were favoured by advertisers for adverts to be broadcast in the rest of the UK had little to do with trustworthiness. It's because in the intensely class-sensitive society of England, Scottish accents are class neutral. When a Scottish person is speaking standard Scottish English, as opposed to Scots, English ears cannot tell if the speaker is working class or middle class. As far as accent is concerned, they don't know the difference between Balmoral and Barmulloch. That's a great advantage to an advertiser who seeks to promote their product in a society riven by class snobbery and an acute awareness of social class.

There is empirical evidence for the acceptability of Scottish accents to a wider UK audience. A poll carried out by the BBC Your Voice project in 2014 found that after "the Queen's English", listeners rated Scottish accents, Southern Irish accents and New Zealand accents most highly of all. All these accents are class neutral to English ears.

Intriguingly the article announcing the death of the Scottish advertising accent appeared in the *Spectator* magazine, whose editor Fraser Nelson has a very special Scottish accent all of his own. As someone who has studied linguistics and phonology, I've always found Fraser's idiosyncratic accent something of a fascination, with its exaggerated diphthongs and irritable vowel syndrome. Yet it remains identifiably Scottish, admittedly it's the Loyd Grossman of Scottish accents, but it's still Scottish.

Fraser's accent does retain postvocalic "r", unlike the accents of certain BBC presenters and former Labour prime ministers, who simply drop "r" in positions where English accents also drop it, but without the compensatory vowel lengthening found in English accents, resulting in peculiar pronunciations like "noth" for "north". North does not rhyme with moth in any English accent. It only does that in Noth British accents like Gordie Broon's.

However there is definitely an unintended irony in the *Spectator*, that bastion of what passes for British Conservative thought, publishing an article saying that patriotic Brits don't want to listen to Scottish voices. To which just about everyone in Scotland replies, "You don't say. Tell us something we didn't already know." The Conservatives have never listened to Scotland, and that is precisely what's going to lead to the end of the UK and the birth of an independent Scotland. When that independent Scotland does come about, it will not only be welcomed by Scots with Scottish accents, but also by Scots with English accents, Scots with Asian accents, Polish accents, German accents and many more. Because unlike the Conservatives, Scotland welcomes diversity and makes it a part of us.

8 September 2018

Desperate Unionist political parties are a threat to our democracy

Theresa May's cabinet is the flat-pack cabinet. It has a few loose screws and it's falling apart. The Tories are completely at a loss over Brexit, openly divided, briefing against one another, plotting and back-stabbing amongst rumours that Theresa May's leadership won't survive long after the party conference season. Labour has been gifted the equivalent of a big political hammer, and just one blow, not even a particularly well-aimed blow at that, will take the whole teetering edifice down. Instead Labour prefers to use that hammer to hit itself in the face.

The Labour leadership has managed to sideline the calls from party membership for a referendum on Brexit. Shadow Chancellor John McDonnell has conceded that there can be a referendum on Brexit, but has ruled out any second Brexit referendum which includes the option of remaining in the EU, which destroys the reason for having the referendum in the first place. The millions of Remainers who had looked to Labour to provide a credible alternative to Brexit will now look elsewhere. If you oppose Brexit, there's little point in voting Labour. They're just as committed to the insane British nationalist project as the Tories, but you'll now be able to get a nationalised train to the job that you'll no longer have after the UK economy tanks.

But continuing in the tradition of the serially inept leadership of the Scottish Branch Office, it's in its Scottish policy where the Labour Party has proven most clueless. Richard Leonard, the man who has most recently got himself trapped in the revolving door of Branch Office leadership, has announced that his party will fight the next general election with a solid manifesto commitment to reject any prospect of a second independence referendum.

Labour has rejected the Claim of Right of 1989, renewed and reaffirmed by its own MSPs in 2012, and again on 4 July 2018 by MPs in Westminster in 2018. That Claim of Right states that the people of Scotland have the sovereign right to determine the form of government best suited to their needs. Yet now Labour is apparently telling us that a future Labour government of Jeremy Corbyn will have a mandate to refuse a Scottish independence referendum even if the Labour Party fails to secure a majority of votes or MPs from Scotland. Labour no longer upholds the Claim of Right. Labour now believes that it's only Westminster which has a sovereign right to determine the form of government best suited to the needs of Scotland, and can do so on the basis of the votes of MPs from outwith Scotland.

The Claim of Right is the document which doesn't merely underpin the devolution settlement, it also represents the political foundation of Scotland's place within the UK. If Labour has unilaterally decided to rip that claim up, then all by itself that counts as a material change of circumstances which justifies a second independence referendum, with or without Brexit. The destruction of the Claim of Right fundamentally alters the relationship of Scotland to the other nations of the UK, and does so without the consent of the Scottish people or their elected representatives.

Independence supporters who lent their votes to Corbyn in the last general election won't make that same mistake in the next general election. Vote Labour, vote to have your democratic rights taken away. It's perfectly OK for a party to oppose independence. Democracy depends on parties having that right. What's not OK is for a party to demand that the right to support independence is taken away from others. That's the death of democracy. Labour is turning itself into the Spanish Partido Popular. Labour tells us that the key theme of their party conference is that socialism in 2018 means extending democracy to every part of society, except for viewers in Scotland.

The obvious question is, "What was Labour thinking?" But the equally obvious answer is that the party wasn't thinking at all. Labour in Scotland can't get past its atavistic hatred of all things SNP in order to consider the implications of its own decisions.

Labour, just like the Tories, repeats the mantra that the result of the referendum of 2014 must be respected. A referendum result can be preserved in stone forever, or it can be democratic. It can't be both. When a people have no right to change their mind in the light of changed circumstances, there is no democracy. That's where we are now with the British nationalist parties in Scotland. They insist that Scotland has no right to change its mind even though circumstances have changed. They demand that the vote they secured in 2014 on the basis of promises that they never kept be respected, so that the electorate have no means of holding them to account. That's not democracy.

The British nationalist parties in Scotland are getting desperate. They can see that the writing is on the wall for their so-called Union that is no Union at all. They know that with English Votes for English Laws, with Brexit, with the farce of the Vow, they have nothing positive to offer to the electorate of Scotland in a future independence referendum. They have destroyed their own best arguments from 2014, the argument that the UK represented the status quo, that it was independence which represented insecurity and instability. They cannot argue that independence is the choice of narrow xenophobic parochial nationalists when they're supporting Brexit.

The best bet of the British nationalist parties, their only bet, for keeping Scotland a part of the UK is to prevent another independence vote from happening at all. They know that when there is another vote on the subject, Scotland will vote to leave this dysfunctional farce of the UK. They can only prevent that happening by stopping a vote from happening. But when you stop the people from having a say, you're no longer a democratic party. The choice facing Scotland now is independence and democracy, or an increasingly anti-democratic future as a silenced and marginalised province of an isolationist UK.

26 September 2018

Scotland in Union should be tucked up in bed with their Yawn avatars

It was Napoleon who said never to interrupt your enemy when they're making a mistake. However there's an important caveat to add to that aphorism, which is, unless your enemy is Scotland in Union, in which case point and laugh. Scotland in Union is best known for the leak of its donors' list to the media, which showed that an organisation billing itself as a grass-roots anti-independence movement is in fact bankrolled by the wealthy and the privileged.

SiU's main activity appears to be organising the so-called Green Ink Brigade of letter writers to newspapers, invariably decrying something or other that the SNP has done and not actually giving a positive argument for Scotland to remain a part of the UK. Members also frequent the comments section of the online editions of newspapers, where they make personal remarks about the writers of articles having the temerity to do public crowdfunding campaigns for their pro-indy work instead of taking the respectable SiU approach, which is to solicit members of the aristocracy and the wealthy in secret for a few grand.

I myself have come under attack from SiU. After publishing a Gaelic map of Glasgow on my blog, a prominent member of SiU took to social media to denounce me as a Gaelic imperialist, a badge I now wear with pride. He was so upset that I had the temerity to produce a Gaelic map of Glasgow, a city where Celtic place names are thick on the ground, that I went and produced a Gaelic map of Edinburgh for no other reason than to annoy him. It's safe to say that with SiU, the independence movement is not dealing with a credible opponent. We are the Interpol to their Keystone Cops. Please, please, please make them the official anti-independence campaign in the next referendum. Scottish politics can be terribly po-faced at times, and we could all do with the laughs.

There's something about so-called grass-roots social media campaigns against independence that is spectacularly inept. This may not be unrelated to the fact that they're typically as organically grass roots as AstroTurf. During the independence campaign we had Vote No Borders, an expensively funded, ahem "grass-roots", campaign with no apparent membership, which for some mysterious reason got itself headlines on the BBC news while real grass-roots organisations supporting independence were sidelined and ignored. It took approximately thirty seconds for independence supporters to rebrand this expensively and professionally developed campaign as Vote Nob Orders, which was a far more accurate summation of what it really represented. We had the slogan UKOK, whose originators obviously never realised was too close to U KOK for comfort. Online anti-independence campaigns are suspiciously phallic. Calling Dr Freud.

The latest social media campaign from SiU is very much in the tradition of this tone-deaf approach to the sensibilities of people who have no prior associations with or loyalties to the message that opponents of independence are trying to get across. Supporters of the organisation have come up with a clever new meme.

Well I say "clever". It's clever in the same way that it's very clever of your new puppy to stand on the newspaper with its front paws while the rear of its body is peeing all over the carpet.

The campaign consists of getting opponents of independence to replace their social media avatars with a circle aping the YES logo used by independence supporters. In the same font, and against a background of the same shade of blue, the logo reads YAWN. It achieved a small amount of notoriety when some clown in the Edinburgh polis used it on the official police Twitter account, an incident which the police assured us was an error and the person responsible will be getting a rocket up the backside which ought to ensure that they won't be yawning for a while.

Apparently the YAWN avatar is supposed to signify the bearer's boredom with talk of another referendum. However the developers of this campaign forgot that boredom is merely a secondary association of the word "yawn". When dealing with slogans, it's vitally important to consider the other associations of the word or words, some of which might be more salient in the minds of readers who don't share your mindset or prior assumptions.

It's a bit like a building services company printing the words BEST ERECTIONS in huge letters on a billboard, then being surprised that most people who see it don't think of quality scaffolding. There was a sunglasses store in the USA whose advertising slogan was "Sitting on faces since 2001", and a one-hour dry-cleaning service which informed the public, "Drop your pants here for immediate attention." Then there was the student TV channel, also in the USA, whose slogan was "Students turn us on". Because that's not creepy and stalkerish at all. What all these logo fails have in common is that the word associations which were forefront in the minds of their creators are not the same as the associations forefront in the minds of people who are not already invested in that business or campaign. That's precisely the same mistake made by SiU.

The primary association of the word "yawn" is of course with sleeping and torpor. Boredom is a secondary association. The avatar fails because those who come to it with no prior knowledge don't immediately associate it with boredom with the pro-independence message of the SNP. They associate it with sleep and with drifting off into a passive unconsciousness. When I first saw this new avatar, I thought that opponents of independence were telling Scotland to go back to sleep. Shut up, go back to sleep Scotland. Let the big boys and girls in Westminster decide your future. This is an avatar that says, "Scotland, it's past your bedtime." Whenever you see someone using this avatar on social media, you should ask them if their mummy knows that they're using the computer.

Independence means a Scotland that is awake and aware and is an active agent in shaping its own destiny. British nationalism means sleeping and passivity. That is the message that SiU is telling us with its logo. The YAWN avatar is more unconsciously revealing of the attitudes of SiU than they are themselves aware. We should encourage them to keep using it. You go back to bed SiU, Scotland is staying up to talk about grown-up stuff. We have our eyes wide open.

3 October 2018

My four-year journey from despair to hope and joy

It's been quite a journey. Four years ago, my partner of twenty-five years passed away. He died on 3 September 2014, just a few days before the independence referendum. Andy died of vascular dementia, a disease which progressed quickly, and which reduced a strong and confident man to a shell of his former self. One of his last actions was to sign his postal vote in the independence referendum. This Englishman, London born and bred, a former Royal Marine and Metropolitan policeman, voted for Scotland to regain its independence.

Andy told me once that he'd seen the British establishment up close. They care nothing for you, he said. They care nothing for working-class people, whether Scottish or English. They only care about themselves, and if it suits their interests they will crush you and rip away from you everything that you hold dear. Scotland, he told me, deserves to be governed by people who love it. And he smiled that wry smile of his, the smile that had made me fall in love with him all those years before. That smile I wept for on 3 September 2014.

Andy never made it to that day of grieving after the vote on 18 September, when I was already dissolved in grief. I know that he'd have been disappointed. But I also know that he would have been so proud of the way in which independence supporters refused to be cowed. We stood up. We declared that we were going to ensure that the British establishment which had threatened, cajoled and vowed its way to a No victory in the referendum was going to be held to account for the promises and commitments that it had made to the people of Scotland.

What I discovered in the days after Andy's death was that I had already done so much of my grieving. Dementia is a cruel disease. It robs those who endure it of everything that makes them who they are, while those of us who love and care for them can only watch helplessly as their loved one's memories, their personality, their character, dissolve in the tears of our grief.

My biggest fear had always been that when he died I would be crushed by the immensity of the loss, but what I discovered was that his passing meant that I was at the end of losing him, I'd already been losing him for years. His death meant I couldn't lose him any more. But his memories stay with me, they inform me and nourish me. The lessons he taught me about strength and personal reliance will always be with me.

I wasn't crushed by the defeat in the referendum either. That campaign had taught a nation how to hope, how to dream of a better future. Those lessons, once learned, will never be unlearned. But I expected that it would be many years before the chance of another referendum would come again. I was prepared for many years, possibly decades, of hard endurance.

A year after the referendum, a year after Andy passed away, hope returned to my own life. Peter and I had been Internet friends for almost twenty years, chatting online as life's journey took us to different places. I had shared with him my fears when Andy was diagnosed, my terrors in the long dark nights when he was having a crisis. He digitally held my hand during the lonely times when Andy's illness took him into distant reveries that no one else could share. I shared my hopes of a better Scotland that might one day be born.

But we'd never met in person. I was in London, then Spain, then Scotland. He was in Connecticut. In late summer of 2015, I went on holiday to the USA to meet him. And that was it. Sometimes you see a person and you know that the connection between you is strong and deep. There was more chemistry than in all of the North Sea's oil and gas fields. It started a series of transatlantic crossings. Peter came here for a visit and fell in love with this grey and damp country with its big heart and landscapes that make you weep with their beauty. We've been back and forth across the Atlantic ever since.

So now, three years later, we're getting married on a beach in Maine. And I know that somewhere, Andy will be looking down with that smile on his face. Hope and joy are still alive, they were only hiding for a wee while. A new life beckons.

What has always struck me as the biggest difference between the independence movement and the campaign to prevent independence, is that it's independence supporters who have the monopoly on joy. Opponents of independence are miserable, they're naysayers, hemmed in by limitations and what we can't do, what we're not allowed to do. They talk so much of poverty because they're defined by poverty of spirit and imagination. The poetry and music, the joy in life, is all with those who support independence, because they're the ones who dream of better things. Hope and joy are still alive, they were only hiding for a wee while.

Here and now, two years after the Brexit vote, Scotland yet again stands on the brink of a historic choice. The independence movement never went away. We were resolved to hold the British establishment to account, and now we will make them pay the price for their arrogance and the contempt with which they've treated the promises and commitments they made to the people of Scotland in 2014 to make us vote No. A better Scotland is coming. A new life beckons.

These past four years have been a journey from grief and despair to hope and joy. You can't live without love, whether you're a person or a nation. We're on a journey to a country that's defined by people who love it. That's all that Scottish independence is about, the right of a country to be governed by people who care for it, who will love it and nurture it. As we get married on that beach in Maine at the end of this month, Peter and I will look across the ocean towards that distant northern country that's home, and see hope on the horizon.

10 October 2018

For Scottish nationalists, the future always looks bright

One of the things that strikes you when you take a break from Scottish politics is how mind-numbingly petty and small-minded British nationalism in this country really is. We have the Labour Party in Scotland turning up to protest against itself, while blaming the SNP for the things Labour did while in office. That's risible enough, but during my recent absence the green ink wing of the doughty defenders of the red white and blue managed to find the SNPbad story to end all SNPbaddery, criticising Nicola Sturgeon when she was on an official trip to Poland for visiting Auschwitz to honour those murdered in the Holocaust. We are dealing here with folk who, if the Scottish government managed to find a cure and prevention for cancer, would embark on a letter-writing campaign complaining about the blow to Scottish health services as oncology units all over the country were closed down.

Having been across the pond for the past couple of weeks, getting better together in a personal union of my own, it was noticeable that the right-wing media over there was trying to distract attention from the mounting crises surrounding Donald Trump by focussing on the entirely imaginary threat represented by a caravan of desperate migrants which is currently walking through Mexico.

People whom you might think possessed some functioning neurones have claimed on national TV that it's possible that this column of desperate and dispossessed Latin Americans fleeing gang violence in Central America – violence which has been produced in no small measure by the USA's war on drugs – might occupy holiday cottages in Minnesota while their rightful owners are away, or that the caravan might contain ISIS terrorists. Trump's administration has gone on record to state that there's no evidence that the caravan doesn't contain ISIS terrorists. Equally there's no evidence that it doesn't contain the Predator alien from the movie who hunted down Arnold Schwarzenegger in the jungles of Central America, but for some reason they've forgotten to mention that on *Fox News*.

While the right-wing American news media is desperately trying to hype something harmless up into a major disaster, the British nationalist media in Scotland is engaged in the exact opposite. Desperately trying to ignore the major disaster that is what passes for Theresa May's Brexit negotiations in case drawing attention to it stirs up support for independence.

When you get a bit of distance from it, what really stands out about British nationalism in Scotland is how miserable it is, how bereft of vision, hope or dreams it is, how it has the imaginative capacity of a tapeworm. It's the political equivalent of being a teenager who's dragged off on a holiday to a wet and dismal seaside town that's seen better days as your maw screams "You'll bloody well enjoy yourself" at you. It's even worse than a holiday cottage in Minnesota occupied by that alien from the Predator movie. All the while you know that your pals are off sunning themselves on an exotic beach in furren pairts. The absolute nadir of this imaginative failure is represented by the misleadingly named Scotland in Union.

Scotland in Union really ought to call themselves something more accurate. They're the people who say they want Scotland to stop and think, and to forget to start again. They're not an organisation which promotes the ideal of a better Scotland within the UK, possibly because a Scotland within the UK has no option but to put up with whatever the rest of the UK inflicts on it. You can't really promote a Union which doesn't exist in the real world. After all, if Scotland really was a valued partner in a family of nations we might have had a modicum of influence on the two-year-long car crash that is Brexit. But we don't, because Scotland isn't a constituent member of a union, it's a subordinate and minority part of a unitary state with devolved bits. Describing that as a union is a bit like describing a chain gang as a conga line. It's like describing orange juice as a solid meal because it's got some unpleasant and unidentifiable floaty bits in it, and to be fair, British nationalists in Scotland do know a lot about orange bits floating about where they're not really wanted.

Scotland as Hostage to Fortune of the Political Interests of a Political Establishment Which Doesn't Really Give a Toss About Us and Won't Listen To Us Anyway would be a considerably more accurate name for an organisation dedicated to maintaining Scotland as a part of the UK, but it's scarcely a snappy title, and is an admission that what the group is up to was always going to be a difficult sell. But then these are the kind of people who would win the EuroMillions lottery and complain that their Auntie Jeanie would expect them to pay for her to have a weekend in Blackpool. Joy and hope aren't exactly their strong points. It's a campaign based on fear and negativity, and all too often on a disdain for anything foreign or different.

It's joy and hope that characterise the Scottish independence movement, because unlike Britishism and its goal of maintaining an inadequate and dreich status quo, the Scottish independence movement looks forward to something better. In my many travels the length and breadth of this country, meeting with independence groups and supporters, not once have I met a single person who wants independence because they're afraid. Not once have I met anyone who wanted independence because they hated anyone, and certainly not our English family, friends and neighbours. Above all, the Scottish independence movement is based in the belief that this country is being sold short by a Westminster govern-ment and the people of Scotland deserve better, are capable of better, and can achieve so much more. Fundamentally, Britishness in Scotland is about looking to the past. Scottish independence is about looking to the future.

And that's why, even though my new husband remains, for the time being, on the opposite side of the ocean, I'm not depressed or downhearted. It's because I know that the future belongs to us, and one day, one day soon, I'll be able to give him the greatest wedding gift of all, the gift of a Scottish passport.

7 November 2018

Independence can't be on the back burner come a general election

Back in 2014, one of the key promises of the Better Together campaign was that it was only by rejecting independence that Scotland could ensure its political and economic stability. Why risk the uncertainties of independence, they said, when you can enjoy the safety and stability of the UK. Of late, the UK has appeared as safe and secure as a flat-pack wardrobe held together with chewing gum, an old hairpin and Theresa May's fond hopes.

British politics have always been characterised by a dangerous and reckless short-termism. Where other countries plan for the years ahead, Westminster can't see further than the next Commons vote. But it's now got so bad that we can't even be certain what's going to happen by the time you've finished reading this article, never mind next week.

The Tory vultures are circling the political corpse of Theresa May. Admittedly it's difficult to distinguish a Tory MP from a vulture at the best of times, but the swivel-eyed Brexit section of the party smells blood and is seeking to replace Theresa May with someone who's as delusional as they are. Sadly for them, and for the rest of the UK, the problem with Brexit isn't Theresa May. The problem with Brexit is Brexit. The only certainty in British politics nowadays is that we're set to be mired in uncertainty for an uncertainly long time to come.

It is entirely possible that the British government won't last much longer. Despite the fact that the one thing that the UK really needs right now is stability and a plan to get out of this Brexmess, sections of the Conservative Party won't hesitate to bring down their own government in pursuit of a hard right crash out of the EU. Meanwhile there seems to be no way out of the Brexit impasse that could gain a majority in Parliament. We could be facing another general election sooner rather than later.

A general election won't solve the problem of Brexit. Jeremy Corbyn certainly doesn't seem disposed to halt it. Last week, the Labour leader said in an interview with a German newspaper that there was no way to stop Brexit happening. He was wrong. Various sources from within the EU have said that they would be willing to halt the ticking clock of Article 50 to allow the UK to have another referendum, and if that referendum produced a majority for staying in the EU, as opinion polls suggest, the EU would be delighted to see the whole sorry mess go away. But Jeremy Corbyn is every bit as committed to Brexit as the most swivel-eyed British Empire loyalist on the Tory backbenches.

It is being widely reported in the British media that there are now only three possible scenarios for the UK. Theresa May's deal, no deal, or no Brexit. That might be the case for the UK, but it's not the case for Scotland. Scotland has an additional possibility, independence. If we are in for an early general election, the SNP needs to make sure that the electorate of Scotland understand that for Scotland, independence is the only realistic and meaningful path out of the disaster of Brexit inflicted upon the UK by a reactionary British nationalism blinded by nostalgia and longing for an empire that's long gone.

The big mistake that the SNP made in the 2017 general election was to try and downplay the issue of independence. The party's attempts to persuade the electorate that the vote wasn't about independence were drowned out by the other parties and the overwhelmingly anti-independence media pushing the message that it was. Ruth Davidson infamously fought that campaign with but one single policy, saying no to another referendum. Saying no to another independence referendum was the Scottish Conservatives' policy on health, education, social security, the economy and foreign affairs.

In a country which had a media which was as evenly split on the topic of independence as the public at large, the SNP might have had a chance of getting their message across. In the Scottish media landscape they had no chance at all. They were caught between the Conservatives seeking to hoover up the votes of everyone who would never support independence under any circumstances, and a Labour Party which was making a pitch to left-wing voters who had been attracted to independence as a means of tackling the social and economic inequalities which blight Scotland. The result was that anti-independence supporters were motivated to go out and vote, but independence supporters were not motivated to vote for the main party of independence.

If there is to be an early general election, the SNP cannot shy away from independence. It must be front and foremost in the party's pitch to the public. The SNP must articulate a clear and compelling case for independence as Scotland's route out of the self-inflicted British disaster of Brexit. It's only independence that offers Scotland the possibility of remaining within the single market and the customs union which is so important to our economy. It's only independence which offers Scotland the possibility of retaining the free movement of people and attracting much-needed inward migration. It's only independence which offers Scotland the possibility of regaining membership of the EU. The SNP is the party of independence. It cannot shy away from that. It needs to own it.

17 November 2018

Anti-independence jibes over Brexit deal for Northern Ireland insult Scotland

There's a deeply alarming line being pushed by certain journalists and politicians who oppose Scottish independence. They are claiming that independence supporters are exploiting the painful and brutal history of Northern Ireland in order to increase support for independence by pointing out that since the UK government is willing to negotiate a special Brexit deal for the Province, then there is no reason at all that it can't do so for Scotland.

Scottish Secretary David Mundell, who hasn't resigned yet, said just a few days ago that the Scottish government was making "crass demands" to be equated with Northern Ireland in the Brexit deal. Assorted anti-independence journalists have gone on social media to insist that Scotland shouldn't expect a special deal because no one in Scotland is blowing anyone up. They support Mundell's view, that Scotland has no right to expect any consideration from the British government. Shut up Scotland, and get back into your shortbread tin with its Union fleg branding.

According to this anti-independence view, Northern Ireland deserves a special Brexit deal because there is a long history there of communal violence, bombing campaigns, riots, and families being burned out of their homes because they had the misfortune to live in a district where their constitutional views were unwelcome. Scotland has no such history, they say, and so we have no right to expect that the British government should negotiate a Brexit deal for Scotland that is specifically tailored to Scotland's needs.

This is quite possibly one of the most insulting and

potentially dangerous arguments against independence that British nationalists in Scotland have ever come out with. They are in effect saying that Scotland doesn't merit any special consideration from the British government because the Scottish independence movement has always been peaceful and respectful of the rule of law. They are implying, in other words, that violence pays.

That's grossly offensive, not just to an independence movement that has always been scrupulously peaceful and dedicated to achieving independence legally and through the ballot box, it's offensive to the people of Scotland. It's telling us that we don't deserve any consideration from the British government because we play by the rules. It's telling us that we shouldn't expect to be listened to, because we respect human rights and the rule of law. It's telling Scotland that because this country is peaceful and has a political culture that abhors violence and illegality that we should expect to be treated more poorly.

In Scotland we are very good at beating ourselves up over all the many and varied things about Scotland that we are dissatisfied with. British nationalists in Scotland are especially prone to this. You know that whenever an opponent of independence tells you that they are a proud Scot, a "but" is immediately following. I'm a proud Scot but... It's as predictable as a Scottish Conservative saying that Scotland doesn't want another referendum.

I'm a proud Scot but... what we're not good at in Scotland is patting ourselves on the back when we've done something to be proud of. We're not good in Scotland at acknowledging those things we do well. We're not great at recognising the things that we're good at.

One of the things that we are extremely good at in Scotland is democracy. When you look at independence movements around the world, they are all too often characterised by violent uprisings, by campaigns of bombing and assassinations, by states of emergency and disappearances, by outright civil war. The Scottish independence campaign is dedicated to peace, to the rule of law, and to achieving independence through debate and discussion.

The Scottish independence movement is defined by a belief that the independent state which a nation wins is defined by the campaign fought to achieve it. If we want a peaceful, democratic independent Scotland which respects diversity and abides by the law, then that's the kind of independence campaign we need in order to win that independent Scotland.

All of Scotland, not just those of us who support independence, should celebrate the peaceful and law-abiding nature of the independence debate, on both sides of the argument. The only convictions for political violence in Scotland have been a far-right extremist who opposes independence, or for threats made on social media, again largely from opponents of independence. The mainstream campaign to oppose independence is, like the campaign to achieve it, defined by a peaceful respect for the rule of law.

There is absolutely no reason why the British government cannot negotiate a separate Brexit deal for Scotland. Theresa May has already established the principle that one part of the UK can be treated differently in order to take into account its needs and the will of its people. There is nothing preventing them from doing the same for Scotland. It's just that they don't want to, because they believe that they can continue to marginalise and ignore Scotland. Those anti-independence journalists who've been tweeting that Scotland doesn't deserve special treatment because Scotland's indy movement is peaceful are doing the Tories' job for them. They are aiding and abetting in ensuring that Scotland continues to be marginalised and ignored within the UK, and they are weakening that so-called Union that they claim to defend. Because if this so-called Union isn't responsive to Scotland's needs, then what's the point of it?

Politicians and journalists who oppose independence should be citing Scotland's peaceful and law-abiding independence movement as a reason why Scotland merits special treatment from the UK government, not as a reason why it doesn't. It's incumbent upon all of us, whether we support independence or oppose it, to demonstrate to Scotland, to the UK and to the world, that peacefulness pays, that respect for the rule of law is rewarding. Scotland is a peaceful country, and all of us have a moral duty, as well as a legal one, to do all that we can to ensure that it stays that way. Opponents of independence are treating Scotland with contempt.

21 November 2018

The Scottish Tories have failed
at the single job they had

Hands up who didn't see it coming? A leaked draft of the Brexit deal which Theresa May hopes to strike with the EU appears to show that, yet again, a Conservative government has sold out the Scottish fishing industry in order to save its Brexit skin. The Scottish Secretary David Mundell, who's not resigned yet, had assured one and all that securing the interests of the Scottish fishing industry was a red line for him and leaderene Ruth Davidson and the rest of Ruth Davidson's Scottish Conservatives™, but it now transpires that the red line wasn't that red after all. At best it's a very pale pink. Possibly mauve. But invisible under normal lighting conditions.

Protecting the Scottish fishing industry was the only advantage from Brexit that the Scottish Conservatives were offering to the people of Scotland. Well, at least protecting the interests of the big fishing boats on the East Coast. According to research from Greenpeace, forty-five per cent of Scotland's fish quota is controlled wholly or in part by just five extremely wealthy families. Protecting interests of the small shellfishing boats on the West Coast who export most of their catch to Europe and rely on frictionless trade, not so much of an interest to the Tories.

The Scottish Conservatives claimed to be standing up for the maritime equivalent of the big Highland lairds and no one else. They were always perfectly happy to sell out every other industry and interest group in Scotland, because apparently the Scottish Conservatives are deeply religious and cod-fearing. The letter that the Scottish Conservative MPs sent to

Theresa May earlier this month said specifically that "access [to fishing waters] and quota shares cannot be included in the Future Economic Partnership". The political declaration now agreed by the British government shows they have been. Ruth Davidson's Scottish Conservatives™ had one job, but they couldn't even manage to do that.

There's that strong voice for Scotland within the UK that they promised you, Scotland. It's a high-pitched squeak that's at a frequency which normal human ears cannot detect, and it's a David Mundell who's not resigned yet even though the British government has ignored his red, no pale pink, no mauve, line. Although to be fair, expecting a man bereft of political principles to resign on a point of political principle was always going to be a big ask.

Ross Thomson is really unhappy. Ross believes he can best represent the interests of his Remain-voting constituency, situated as it is in a Remain-voting country, by pressing for the kind of Brexit that could only be achieved by towing Britain somewhere into the mid-Atlantic and becoming the fifty-first state of the USA. Ross is furious. However being the subject of Ross Thomson's anger is rather like being savaged by a toothless chihuahua with an incontinence problem, so it's not like it's going to make any difference. In that respect he's the typical Tory, making no difference and having no effect.

The reality is that the bulk of the British fishing catch is sold to Europe, and it's vital for the fishing industry to have preferential access to European markets. Seventy-five per cent of the UK fishing catch is exported, the overwhelming majority of which goes to EU countries. That export trade relies upon fast and friction-free trade. The fact is that the UK doesn't eat anything like enough of the fish it catches to support its own fishing industry, one of the biggest in Europe.

UK boats catch species of fish that people in the UK don't eat, and in return the UK imports large numbers of the fish that people in the UK do eat, mostly cod and haddock. Scottish boats could catch a lot more cod and haddock in

Scottish waters, but only at the expense of destroying the precarious and precious fish stocks. The large companies which control almost half the fishing quotas have shown in the past that they are mainly interested in short-term profit and have no great regard for the long-term future of the fishing stocks. You know that phrase, there's plenty more fish in the sea? Well, there isn't. The eventual outcome would be the decimation of Scottish stocks of cod and haddock, and an abundance of fish species that people in Scotland and the rest of the UK don't eat and which can no longer be exported.

This network of fishing nets depends upon frictionless trade with the European single market. The price of continuing access to European markets was always going to be access for EU vessels to UK waters. That was always going to be the deal, and it was foolish and mendacious of the Conservatives to pretend to fishing communities that they could have their fishcakes and eat them.

The Scottish Tories have proven now that they are utterly incapable of protecting Scottish interests within the UK. Their failure demonstrates that not even the strongest proponents of the so-called Union can extract any gains for Scotland within that Union. Whenever there is a conflict of interest between what is good for Scotland, and what is good for the rest of the UK, Scotland always loses. The Scottish Conservatives have all by themselves demonstrated that the UK doesn't work for Scotland. All they received is a slap on the face with a wet fish.

24 November 2018

Why rallies and marches matter
for Scottish independence

If 2017 was the year when the independence movement was stalled by the gains made by the Conservatives in that year's Westminster general election, 2018 will be remembered as the year when the independence movement regained its momentum and made its strength felt in the streets. 2018 was punctuated by a series of pro-independence marches and rallies across the length and breadth of Scotland, culminating in the massive march in Edinburgh last October when many tens of thousands marched through the Scottish capital in order to assert the absolute right of the people of Scotland to determine the form of government best suited to their needs.

I was privileged enough to be asked to speak at the rallies that took place after the marches in Stirling and Bannockburn on 23 June, and the Inverness march and rally on 28 July. The Inverness march was the greatest concentration of people demanding Scottish independence that the capital of the Highlands had witnessed since the Jacobite Wars of the eighteenth century, but unlike those events, this year's march and rally was like all the others entirely peaceful and good-natured.

I had also been asked to speak at the march and rally in Dumfries on 2 June, but unfortunately at the last moment I wasn't able to get there due to car trouble. That was particularly disappointing, as there is an active and vital independence movement in the south of Scotland, one which is often overlooked by a Scottish media which, with the honourable exception of *The National*, isn't great at representing the independence movement at the best of times.

Mark Twain said that there are only two types of public speaker, those who are nervous about speaking in public, and those who lie about not being nervous about speaking in public. It is indeed daunting to stand before a crowd of thousands of people and speak. According to a number of studies, fear of public speaking is the most common fear. It's even more common than a fear of snakes, horrible wee beasties, and poisonous spiders. Which means that it's scarier to speak in public than it is to confront yer average Tory politician. The very worst thing that can befall you when you are addressing a large crowd of people is that all of a sudden your mind goes blank, but if that does happen all you have to do with a pro-independence crowd in Scotland is to remark that you've suddenly discovered what it feels like to be Ross Thomson.

Scottish Conservatives are very quick to condemn pro-independence events for causing traffic disruption. Those same people are silent during the annual shame of Orange parades, which not only cause traffic disruption but which celebrate sectarianism and exclusion. If the likes of Ruth Davidson and Murdo Fraser want us to pay any heed to their carping about independence marches, then they can start by condemning the hate-filled parades of Union fleggery, parades which unlike pro-independence marches and rallies are associated with violence, drunken disorder and fighting in the streets.

Opponents of independence also scoff because Scotland's independence movement doesn't attract as many on to the streets as the Catalan movement does. They condemn us for bringing too many on to the streets, they condemn us for not bringing enough on to the streets. The Catalans are able to mobilise hundreds of thousands for a number of reasons. Firstly there's the not insignificant issue of the climate. You can organise an outdoor event in Catalonia and be reasonably confident that the weather in a couple of months' time is going to be warm and sunny. In Scotland you don't know what the weather is going to be like in a couple of hours, never mind in a couple of months. Because of its climate, Catalonia, unlike Scotland, has a tradition of outdoor public events.

However there is also a more significant reason. Like Scotland, Catalan public opinion is divided on the issue of independence. In both countries approximately half the population supports independence. The difference is that in Catalonia the Catalan media is also equally divided on the question of independence. In Scotland we have thirty-eight daily and Sunday newspapers, but only *The National* and its Sunday sister support independence. Where Catalonia has five TV channels of its own, Scotland has no control of broadcasting and no public service broadcaster of its own.

When there is going to be a large-scale public event in Catalonia, their media tells people about it in advance. Irrespective of your view on the constitution it is news that there's going to be a big public event. When you know about it in advance, you can then make up your own mind about whether you choose to participate or not. In Scotland we get at best a grudging few seconds on the BBC Scotland news after the event. Again with the honourable exception of *The National*, we are entirely dependent on social media to publicise pro-independence events. Given all that, the remarkable thing is not that Scotland's independence movement doesn't attract the same numbers on to the streets as the Catalan movement, the remarkable thing is that so many people in Scotland still turn out for pro-independence marches and rallies.

There are also those in the independence movement who scoff at marches and rallies. They point out from their social media accounts that no one is converted to the cause of independence because someone marches down the high street carrying a saltire. And this would be true. Mind you, it is also true that neither is anyone converted to the cause of independence because a self-righteous person is being self-satisfied, smug, and is flaunting their moral superiority on Twitter. But hey, horses for courses.

People who say that no one is converted to independence because of a march and therefore marches are pointless are missing the point. The point of a march and rally isn't to convert No voters to a Yes vote. The point is to make a public show of strength of the independence movement in a country whose media is overwhelmingly opposed to independence, and which systematically ignores and sidelines any news or developments which are good for the independence cause.

There was a perfect example of that last week. After years of giving front-page lead stories to minor and marginal Spanish politicians who have hinted that Spain may not look favourably on a Scottish application for EU membership, those same newspapers and broadcast media ignored the remarks from the Spanish foreign minister who stated bluntly that Spain would not veto Scottish membership of the EU. It was a development which was positive for the independence campaign, yet far from ensuring that the people of Scotland were fully informed about the death of a matter which the Scottish media had turned into a major concern, the story was ignored.

That's the kind of reason why it's vital for ordinary grass-roots independence campaigners to keep marching, to keep organising public events, to keep demonstrating a public presence. When the media wants to sideline you and ignore you, you need other peaceful and lawful means of showing the people of Scotland that you not only exist, but that the movement counts on the support of a significant part of the Scottish population. That's important because it's opponents of independence who have their views normalised and supported by the media, leaving independence supporters isolated. A march and rally attended by tens of thousands proves to those isolated supporters that they are not alone, that they are a part of something bigger, something massive.

The marches and rallies also exist in order to boost the morale and enthusiasm of those who are already involved in the campaign. That's vitally important. A successful campaign needs to look outwards, in order to attract new supporters, to change minds and opinions, but it also needs to look inwards, to support, encourage and enthuse those who are already involved in the campaign. It's those existing supporters who are the ones who will be doing the persuasion, who will be working to assuage the doubts of the undecided and to change the minds of soft-No voters. They're going to do better at that when they know that they are a part of a mass movement of like-minded people. That's doubly important when the media doesn't reflect the true extent of Scottish public opinion on independence.

As we go into 2019 and Brexit looms, a Brexit which is being imposed on Scotland against its will, it's vital that we continue to march, to rally, to show that this movement of ours will always speak up for Scotland. We are in every town and village, in every street, in every community. There are going to be many more marches and rallies in the coming year, and as Scottish anger about Brexit grows, some of them are going to dwarf those which have already taken place. The streets are ours, and so is Scotland's soul. We are marching to independence, marching to a better Scotland.

3 December 2018

Theresa May's lies on devolution just insult our intelligence

Please make it stop. Please make it go away. We're in for another week of drama, recriminations, tantrums and idiotically childish behaviour, and I'm not even talking about the British nationalist media in Scotland's obsession with SNPbad stories. No, this is the drama, recriminations, tantrums and idiotically childish behaviour that has come to define and characterise that British state whose security and stability Scotland was told it could enjoy. Back in 2014 the Better Together campaign never clarified that they meant secure in the sense of being locked up in a Victorian asylum with Jacob Rees Mogg and his fantasies of taking on Napoleon.

There are few things more galling than having your intelligence insulted by idiots. That however is now the main strategy of Theresa May's ship of fools. We have a government and a prime minister which trade in fantasy with a currency of lies. That must be what they meant when they told us that Brexit was going to unleash a new global Britain making favourable trade deals around the world.

In her speech on Monday, standing in front of some pottery that looked suspiciously like chamber pots, which would be appropriate containers for the contents of her speech, Theresa May warned of the negative consequences on British democracy if the House of Commons voted Brexit down. She said, "imagine if an anti-devolution House of Commons had said to the people of Scotland or Wales that despite being in favour of a devolved legislature, Parliament knew better and would over-rule them."

In Scotland and Wales we don't actually have to imagine that. It has really happened. In the case of Scotland not once, but three times. It happened in 1979 when the House of Commons voted down Home Rule even though the Scottish referendum that year voted in favour of a Scottish Assembly with a very similar majority to the majority in the UK which voted for Brexit in 2016. It happened after the 1997 referendums when Theresa May was amongst those Conservatives who voted against devolution even though the referendums in Scotland and Wales had produced results in favour.

More pertinently however, it happened again in the aftermath of that Brexit vote when Theresa May's own government used the Brexit decision as an excuse to undermine the very foundations of the 1997 devolution settlement , a settlement which the people of Scotland had supported by a very large margin in that year's referendum. Theresa May's own government has unilaterally over-ruled the Scottish Parliament's bill to protect the devolution settlement following Brexit. Her own government has taken it upon itself to decide which reserved powers it's going to take back to itself, and even gave itself the power to do so retrospectively. Theresa has no problems over-ruling Scottish referendums.

Yet now we have Theresa May telling the UK how awful it would be for the result of a popular referendum to be voted down by politicians in the House of Commons. The hypocrisy is strong in this one. Which is in fact the only way in which her government could be described as strong. If Theresa May had displayed even a fraction of the same respect to the outcome of Scotland's devolution referendum as she claims must be given to the outcome of the Brexit vote, then Scotland wouldn't currently be looking towards another independence vote.

In effect, the Prime Minister herself has just told us that in the UK some referendums are more important than others, some electorates are more important than others and some constituent parts of the UK are more important than others. Only some referendums results need to be respected and implemented by the House of Commons, and those don't include Scottish ones. Naturally this story is dominating the anti-independence Scottish media which is determined to protect and defend Scotland's place within the UK and to stand up for Scotland within the UK. Oh wait. No. It's not about how bad the SNP is.

We've gone from no deal is better than a bad deal to warnings from the British government that a rejection of Theresa May's deal would result in the apocalypse. Government strategy this week has been reduced to holding up a cute ickle puppy in front of Conservative backbenchers and warning them that if they vote down Theresa May's deal then the puppy will become a staple food item. At least for those who can still afford meat.

This tactic has been wildly successful, if you define success as failing miserably that is. Theresa May can do that since she is happy to say that black is white and up is down, that Windrush isn't her fault, and she loves and respects Scotland as a partner in her precious union. It's such a successful strategy that Gavin Johnson has resigned, and he was the Tory Whip responsible for dragging around the immature little creature by the scruff of the neck. Which is, entirely coincidentally, also a good description of Ross Thomson's career in politics has gone so far.

Thankfully Labour are giving the Tories some stiff competition, but only in the sense of being mistaken for a corpse. The Shadow Scotland Secretary Lesley Laird, or to give her her correct title, the Shadow Scotland Secretary Lesley Laird Who?, was interviewed on the TV and avoided saying whether her party would campaign for or against Brexit in the event of that snap General Election which the Labour party is so keen on. Although to be fair it's a bit unreasonable to expect Lesley to know the answer to that question since no one else does either.

There are precious few certainties in British politics any more. The prime minister is now warning that Brexit might not happen at all. She's saying that like it would be a bad thing. The only certainty is that her deal is about as likely to attain a majority in the Commons as her government is likely to get through the week without lying, threatening or bullying. Then the gods alone know what will happen next. This is what passes for strong and stable government in the UK these days. Are you feeling secure?

15 January 2019

Scotland must realise the
Labour Party can't save us

It's like we're all trapped in a never ending episode of Mr Bean in which he's joined the Orange Order, and keeps marching repeatedly into a glass door. This is a government whose sole achievement is the ability to be both creepily threatening and unintentionally hilarious at the same time.

Reports over the weekend claimed that the government have emergency plans to relocate the Royal Family in the case of civil unrest because of Brexit. It's just a shame that they don't have the same consideration about the personal welfare of everyone else. The UK in which the British nationalists promised in 2014 that Scotland would be an equal and valued partner has turned out to be a unitary state in which Scotland is sidelined and marginalised, and where there are plans to put the army on the streets in order to subdue the people.

We have the most calamitous and incompetent British government in modern history. We have over the past few months witnessed the Conservatives risk pauperising much of the UK in pursuit of the English nationalist fantasy of the Brexit unicorn. Despite claiming that the point of Brexit is to restore the sovereignty of the British parliament, Theresa May's government has at every turn sought to sideline parliament and avoid the scrutiny of MPs. It has been determined to avoid being held to account. It has trashed what passes for a British constitution, it has wrecked the devolution settlement, but even worse it has cynically risked the Good Friday Agreement with its venal pandering to the DUP.

It seems that to this British government, the only views

in Northern Ireland which matter are those of the most intransigent and backward hard-line Ulster Unionism. The only views in Scotland which count are those which tug a forelock and subordinate themselves to Greater Englandshire. This is a British government which is more willing to meet with an Orange Lodge than it is with the Scottish Government. Yet despite its insistence on protecting Theresa May's favourite fairy story, her so-called Precious Union, a united Ireland and an independent Scotland are closer than ever. Its strategy for keeping Scotland and Northern Ireland within the UK is to stick its fingers in its ears and chant the Sash. This is a historic failure for a government and a party which prides itself on protecting the unity of the UK. If Theresa May wants to protect and defend her preciousssssss, she's doing a spectacularly poor job of it. Even on their own terms, British nationalists are a failure.

On any rational measure, this is a British government which is failing. And yet according to the latest opinion poll for *The Observer*, the Labour party trails them in the polls and support for the official opposition has crashed by 6%. The latest poll puts the Conservatives on 41% and Labour on 34%. If by some miracle Jeremy Corbyn did succeed in getting his snap General Election, on current polling figures he'd lose it. It's not just Theresa May which is failing, it's also the Labour party and the British political system.

It is clear now to anyone who has been paying attention that the strategy of the Labour leadership is to allow Brexit to happen, and then because things are so dreadful, the people will vote against a Conservative government and return a Labour one. Jeremy Corbyn will then have the Brexit that he wants, and he'll be able to blame the Tories for it even though he's done precious little to stop it happening. Jeremy will be Prime Minister of the ruins of Britain. It's obvious where his sympathies lie. This is a Labour leader who last year sacked those Labour MPs on his front bench who campaigned for another EU referendum, but who has given a knowing wink to those front benchers who voted last week against the Cooper amendment which attempted to delay Brexit.

But hey, there might be a Labour government amidst the rubble – well, if he can turn round the opinion polls and get his message through despite the right wing press. Never mind that jobs will be lost, opportunities squandered and futures trashed. It's breathtakingly cynical, even from a party for which triangulation and abstention substitute for principle. Jeremy was elected because he promised to be the Labour leader who would listen to the grassroots of his party, but we've now discovered that this only applies as long as the grassroots agree with Jeremy.

It's so bad that the Labour party in Scotland is losing members more quickly than a zombie horde being mown down by a combine harvester. It's so bad that, according to a report over the weekend, some of the party's own MPs are plotting to leave the Labour party and found a new party of their own. When a party's own membership and elected representatives have lost faith in it, it's going to be very difficult for that party to persuade the rest of us to believe in it. Welcome to Ukania, where there's nothing to believe in except unicorns, the magic pot of gold at the end of the Brexit rainbow, and a sunlounger that's draped in a union fleg so the Germans can't get it.

Throughout all of this, the Labour leadership is showing exactly the same consideration for the needs and wants of Scotland as the Tories. It's not often in politics that something can be exactly quantified, but zero is as exact as you can get. Labour isn't acting in the interests of Scotland. It's acting as the enablers of the worst face of British nationalism. It preaches internationalism, and practises immigration controls and the end to freedom of movement.

Remember what your mammy told you. Remember what ought to be the motto for the Scottish independence movement. If you want something done, you need to do it yourself. If Scotland wants to get out of this mess that has been created by the British political establishment, we need to do it ourselves. Because the Labour party sure as hell isn't going to do it for us.

5 February 2019

BBC's Question Time farce is nothing new for independence movement

Yet again the BBC has succeeded in its mission. Well, that is if you define its mission as alienating, angering, and antagonising a large segment of the population of Scotland. The BBC couldn't have done a better job if it had done it deliberately. In fact it's done it so well that there are many people in Scotland who are convinced that the BBC has indeed done it deliberately. And worse, that it continues to do so as a conscious policy.

The anger and outrage created by Thursday's episode of BBC Question Time didn't come out of nowhere. The programme managed to create the impression to the wider UK public that Motherwell, a town with an SNP MP and constituency MSP, a town which is part of a council area where a majority voted for independence in 2014, is in fact a bastion of support for the Conservatives and Brexit, and is repelled by the very notion of an independent Scotland. It was an even less accurate depiction of the Scottish political landscape than the BBC weather map.

This inaccurate representation of Motherwell found its figurehead in the personage of Billy Mitchell, a far right supporter of sectarian organisations, Trump and Brexit, who has managed to appear on BBC Question Time almost as often as the SNP. Most of the subsequent discussion has focussed on how this marginal figure whose views are far from the mainstream in Scotland has managed to appear so frequently on BBC debate programmes. In fact we've since discovered that he's also managed to get into the audience for the Scottish debate programme being piloted for the

BBC's new underfunded McGhetto channel.

It's not easy to get on these programmes, as any independence supporter can attest. In my travels around Scotland meeting independence activists, I have met several individuals who have tried but failed to get into the audience for BBC Question Time, never mind getting to ask a question. With the new BBC Scottish channel about to launch, I've not met anyone amongst my extensive contacts in the independence movement who has been invited onto any of the new programmes which the channel promises.

I know that my own name is mud with BBC Scotland management. I am one of those people whom Ken McQuarrie once referred to as "those bastards from Newsnet", so I'm not surprised that I've never been asked to appear on any of the new programmes which this new channel is developing. However none of those many people I know who are prominent within the independence movement have been contacted by anyone from the BBC about the new channel either. It seems that the new channel is going to be the same as the old one.

Yet some marginal far right figure repeatedly manages to get onto BBC debate shows. This does not inspire confidence. Either the BBC has a serious issue with its vetting and selection procedures, or it is indeed biased towards marginal figures with right wing British nationalist opinions and biased against those who represent a mainstream political viewpoint in Scotland. One of those explanations must be true. Neither of them paint the BBC in a good light.

However Billy Mitchell popping up on the BBC's Scottish debate shows is the least of the issues with the Corporation. If this had been an isolated occurrence, or if it had been merely an issue about one person, then there would not have been the outrage and anger that Thursday's programme produced. The reason that so many people were so annoyed and so offended by the Motherwell edition of Question Time is because it's not an isolated incident. It's part of a long pattern of perceived anti-independence bias from a broadcaster which demands that independence supporters, along with the rest of the population, pay for it.

There was a similar outpouring of disbelief, anger and dismay when Question Time visited Dundee and managed to create the impression that Yes-voting working-class Dundee, that bastion of the independence movement, was in fact full of plummy voiced Tories who supported Brexit. There was widespread indignation when it came to light that one of the programme's reseachers who was responsible for audience selection was sharing far right and British nationalist postings on social media. Nothing was done then, and it's unlikely that anything will be done now.

We have in the BBC a large media organisation, moreover one which relies upon public funds, which has managed to alienate half of its target audience. I've made this point before, but it bears repeating : when there is a widespread and persistent loss of trust in a public-service broadcaster by the public, that's the fault of the broadcaster, not the public. The onus is on the BBC to address and remedy the situation. If it does not, then the number of people in Scotland who are convinced that it's a deliberate policy on the part of the BBC will continue to grow. Scotland already has the highest proportion of residences in the UK which don't pay the licence fee. That number is only likely to increase.

The issue here is not with individual BBC journalists or staff. The issue is with a persistent perception of anti-independence bias from a broadcaster which we are all expected to pay for. It's one thing to believe that, say, Sky News is biased against Scottish independence, but you don't have to pay for Sky News. What really sticks in the craw of so many in Scotland is that there is a perception of anti-independence bias from the BBC, but that the BBC expects independence supporters to pay for it. It's little more than the BBC poll tax.

However it's not just the BBC which is letting down the

people of Scotland. So is the Scottish government. Nothing will change about the BBC in Scotland until the subject of broadcasting becomes a political issue. It needs to be a major public issue in Scotland that this country is unique amongst self-governing nations and territories in not having its own public service broadcaster. It needs to become an issue that it's those who refuse to allow Scotland to have its own public service broadcaster who are making the unreasonable case, not those of us who are only arguing for something that every other self-governing nation already has. That takes the Scottish government. The Scottish government needs to stop being passive in the face of the BBC's refusal to represent the Scotland that really exists, instead of the Scotland that British nationalists would like to exist.

12 February 2019

Indyref "no" from May is no problem

If it wasn't for the fact that I've got considerably less hair, a much larger stomach and popular music is rubbish, there are days when I wake up and wonder if Scotland has fallen through a hole in the fabric of space-time and has ended up back in the 1980s.

Thirty years ago this month was the first meeting of the Scottish Constitutional Convention, led by the late Canon Kenyon Wright. The Convention was set up in order to tackle the refusal of Margaret Thatcher's government to accede to the will of the Scottish people, as expressed through their elected representatives, for the establishment of a Scottish Parliament. At that famous meeting, Canon Wright declared, "What if that other voice we all know so well responds by saying, 'We say no, and we are the state'? Well we say yes – and we are the people."

The Scottish Constitutional Convention crafted a document which came to be known as A Claim of Right for Scotland, or the Scottish Claim of Right. The Claim stated the "sovereign right of the Scottish people to determine the form of Government best suited to their needs". The document was signed and endorsed by a large majority of Scottish MPs, including Gordon Brown. It was not endorsed by the SNP at the time, as the Scottish Constitutional Convention had, at the behest of its Labour and Lib Dem representatives, refused to allow independence to be discussed as an option.

In 2012, the document was presented to the Scottish Parliament by the SNP Government. This time it was endorsed and supported by the SNP, which over objections from Labour and Lib Dem members noted that its reasons for not backing the Claim in 1989 were well documented. Nicola Sturgeon, who was then Deputy First Minister, called on all the parties in Holyrood to recommit to the principles of the Claim of Right.

On 4 July 2018, the current Westminster Parliament also officially endorsed the Claim of Right. Presented to the House of Commons as an opposition motion by the SNP, it was accepted and endorsed without a vote. With that decision, both of Scotland's parliaments officially accepted and endorsed the sovereign right of the people of Scotland to determine the form of government best suited to their needs. There was no additional rider specifying "subject to a veto by the British Prime Minister".

The purpose of the Claim of Right was to assert the traditional sovereignty of the people of Scotland. It sought to make Scottish popular sovereignty a political reality in the face of the opposition of a Conservative government to the will of the people of Scotland as expressed through their elected representatives. That's the position Scotland was in in 1989, and that's the position Scotland is in thirty years later.

In fact we are in a worse situation, as this weekend Labour's leader in Scotland, Richard Leonard, opined that a future Labour government wouldn't consent to an independence referendum either. Richard is either unaware of his own party's endorsement of the Scottish Claim of Right, or he's ignorant of it. In either event he's consigning the Labour party in Scotland to irrelevance.

This week Conservative sources made it known that within a few weeks they expect Nicola Sturgeon to press Theresa May for her assent to a Section 30 order to allow an independence referendum to go ahead, in accordance with the mandate that the Scottish electorate have given to the current Scottish Government. The Conservatives have made it clear that Theresa May will refuse. We have a British Prime Minister who has abrogated to herself the sovereign right of the Scottish people to determine the form of government best suited to their needs. That's precisely why the Claim of Right was necessary in the first place.

The difference between 2019 and 1989 is that Scotland has had decades of experience in resisting the overweening power of a Westminster that ignores the will of the people of Scotland. We have a Scottish Parliament, we have democratic avenues open to us which were not available thirty years ago. Equally importantly we have a mass grassroots independence movement which can count on hundreds of thousands of activists.

Theresa May can say no if she likes, but she doesn't get to have the final say on the right of the Scottish people to choose their form of government. The Scottish government can test the legality of a consultative referendum in the courts. Any future election in this country can be transformed into an effective referendum on independence. One way or another, the people of Scotland can have a democratic and legal say on their future, and Theresa May can't stop it.

If the Prime Minister wants to maintain the fiction that Scotland really is a partner in a family of nations, it's very much in her interests to cooperate with a referendum. If she doesn't, she merely gives the independence campaign the greatest argument for independence of all – that a Scotland which needs the permission of a Conservative Prime Minister in order to ask itself about its future isn't a partner in a union at all. It's a subject nation.

During the independence referendum Canon Wright came out as a supporter of independence. Scotland has outgrown devolution, he wrote in an article in the Scotsman newspaper. In that piece he remarked that "devolution is power by gift; or, perhaps, it is really power on loan, for gifts can't be taken back. Power devolved is power retained." And he warned that in the event of a No vote the UK was likely to drag Scotland out of the EU against its will. The Canon passed away in 2017, he lived long enough to witness his fears come true. Worse, because Westminster has indeed decided to take back part of its loan. He knew that as long as Scotland remains a part of this so-called union, that this country will continue to be subjected to policies and decisions made in London by politicians who are neither interested in the views of the people of Scotland nor disposed to take account of them. Politicians who do not have the interests of the people of Scotland at heart.

On 4 July 2018, the House of Commons officially endorsed the Claim of Right, yet like so many decisions taken by the House of Commons Theresa May feels free to ignore it. So here Scotland is again, caught in the British time warp. We are still being told by Westminster politicians that Scotland is prostrate and powerless before a Prime Minister who was not chosen by the people of Scotland, but acts like an absolute monarch.

Thirty years on from the Claim of Right, Theresa May says no to a mandate for an independence referendum given to the Scottish Parliament by the people of Scotland. Well we say yes – and we are the people.

5 March 2019

It's wrong to say Brexit has achieved nothing

Another week, another decisive vote on Brexit in the House of Commons. Is it possible to have a decisive vote that doesn't actually decide anything? It's become a modern philosophical question on a par with if a tree falls in the forest does it make a sound if there is no one there to hear it. Although if a tree fell and pole-axed the Brexit process you'd be deafened by the cheering from Scotland. Even those of us who have been paying attention and are managing, just about, to refrain from banging our heads against a wall at the sheer pointless frustration of it all have lost count of the number of decisive votes that the House of Commons has held on Brexit and still there's no decision on anything, except the general uselessness of British politics. Which is a start.

It is theoretically possible that Theresa May will manage to get her deal through the Commons this week. However it is also theoretically possible that David Mundell will resign on a point of principle, that doesn't mean it's at all likely to happen. Mind you, there is, lost somewhere amongst the infinite number of universes that make up the multiverse, one universe in which a version of David Mundell found he had enough of a principle on which to resign. Admittedly that was in a universe in which we are governed by sentient sea-squirts who consume their own brains as they age and he'd forgotten what the principle was by the time he'd resigned. So that universe is not that much unlike this one really, we just have less sentience in our rulers.

This will be the second attempt by the government to get Theresa May's deal through the Commons. The first time it went down to a historic defeat and lost by 230 votes. The signs are that this time it will be rejected by a similar number. In fact there are even some commentators who warn that this time the deal could be rejected by an even larger number of votes than the last time.

After the previous rejection, Theresa went back to Brussels in order to negotiate sufficient changes to the deal to allow it to attract the support of the spittle-flecked Brexit extremists in the European Research Group who were always unlikely to be satisfied with anything short of abject surrender from the EU and Jean Claude Juncker's head on a stake. It was always going to be an exercise in futility, but all the British government has managed to come back with is an EU that's now even more fed up with it than it was before. Considering how fed up the EU was previously, that's quite an achievement.

Also this week in the Commons, the SNP will present its own amendment calling for the British government to recognise that Scotland voted to remain, and that should Brexit go ahead then Scotland should have the right to decide its own future via an independence referendum. The amendment will remind the House that it supported the Scottish Claim of Right which asserts the sovereignty of the people of Scotland and their right to choose the form of government best suited to their needs.

The SNP amendment is even more likely to be voted down by the Commons than Theresa May's deal. It will be voted down by MPs from outwith Scotland, many of whom fulminate in the Commons about the iniquity of the UK being dictated to by the EU. Those same MPs would howl in outrage if non-British MEPs in the European parliament rejected the right of the UK to hold its EU referendum without the permission of the EU, but they are perfectly happy to withhold the same right from Scotland. That in a nutshell is British exceptionalism.

The SNP's amendment is important for Scotland, but it's a sideshow to the main event. This is the week when we are promised that the can which Theresa May has been kicking down the road finally runs out of road.

In the likely event that Theresa May's deal fails again, the Commons will vote the following day on whether to rule out a no deal Brexit. Should that happen, then the next step will be to vote for an extension to Article 50. Theresa May will then have to return to Brussels to beg for extra time for the UK to try and sort itself out. The problem however is that although the Commons fetishises its supposed absolute sovereignty, it's not within the power of the House of Commons to grant itself an extension to Article 50.

That power lies with the EU, and any one of the 27 EU member states could decide to veto it unless they can be persuaded that the extension serves a real purpose. The Ireland which Britain has so casually traduced and ignored throughout the Brexit process is one of those states. That's the difference that independence makes, a difference which shows the reality of Scotland's supposed place at the top table within the UK as nothing more than a bad and unfunny joke.

The EU is not likely to look favourably on a UK which seeks a short extension to Article 50 just so that British politicians can continue to argue amongst themselves and negotiate something that the EU has already told them is off the table. British exceptionalism will finally be forced to confront the reality of a UK which doesn't get to call the shots.

By the end of this week the fog will have lifted, or not. But it's not true to say that Brexit hasn't achieved anything. It has exposed the true nature of the UK as a unitary state which is a union in name only, a so-called union which treats Scotland as a pretty bauble to bedeck the crown of British exceptionalism. Brexit teaches us that the British state is intellectually and politically bankrupt, trading on past glories and saddled with institutions which are unfit for purpose. The lesson of Brexit is that Scotland is trapped in an abusive relationship by a British state that threatens it, gaslights it and keeps it in a constant state of insecurity and uncertainty.

That will remain the case whether Brexit can be avoided or not.

12 March 2019